- A  in the text denotes a highly recommended sight
- A complete A–Z of practical information starts on p.221
- Extensive mapping at end of text

Berlitz Publishing Company

Princeton   Mexico City   London

Copyright © 1998, 1994 Berlitz Publishing Company, Inc.,
400 Alexander Park, Princeton, NJ 08540, USA
24-25 Nutford Place, Suite 120 London W1H 5YN UK

Berlitz Trademark Reg. U.S. Patent Office and other countries
Marca Registrada

Text:	Jack Altman
Editor:	Barbara Ender
Photography:	Monique Jacot, Mireille Vautier, Claude Huber, PRISMA/Schuster GmbH, PRISMA/Etienne, Loomis Dean, Erling Mandelmann
Layout:	Media Content Marketing, Inc.
Cartography:	Falk-Verlag, Munich

We would like to express our warmest thanks to Laure Bachy, Claire Teeuwissen, Geneviéve Vincent, Pierre Carta, Nicholas Campbell, and Gérard Chaillon for their assistance in the preparation of this guide.

Although the publisher tries to insure the accuracy of all the information in this book, changes are inevitable and errors may result. The publisher cannot be responsible for any resulting loss, inconvenience, or injury. If you find an error in this guide, please let the editors know by writing to Berlitz Publishing Company, 400 Alexander Park, Princeton, NJ 08540-6306.

ISBN 2-8315-6416-6

Printed in Switzerland by Weber SA, Bienne

040/107 RP

CONTENTS

France and the French   8

A Brief History   18

Where to Go   40

Getting Around 42
Paris and Vicinity 45
    Paris 46
    Ile-de-France 77
Northeast 85
    Picardy 85
    Champagne 89
    Lorraine 91
    Alsace 92
    Burgundy 102
    Jura 114
Northwest 116
    Normandy 118
    Brittany 132
    Loire Valley 139
Southeast 146
    Savoie 147
    Rhône Valley 150
    Provence 153

Côte d'Azur 163
Corsica 171
Southwest 174
Périgord 174
Atlantic Coast 181
Pyrénées 184

What to Do 192

Sports 192
Entertainment 198
Shopping 202

Eating Out 207

Index 216

Handy Travel Tips 221

Maps

France 6–7
Paris Metro 249
Paris 250–251
Northwest and Ile-de-France 252–253
South 254–255
Northeast 256

FRANCE

FRANCE AND THE FRENCH

Modest people, as Winston Churchill once said of a political opponent, often have much to be modest about — but nobody has ever accused the French of modesty. Behind their carefully constructed grouchy façade, this race of perpetual malcontents clearly believes that France is the most splendid place on earth. Even their most fervent detractors have a hard time trying to prove them wrong.

If the French do complain so much, perhaps it's because they feel they always deserve even better. In a modern world where everyone is obsessed with being at the cutting edge of technology, the French still find it important to do a little polishing, too.

Not that they're duds in modern industrial achievement. Just

The zest and sparkle of French life in a fountain at Paris's Palais-Royal.

Still the backbone of France, farmers like this have little time for frivolous Saint Tropez.

in the field of public transport, for instance, sophisticated French subway systems are exported to major cities on every continent; Concorde, the supersonic plane they built with the British, has proved to be a great success; and their high-speed train, the TGV, is widely considered the best in the world.

The French are generally much more efficient than their international reputation suggests. Service in hotels and restaurants is good; and the road network is excellent. But the French cannot live by nuts and bolts alone. Quality of life remains their paramount preoccupation. No accident that they are best known for their food and wine, their clothes and perfumes, their dashing art and monumental architecture. French civilization is essentially an exercise in enlightened self-indulgence.

They're always looking for some way to turn the ordinary into something special. And it's all for their own pleasure and the world's admiration. It's amazing the magic a French girl can perform with a comb in her hair or a simple cotton scarf around her neck. Remember what happened to good old American blue jeans: they were taken up by the French and converted into a thing of high fashion.

Give them a couple of eggs and they won't just boil them, fry them, or make an omelette (all of which they're quite prepared to do superlatively) — they feel obliged to produce a delicate soufflé or a rich hollandaise sauce that makes an egg proud to be an egg. Even hamburgers have been stretched by one fast-food chain into a more manageable long bun, apparently inspired by the traditional *baguette* sandwich.

The French just won't leave well alone, and occasionally they're inclined to overdo it. You may consider their formal, geometrically planned gardens a pompous distortion of nature, or their triumphal arches and grandiose palaces just a little bit pretentious. However, this tendency to show off — frowned upon in more sober lands and affectionately dubbed *la frime* in France — may be an irresistible desire to celebrate the riches with which nature has endowed the land.

France is blessed with an astonishing variety of landscapes. The stark, rough, dazzling expanses of naked rock and arid ruddy soil of some parts of Provence could easily be the setting for an American Western. But that's just as typical of France as the more conventional image of rolling green meadows bounded by straggling hedgerows beside a shady, arrow-straight avenue lined with plane trees, with a village clustering around its church visible on the horizon.

The country is a veritable compendium of European geography, modified by a "French touch." The plains and plateaux of Picardy in

From off the beaten path, glamorous Saint Tropez appears as just a small fishing town tucked between the hillside and the harbour.

the north and Alsace to the east are the logical conclusion of the central European steppes. The wide-open spaces lend themselves to large-scale agriculture (they have also in the past proved all too convenient as battlefields) before ending in the gentler, rolling green fields of Normandy to the west or the vineyards of Burgundy that herald the beginnings of the south.

The Alps of Savoie and the Dauphiné extend the gigantic chain that rises from Austria across Germany and Switzerland to peter out in the rugged little *Alpilles* of Provence. The olive trees and vineyards, umbrella pines and cypresses of this Provençal countryside and the lazy beaches of the Côte d'Azur are a natural continuation of the classic Mediterranean landscape, till it gives way to the formidable barrier of the Pyrénées near the frontier with Spain.

With those mountain ranges protecting the eastern and southern frontiers, the mild Atlantic winds penetrate deep inland, bringing with them all the rain and sun needed for a highly productive agriculture, while avoiding the extremes of a continental climate.

Inland from the Atlantic coast — Aquitaine, Dordogne, Périgord — the southwest is rich in farming and vineyards. It's the land of good duck and goose, of fine Bordeaux wines. At the country's western edge, Brittany's spectacular craggy shoreline has earned the region a reputation for rough weather. In fact it enjoys the mildest of climates, even in winter, and offers the surest of bets for its seaside resorts in summer.

The kings and counts and feudal lords have gone from the Loire Valley and the forests and marshes of Sologne, but the hunting and fishing country remains. At the country's heart, slightly north of the geographical centre, Paris nestles in a basin ideal for industrial and commercial enterprise, comfortably surrounded by the forest and farmland of the Ile-de-France. And the Champagne area lies conveniently to the east to help celebrate its successes.

If the land itself is the most obvious source of a Frenchman's pride, the nation's cultural wealth is just as important. Philosophy and the fine arts do not intimidate the French as something to be confined to a small élite. For most people, "intellectual" is not the dirty word it seems to be in so many other countries. One of the most popular television shows devotes an hour and a half every week to talking, very entertainingly, about nothing but books. The museums do better business than the football stadiums, and crowds flock to theatre and music festivals in spring, summer, and autumn all over the country. Even popular arts such as advertising, the cinema, comic strips, and fashion are elevated to the level of high culture, with their own museums and festivals.

An active government cultural policy in recent years has preserved the architectural monuments of the "national patrimony" from the ravages of time, weather, war, revolution, and the barbaric assaults of building speculation. The Palace of Versailles has been refurbished to sparkle as in the days of Louis XIV, the Louvre Museum reorganized for an ambitious expansion. The simplicity of Romanesque village churches and the grandeur of Gothic cathedrals can more and more be appreciated at their best. And even the ruins of Roman towns and medieval monasteries have come alive again as the sites of open-air concerts or theatre.

One major boon for the visitor has been the steady replacement of most of those boring uniformed guides, who recited lifeless facts and figures about abbeys or palaces like melancholy parrots, by bright young art historians who are enthusiastic about the places they work in and their areas of knowledge. Their descriptions are fresh and informative, and they're glad to answer questions that go beyond the brochure or guide book.

The country offers plenty of outdoor enjoyment, too: swimming and other water sports, or just sunbathing, on the beaches of Normandy and Brittany or the famous resorts of the Côte d'Azur (the French would like to discourage that Italian word "Riviera"); first-class skiing in the Alps and Pyrénées; canoeing down spectacular gorges in the Ardèche; and marvellous hiking around the country's national parks and nature reserves. Evidence that France is far from being a country of hidebound highbrows is the fact that the Marne Valley, east of Paris, was selected for Europe's first Disneyland.

The people are as varied as their landscape, but don't let anyone tell you the French national cliché is a myth. The red-nosed, moustachioed fellow with a beret on his head, a crumpled cigarette drooping from his lip, and a long *baguette* or two under his arm certainly *does* exist and can be seen in all regions of the country. The French themselves have long acknowledged that all those who are not like him have a brother-in-law who is. But there's all the difference in the world between the prudent, close-mouthed Norman and the vociferous, easy-going Provençal, between the pious Breton and the pagan sophisticates of Paris.

For a people so fiercely proud of their identity, with all the recurrent waves of xenophobia

These women of Anjou keep local traditions alive.

that such nationalism encourages, the French are a marvellously rich mixture — another compendium of the European map, this time in an ethnic sense. Up in Picardy the Flemish influence is unmistakable; and although Alsace may celebrate Bastille Day at least as proudly as any other French province, its cuisine, wines, and dialect all reveal a profoundly Germanic influence. The Côte d'Azur and Corsica both have a distinctly Italian flavour, and the people north of the Pyrénées are not so very different from their Spanish cousins to the south. Then there are the Celts of Brittany, the Norsemen of Normandy, the Basques of the Pays Basque….

As the land of the Declaration of the Rights of Man, France has never for long resisted welcoming political refugees. There were Polish, German, Italian, American, and British deputies in the National Assembly of the French Revolution. Russians fled to France from the Tsar and Stalin, Spaniards from Franco, Jews from Hitler, Armenians from the Turks, Lebanese from the civil war in Beirut.

However, it's in the artistic field — as a pole of attraction rather than a refuge from persecution — that France has happily made a mockery of its own suspicion of foreigners. Not by accident did Van Gogh come from the Netherlands, Picasso from Spain, Max Ernst from Germany, and Chagall from Russia to make their home in France. One of France's greatest poets of the 20th century, Wilhelm Kostrowitsky, better known as Guillaume Apollinaire, was born in Rome of a Polish mother and an Italian father. Irishman Samuel Beckett happily wrote plays in French. And Kenzo, Lagerfeld, and Cerruti design in the international but inexorably Paris-based language of *haute couture*.

Despite occasional tensions, perhaps inevitable in times of economic uncertainty, today French people increasingly recognize that the immigrant workers from France's former colonies — Algerians, Tunisians, and Moroccans — enrich the national culture, and add spice to the country's cuisine. Not least of all, they add even more flavour, colour, and music to that greatest of French assets, the street scene — the sheer light and movement of life itself.

FACTS AND FIGURES

Geography: With a land mass of 547,000 square km (213,000 square miles), France is by far the largest country in Western Europe, a hexagon neatly measuring approximately 1,000 km (620 miles) from north to south and another 1,000 km from east to west. It is bounded by three seas (the English Channel, the Atlantic, and the Mediterranean) and three mountain ranges (the Pyrénées , the Alps, and the Jura), with the Rhine river and Flanders plain to the northeast. The country's four main rivers are the Loire, running west to the Atlantic from the plateau of the Massif Central; the Seine, flowing northwest from Burgundy through Paris to the Channel; the Garonne, flowing down from the Pyrénées past Toulouse and Bordeaux to the Atlantic; and the Rhône, which starts in the Swiss Alps, then turns south at Lyon and flows down to the Mediterranean.

Highest peak: Mont Blanc (Alps) 4,807metres (15,800 feet).

Population: 57,000,000, including 5,500,000 non-French (principally North African, Portuguese, Italian, and Spanish).

Capital: Paris 2.2 million (metropolitan area 9 million).

Major cities: Marseille (800,500), Lyon (415,000), Toulouse (359,000), Nice (342,200), Nantes (245,000), Strasbourg (250,000), Bordeaux (210,300).

Government: Under the Constitution of 1958, every 7 years France's Fifth Republic elects a president, who exercises executive power with a prime minister and cabinet of ministers. The legislature is divided between the National Assembly, elected by universal suffrage every 5 years, and a largely subordinate Senate, chosen every 9 years by an electoral body of deputies and regional councillors. At local level, the 1982 decentralization law reorganized the country's 96 departments into 22 regional councils.

Religion: Predominantly Catholic (45,600,000), while Muslims are estimated at 3,000,000, Protestants at 1,000,000, and Jews at 600,000.

A BRIEF HISTORY

Neanderthal man was what anthropologists term a *homo sapiens* (literally a man who knows) — but the most famous Stone Age Frenchman, Cro-Magnon, was a *homo sapiens sapiens* (a man who knows he knows). From that Stone Age caveman, whose remains were dug up by railway workers in the Dordogne, down to Charles de Gaulle with his "certain idea" of what France ought to be, and beyond, the French have always wanted to know what it means to be a Frenchman. Their history has been a constant quest for national identity, a conflict between strong regional loyalties and the central authority of a Cardinal Richelieu, King Louis XIV, Emperor Napoleon, President de Gaulle — or his successors.

Round about 2000 B.C., Celtic tribes — probably from eastern Europe — came looking for greener pastures in the areas that are now Franche-Comté, Alsace, and Burgundy. At the same time, migrants from the Mediterranean countries were trickling into the south.

The first recorded settlement was the trading post set up by Phocaean Greeks from Asia Minor at Massalia (Marseille) around 600 B.C., followed by other ports at Hyères, Antibes, and Nice. But the Greeks developed few contacts with the interior beyond a little commerce in olives and wine with the Celts of Burgundy. When their position was threatened by Ligurian pirates at sea and bellicose tribes from their hinterland, the merchants of Marseille called on Rome for help.

From Gaul to France

In 125 B.C., the Romans came in force, conquered the "Gallic barbarians" and set up a fortress at Aquae Sextiae (Aix-en-Provence). They took advantage of this new stronghold to create Provincia (now Provence), stretching from the Alps to the Pyrénées , in order to guarantee communications between Italy and Spain.

When this province was endangered by fresh attacks from the north, Julius Caesar himself took charge, conquering practically the whole of Gaul by 50 B.C. Caesar drew Gaul's northeastern frontier at the Rhine, taking in present-day Belgium, and warned that the Germanic tribes across the river — the Franks, Alamans, and Saxons — would always threaten the security of the frontier.

The Romanization of Gaul exiled the most energetic warriors to defend the outposts of the empire, while their families settled down to work the land, or build towns such as Lyon, Orange, Arles, and Nîmes, and the first great highways between them. At the same time, merchants built up a thriving trade with the rest of the empire. The pattern for the peasantry and bourgeoisie of France was thus established.

Christianity was introduced into Gaul in the first century A.D., but was not really accepted until 391, when it became the empire's official religion. Large-scale conversions were led by Martin de Tours, a soldier turned bishop. (Sword and cross were to form a regular alliance in French history.) The new religion soon cemented national solidarity in the face of more barbarian invasions, this time by the Franks.

Gallic unity collapsed with the crumbling Roman empire. King Clovis, the leader of the Franks, defeated the Roman armies at Soissons in 486 and won the allegiance of most Gallo-Romans by converting to Christianity ten years later. With Paris as his capital, he extended his rule to the Mediterranean. But the realm was divided up among his heirs and progressively fragmented by the rivalries of the Merovingian dynasty that battled for power over the next 300 years.

Spain's Arab rulers exploited this disunity to sweep north across Gaul, controlling Languedoc, Dordogne, and a large part of Provence, before being defeated at Poitiers in 732 by the army of Charles Martel, bastard son of Pépin of Heristal.

Even the mighty Charlemagne, king of the Franks from 768 to 814, did not manage to create an enduring national unity: his sons fought for the spoils of his empire. This time it was the Normans from Scandinavia who took advantage of the Carolingian dynasty's divided kingdom, pillaging their way inland along the Loire and the Seine, and plundering Paris in 845. In addition, Saracens invaded the

Provençal coast from North Africa, and Magyar armies attacked Lorraine and Burgundy. To keep the support of the nobles' armies, the kings had to give the nobles more and more land. Consequently, the realm broke up into the fiefdoms of the feudal Middle Ages, precursors of the country's classical provinces — Provence, Burgundy, Normandy and Brittany, etc.

In the central region, from the Loire Valley to Belgium, Hugues Capet succeeded in achieving a precarious ascendancy, and was crowned the first king of France in 987. As had happened at the fall of the Roman Empire, the Christian Church provided the essential element of national unity. Hugues was anointed at Reims with an oil said to have been brought to earth by the angels, thus establishing kingship by divine right for the French.

Middle Ages

It was this alliance with the Church that served as the underpinning of regal authority. In exchange for the anointment, the Church was enriched with lands and the right of taxation by tithe, a fraction of the peasants' seasonal produce.

After the more sober spirituality of the Romanesque churches, the soaring Gothic cathedrals of Chartres, Paris (Notre-Dame), Bourges, and Amiens were at once monuments to the glory of God and testimony to the sheer power, spiritual and temporal, of the Catholic Church.

France, dubbed by the pope "eldest daughter of the Church," took the lead in the Crusades against the "infidels" in Palestine, stopping off on the way across Europe to massacre Jews and heretics. Louis IX, the ideal of the Christian king for the justice he handed down to his subjects and for the Crusades he led to the Holy Land, was sainted after his death in Tunis in 1270. When, in 1309, things grew too hot for the popes in Italy, it was therefore quite natural for the papacy to move to Avignon, where it stayed some 70 years.

France's other major preoccupation was England. In 1066, as probably more British than French schoolchildren know, Duc Guillaume of Normandy crossed the English Channel and became William the Conqueror. For the next 400 years, English and French monarchs fought over the sovereignty of various pieces of France — among them, Aquitaine, Touraine, Normandy, and Flanders.

It's a tiresome tale of much-tangled marital alliances and military victories more important to national morale than to resolving the perennial conflict — such as Bouvines (1214) for the French, Crécy (1346) and Agincourt (1415) for the English. It took a teenager from Lorraine, Jeanne d'Arc (Joan of Arc), to pull the French into good enough shape to resist the English at Orléans. For her pains, the English burned her to death in Rouen in 1431, but her martyrdom stirred national pride sufficiently to boot the English out of France 20 years later.

But the noble national cause was not the first concern of the ordinary Frenchman. Wars were just another hardship, taking sons away from the farm to fight, while the armies — French as much as foreign

In Carcassonne's dungeons, the only things missing are dragons and damsels in distress.

— ravaged the land or pillaged the towns. During war and peace alike in this feudal age, the Church and the aristocracy continued to claim their respective portions of the peasants' labour, leaving barely enough for mere subsistence. And all too frequently, a cycle of drought, famine, and plague would decimate the population. A Dordogne farmer rarely took time off to find out who his current monarch was.

In any case, large portions of France were independently controlled by powerful dukes whose allegiance to the king was only nominal. The unity of France was still a long way off.

Ancien Régime

Absolutism was the dominant feature of what post-Revolutionary France called the *Ancien Régime*. The monarchy noticeably began to come into its own with François I (1515-47). He strengthened the central administration and abandoned an initially tolerant policy towards the Protestants. A debonair Renaissance prince, he introduced a grand style at court.

François brought Leonardo da Vinci to work at Blois, and Rosso and Primaticcio to decorate Fontainebleau. He also commissioned paintings by Raphael and Titian for the royal collections that are now the pride of the Louvre. A new opulent architecture blossomed with the châteaux of the Loire and around Paris. On the international scene, after he had crushed the Duke of Milan's army at Marignano, and formed a showy alliance with Henry VIII of England, his European ambitions were halted by the German Emperor Charles V. François even suffered the indignity of a year's imprisonment in Madrid, following a resounding defeat at Pavia in 1525.

The bloody 16th-century conflicts between Catholics and Protestants throughout Europe centred more on political and financial intrigue than questions of theology. The French Wars of Religion pitted the Catholic forces of the regent Catherine de Médicis against the Protestant (Huguenot) camp headed by Henri de Navarre. Their crisis came on 24 August 1572, with the infamous Saint Bartholomew's Day Massacre. Two thousand Protestants, in Paris for Henri's wedding to Catherine's daughter Marguerite de Valois, were killed. The general massacre of Protestants spread to the countryside, and by October another 30,000 had lost their lives.

The conciliatory policies that painfully emerged after the bloodshed brought the Prince of Navarre to the throne as Henri IV (1589-1610), but not before promising to convert to Catholicism. The enormous personal popularity of this good-natured but tough king from the Pyrénées proved vital for healing the wounds from the bitter wars. The Edict of Nantes was signed in 1598 to protect the Protestants, and five years later the Jesuits were allowed back into France. But Henri won the hearts of the French people most by finding the time to establish a reputation as an incorrigible womanizer — becoming known to posterity as the *Vert Galant* — until he was stabbed to death by a Catholic zealot.

Joan of Arc remains a powerful symbol of French nationalism.

The country floundered in intrigue under the regency of Marie de Médicis, mother of the young Louis XIII, until Cardinal Richelieu took charge as prime minister in 1624. Directing national policy until his death in 1642, he reasserted the authority of his king against both the conservative Catholics who surrounded the queen mother, and the Protestant forces that were fiercely defending the privileges granted them by the Edict of Nantes. With his successful siege of the Protestant stronghold at La Rochelle, the cardinal neutralized the threat of their military strength while guaranteeing their freedom of worship.

Richelieu's major achievement was the greater centralization of royal power, laying the foundations of the strong sense of national identity that has characterized France ever since. He tightened the king's control over legislation and taxes, enraging the Vatican by daring to impose a new levy on the Church. More powerful royal stewards were sent out to diminish the autonomy of the regional *parlements*, councils with judicial rather than legislative functions, dominated by the high clergy and the nobles. The cardinal also created the Académie Française in 1635 to ensure the purity and clarity of the French language through its *Dictionnaire* and its *Grammaire*.

Promoting overseas trade and the founding of a navy, Richelieu also launched France somewhat belatedly on the road to empire with the colonization of Guadeloupe and Martinique in the Caribbean. In Europe, the Catholic cardinal, master of *Realpolitik*, was not above supporting the Protestant Swedish, Danish, and German forces in the Thirty Years' War against the Catholic Austrians, Italians, and Spanish. All that mattered was that it served France's interests.

Richelieu's protégé Mazarin, another cardinal, took over the job of prime minister during the minority of Louis XIV. The court and

---

Too Much Starch?

Executing a king's assassin was no simple business, least of all when the king was as beloved as Henri IV.

For an ordinary capital offence during those pre-Revolutionary times, hanging did the trick — the more dignified decapitation by axe being reserved for those of noble blood. But a regicide, even when he had been found guilty and sentenced to public execution, had to be tortured and, still alive, "quartered" by four horses each attached to an arm or leg. His remains were then cremated by the executioner.

In the case of Henri's murderer, François Ravaillac, the frenzied crowd in front of Paris town hall set upon his remains, and only his shirt was left over for cremation.

regional aristocracy were infuriated by the Italian-born churchman's intimate relationship with the king's mother, Anne of Austria. Nor did they like his astounding knack for amassing a vast personal fortune while managing, very efficiently, the affairs of state. But most of all, they despised the way he eroded the nobles' power and smoothed the path to an increasingly absolutist monarchy.

The revolts of the *Fronde* forced Mazarin, Anne, and the boy-king to flee from Paris in 1649. However, the royal family's triumphant return three years later, with the rebellious nobles crushed, saw the monarchy stronger than ever.

Louis XIV drew his own conclusions from Mazarin's careful coaching in the affairs of state. When he began his personal rule in 1661, at the age of 23, there was no question of a new prime minister impinging on the royal prerogative. Adopting the unequivocal symbol of the sun, Louis was to be outshone by no one. Counsellors were wholly subservient. Louis never once convened the parliamentary assembly of the *Etats généraux*, even though its powers were minimal. He moved the court to Versailles, not only to get away from the troublemakers of Paris, but to impoverish the nobility, by forcing them to contribute to the crippling luxury of his palace, with no other function than to support the king in time of war.

It's all too easy to be bedazzled by the brilliance of life at Versailles, by its architectural splendour, and most of all by the sheer hypnotic power of Louis XIV's cult of self-glorification. In his lifetime, many petty European princes tried to imitate Louis's style with their own little Versailles, complete with court artists and sycophants. It took French historians a long time to resist the glitter and come to terms with the less attractive realities of what that style cost the nation.

To enhance his glory, the Sun King turned to foreign conquest. The devastating military expedition he launched across the Rhineland and Palatinate, and the series of largely fruitless wars with Spain, Holland, England, and Sweden did not endear him to the European people. Moreover, they left France's once-thriving economy in ruins.

At home, his authoritarian rule required a brutal police force. Taxes soared to pay for his wars, and more and more peasants had to abandon their fields when press-ganged into his armies. Influenced in later life by the Catholic piety of Madame de Maintenon, his mistress and subsequently secret wife, Louis put an end to religious freedom for Protestants by revoking the Edict of Nantes. In the face of forced conversions, the Protestant Huguenots — many of them the most talented bankers, merchants, and artisans of their generation — fled to Switzerland, Germany, the Netherlands, England, and Scandinavia.

The reaction to Louis XIV's death in 1715, a sigh of relief, was almost inevitable. Having outlived his children and grandchildren, he was succeeded by his five-year-old great-grandson, Louis XV. But government was in the hands of the late king's cultured, libertine, and atheist brother, Philippe d'Orléans.

Royal Mistresses

Since royal marriage was an affair of state rather than of the heart, the king of France made no bones about having mistresses, too. One of them was given formal precedence as *maîtresse en titre* (titular mistress). She wasn't always a giggle, as Louis XIV discovered with the sanctimonious pillow-talk of Madame de Maintenon.

As the last person to see the king before he went to sleep, the royal mistress was ideally placed to whisper more than sweet nothings in his ear and inevitably acquired a taste for politics.

Ambitious families competed to get one of their daughters into the royal bed, and Louis XV entertained three Nesle sisters, one after the other, until the youngest, Madame de Châteauroux, got the titular job. She was succeeded by the most famous mistress of them all, Madame de Pompadour. With her famous high-flying hair-do, the extravagant Pompadour was a great patron of the arts, promoting the painting career of François Boucher and protecting Voltaire from his many court enemies.

Madame du Barry, who rose to royal favour literally from the streets, was Louis XV's last and loveliest *maîtresse en titre*, and perhaps the only one reluctant to get involved in politics —particularly in 1793 when she was carried screaming to the guillotine.

After the morose twilight years of the Sun King, life perked up with the satiric pen of Voltaire and the erotic fantasies of Watteau's paintings and Marivaux's comedies. The court moved back from Versailles to Paris. The generally lazy regent gave a bunch of incompetent nobles too much of a say in the running of the state. Regional *parlements* obtained the right to present remonstrances, the thin end of a wedge to weaken the monarchy.

The easy-going Louis XV was called, at least in the first half of his reign, the *Bien-Aimé* (Beloved). The king seemed more interested in his mistresses than in running a tight ship of state. Despite this (or perhaps because of it) the economy recovered, the overseas empire expanded in the East and West Indies, arts, and letters flourished in this age of enlightenment.

But the new voices were a clear threat to the established order. Diderot's *Encyclopédie* championed reason over traditional religion, Rousseau discoursed on the origins of inequality, Voltaire shot at everything that didn't move.

Revolution and Napoleon

Louis XVI, grandson of Louis XV, found himself attacked on all sides. The intransigent aristocracy and high clergy were anxious to protect their ancient privileges; a burgeoning bourgeoisie longed for reforms that would give them a larger piece of the national pie; the peasantry was no longer prepared to bear the burden of feudal extortion; and a growing urban populace of artisans groaned under intolerable hardships, symbolized by the fluctuating price of bread.

At the assembly of the *Etats généraux*, convened for the first time in 175 years, it was clearly the king's enduring absolutism rather than the throne itself that was under fire. For reactionary nobles, the king was the guarantor of their hereditary status. Liberal reformers wanted a constitutional monarchy similar to England's, not a republic. Even the grievances drawn up by the peasants and townspeople insisted on continuing devotion to the king himself.

Two months later, the blindness of the king's conservative advisors and his own weakness and vacillation led to the explosion of centuries of frustration and rage — which culminated in the storming of the Bastille, the régime's prison-fortress in Paris. On that fateful day, 14 July 1789, the king went hunting near his château at Versailles and at the end of the day wrote in his diary "*Rien*" ("Nothing").

A National Assembly voted a charter for liberty and equality, the great Declaration of the Rights of Man and of the Citizen. The aristocracy's feudal rights were abolished, the Church's massive landholdings confiscated and sold off.

Rather than compromise, the king fled Paris in a vain effort to join up with armed forces hostile to the Revolution. With Austrian and German armies massing on France's frontiers and the forces of counter-revolution gathering inside the country, the militant revolutionary Jacobins led by Maximilien de Robespierre saw the king's flight as the ultimate betrayal. A Republic was declared in 1792, and Louis XVI was guillotined in 1793. His son Louis XVII died in obscure circumstances under the Revolutionary government, probably in 1795.

Under pressure from the poorer classes, who did not want the Revolution appropriated for the exclusive benefit of the bourgeoisie, the

The gigantic palace of Versailles is a perfect expression of Louis XIV's talent for self-glorification.

Jacobin-led revolutionary committee ordered sweeping measures of economic and social reform, which were accompanied by a wave of mass executions, the Terror, aimed at moderates as well as aristocrats. Despite his attempts to quell the extremists, Robespierre was overthrown and guillotined in the counterattack of the propertied classes.

During their *Directoire*, a new wave of executions — the White (royalist) Terror — decimated the Jacobins and their supporters. But the bourgeoisie, fearing both the royalists and their foreign backers, turned for salvation to a Corsican soldier triumphantly campaigning against the Revolution's foreign enemies — Napoleon Bonaparte.

In between defeating the Austrians in Italy and a less successful campaign against the British in Egypt, in 1795 Bonaparte returned to Paris to crush the royalists, and four years later he staged a coup against the *Directoire*. He was just 30 years old.

In the first flush of dictatorship as First Consul, he established the Banque de France, created state-run *lycées* (secondary schools), and gave the country its first national set of laws, the *Code Napoléon*. The centralization dear to Richelieu and Louis XIV was becoming a reality.

The supreme self-made man, in 1804 Bonaparte became Emperor Napoleon at a coronation ceremony in which he took the crown of golden laurels from the pope and placed it on his own head. He managed to pursue simultaneously foreign conquests in Germany and Austria and domestic reforms that included a modernized university and police force and proper supplies of drinking water for Parisians. During his disastrous campaign in Russia, he found time in Moscow to draw up a new statute for the *Comédie-Française* (the national theatre), which had been dissolved during the Revolution.

The nationalism that Napoleon invoked in his conquest of Europe's *Ancien Régime* turned against him in Spain, Russia, and Germany. The monarchies regrouped to force him from power in 1814. Nevertheless, he made a brilliant but brief comeback the following year — before an alliance of British, Prussian, Belgian, and Dutch troops inflicted the final defeat at Waterloo.

Kings and Emperors Depart

More intelligent than his executed brother, Louis XVIII tried at first to reconcile the restored monarchy with the reforms of the Revolution and Napoleon's empire. But his nobles were intent on revenge and imposed a second, even more violent, White Terror against Jacobins and Bonapartists, including some of Napoleon's greatest generals.

Louis's reactionary successor, brother Charles X, was interested only in renewing the traditions of the *Ancien Régime*, even having himself anointed and crowned at the ancient cathedral of Reims. But the middle classes were no longer prepared to tolerate the curtailment of their freedom, nor the worsening condition of the economy in the hands of an incompetent aristocracy. They reasserted their rights in the insurrection of July 1830 — the kind of liberal revolution they would have preferred back in 1789 — paving the way for the "bourgeois monarchy" of Louis-Philippe.

This last king of France, heir of the progressive Orléans branch of the royal family, encouraged the country's belated exploitation of the Industrial Revolution and the complementary extension of its overseas empire in Asia and Africa (Algeria had been occupied just before the 1830 revolution). But the new factories created an urban proletariat, clamouring for improvement of its miserable working and living conditions. The régime's response of ferocious repression and other ineptitudes led to a third revolution in 1848, with the Bonapartists, led by Napoleon's nephew, emerging triumphant.

The Second Republic ended four years later when the man whom Victor Hugo called "Napoléon le Petit" staged a coup to become Emperor Napoleon III. Determined to cloak himself in the legend of his uncle's grandeur, he saw his own role as that of champion of the people. But he used harsh anti-press laws and loyalty oaths to quell the libertarian spirit that had brought him to power.

The economy flourished thanks to the expansion of a vigorous entrepreneurial capitalism in iron, steel, and railways, augmented by overseas ventures such as the Suez Canal. Despite the emperor's obsession with the new "Red Peril" — the 1848 Communist Manifesto of Marx and Engels, which was being circulated in Paris — he could not prevent such social reforms as the workers' right to form unions and even to strike.

With the excessive enthusiasm that characterized the age, Baron Haussmann's urban planning barrelled its way through old Parisian neighbourhoods to create a more airy and spacious capital. Similarly, architect Viollet-le-Duc often went overboard restoring some of the great Gothic cathedrals and medieval châteaux in ways their original creators had never imagined.

Victor Hugo, in exile in Guernsey, was writing *Les Misérables*, while Baudelaire was working on *Les Fleurs du Mal,* and Offenbach was composing acid but jolly operettas, such as *La Belle Hélène*. Courbet was painting his vast canvases of provincial life, and Manet his *Déjeuner sur l'Herbe*.

Napoleon's battles celebrated on the Arc de Triomphe have given way to the sweeter things of life.

Life was generally looking up. The bourgeoisie showed off its new prosperity with extravagant furnishings, silks, satins, and baubles, and in 1852 Paris opened its first department store, Au Bon Marché. In this optimistic society, with its high level of social critique and constant pressure for improvement, France was assuming its true national identity.

But Germany had an account to settle. In 1870, Prussian Chancellor Bismarck exploited an abstruse diplomatic conflict with France to bring the various German principalities and kingdoms together into a fighting force well equipped for war. After a lightning victory over the ill-prepared French armies, the German nation, or Empire (*Reich*), was founded under Kaiser Wilhelm I in the Palace of Versailles. The confiscation of Alsace and Lorraine avenged the old but unforgotten scars left by Louis XIV's devastation of the Rhineland and Palatinate, and by Napoleon's more recent invasion.

The Third Republic

Defeat shattered the Second Empire. While the new Third Republic's government under Adolphe Thiers negotiated the terms of surrender, the workers' communes refused to capitulate. In March 1871 they took over Paris and a few provincial cities, and held out for ten brave but desperately disorganized weeks. In the end they were brutally crushed by government troops, and order was restored.

France resumed its industrial progress, quickly paid off its enormous war-reparations debt to Germany, and expanded its overseas empire in North and West Africa and Indochina. Rediscovered national pride found its perfect expression in the great Eiffel Tower thrust up into the Paris skies for the international exhibition of 1889.

Left and Right

The ideological divisions of "left" and "right," today adopted all over the world, derive from the seating arrangement of the National Assembly that legislated the French Revolution. Quite simply, supporters of the Revolution sat on the left and opponents on the right.

Within the ranks of the Revolutionary left, what the British might now call the "militant tendency" sat up on the high benches, the *montagne* (mountain), while the moderates sat down in the *marais* (marshes).

In 1874, the first exhibition of Impressionism had blown away the dust and cobwebs of the artistic establishment. Novelist Emile Zola poured forth diatribes against industrial exploitation. Rodin, more restrained, sculpted masterpieces such as *le Penseur* (The Thinker). Leading the "republican" hostility to the Church's entrenched position in the schools, in 1882 Jules Ferry enacted the legislation that has formed the basis of France's formidable state education system ever since.

On the right, nationalist forces were motivated by a desire to hit back at Germany, seeing all contact with foreigners or any form of "cosmopolitanism" as a threat to national honour and integrity. For many, the Jews were the embodiment of this threat — Edouard Drumont's vehemently anti-semitic *La France juive* (Jewish France) was a runaway national bestseller. It appeared in 1886, eight years before Captain Alfred Dreyfus, an Alsatian Jew in the French Army, was arrested on what proved to be trumped-up charges of spying for the Germans. In a case that pitted the fragile honour of the Army against the very survival of French republican democracy, the captain had to wait 12 years for full rehabilitation.

The desire for revenge against Germany remained. And as Germany's own imperial ambitions grew, competition for world markets became intense. Most of France went enthusiastically into World War I, and came out of it victorious and bled white. With the 1919 Treaty of Versailles, France recovered Alsace and Lorraine; but 1,350,000 men had been lost in the four years of fighting. The national economy was shattered, and political divisions were more extreme than ever.

In face of the fears aroused by the Russian Revolution of 1917, the conservative parties dominated the immediate post-war period, while a new French Communist Party, loyal to Moscow, split with the Socialists in 1920. France seemed less aware of the threat from Nazi Germany, allowing Hitler to remilitarize the Rhineland in 1936 in breach of the Versailles Treaty, a step Hitler later said he had never dreamt of getting away with.

In the 1930s, extreme right-wing groups such as Action Française and Croix-de-Feu (Cross of Fire) provided a strong antidemocratic undercurrent to the political turmoil of financial scandal and parliamentary corruption. The bloody 1934 riots on the Place de la Concorde in Paris offered a disturbing echo to the street fighting of Fascist Italy and Nazi Germany.

The left-wing parties responded by banding together in a Popular Front, which the Socialists led to power in 1936. Within the first few weeks, Léon Blum's government nationalized the railways, brought in a 40-hour week, and instituted the workers' first holidays with pay. But the Communists broke the alliance after Blum first failed to support the Republicans in the Spanish Civil War and then — faced with financial difficulties — put a brake on the reforms.

War and Peace

Blum's government collapsed in 1938, and the new prime minister, Edouard Daladier, found himself negotiating the Munich agree-

---

No Small Affair

Over and above a judicial error, the Dreyfus Affair crystallized the passions that had burst into the open with the French Revolution, the conflicts between order and justice, conservatism and progress. It was no accident that the association formed by the Dreyfusards was named the *Ligue des droits de l'homme* (League of the Rights of Man), still in existence today to defend the historic Declaration of 1789.

Not least of all, the peculiar prestige that intellectuals have enjoyed in French society derived directly from their contribution to the Jewish captain's vindication, epitomized by Zola's decisive newspaper article *"J'accuse"* ("I accuse"). Coming down from their ivory tower, writers and academics demonstrated they could have a direct influence on public events. Elsewhere, "intellectual" is often an insult hurled at an educated troublemaker by his opponents. His French equivalent may be heard unashamedly beginning his tirades: *"Moi, intellectuel…"* ("An intellectual myself…").

ments with Hitler, Mussolini, and Britain's Neville Chamberlain. A year later, France was once again at war with Germany.

Relying too complacently on the defensive strategy of the fortified Maginot Line along the northeast frontier with Germany (but not facing Belgium), the French were totally unprepared for the German invasion across the Ardennes in May 1940. With fast-moving tanks and superior air power, the Germans reached Paris 30 days later. Marshal Philippe Pétain, the hero of World War I, capitulated on behalf of the French on June 16. Two days later, on BBC radio's French service from London, General de Gaulle appealed for national resistance.

Compared with other occupied countries such as Belgium, Holland, and Denmark, France's collaboration with the Germans is an inglorious story. Based in the Auvergne spa town of Vichy, the French government often proved more zealous than its masters in suppressing civil liberties and drawing up anti-Jewish legislation. It was French police who rounded up the deportees for the concentration camps, many of them denounced by French civilians seeking to profit from the confiscation of property. The fighters of the underground Resistance movement were heroic, but they were a tiny minority, a few of them conservative patriots like de Gaulle, most of them socialists and communists, and also a handful of refugees from Eastern Europe.

Deliverance came when the Allies landed on the beaches of Normandy on D-Day (6 June 1944). De Gaulle, with his canny sense of history, took an important step towards rebuilding national self-confidence by insisting that French armed forces fight side by side with the Americans and British for the liberation of the country, but, above all, that the French army be the first to enter Paris itself.

After the high emotion of de Gaulle's march down the Champs-Elysées, the business of post-war reconstruction, though boosted by the generous aid of the Americans' Marshall Plan, proved arduous, and the wartime alliance of de Gaulle's conservatives and the Communist Party soon broke down. The general could not tolerate the political squabbles of the Fourth Republic and withdrew from public life.

The Louvre houses Delacroix's "Liberty Guiding the People."

Governments changed like musical chairs, but the French muddled through. Intellectuals debated in Paris's Left-Bank cafés whether Albert Camus was correct in writing that it was less important to be happy than merely to be conscious of what is going on. And, as Jean-Paul Sartre argued at the next table, "There's nothing in heaven, neither Good nor Evil, nor anybody to give me orders."

The French empire was collapsing. After France's fruitless last stand in Vietnam, Pierre Mendès-France wisely negotiated an Indochinese peace settlement. He gave Tunisia its independence and handed Pondicherry over to India, but was ousted from office as hostilities broke out in Algeria.

De Gaulle returned from the wilderness in 1958, ostensibly to keep Algeria French. But he'd seen the writing on the wall and brought the war to an end with Algerian independence in 1962. His major task was to rescue France from the chaos of the Fourth Republic. The new constitution, tailor-made to de Gaulle's authoritarian requirements, placed the president above parliament, where he could pursue his own policies outside the messy arena of party politics.

De Gaulle's visions of grandeur, and of a country independent of America's NATO and the Soviet Union's Warsaw Pact, gave France a renewed self-confidence. One of his great achievements was the close alliance with West Germany, overcoming centuries of bloodshed between the two peoples.

But with self-confidence came smugness, and the French bourgeoisie was given one of its periodic frights with the massive student rebellions of 1968. The "events of May" that erupted in Paris's Latin Quarter and swiftly spread through the country disturbed de Gaulle enough for him to fly off to seek reassurance with his troops stationed in West Germany.

As it turned out, people were reluctant to make a complete change until 1981, when the forces for reform gathered sufficient strength to elect François Mitterrand as the Fifth Republic's first Socialist president. Like the Popular Front in 1936, the new government began with a quick-fire set of reforms — a broad programme of nationalization, abolition of the death penalty, raising the minimum wage, and the introduction of a fifth week of holiday with pay — until the impact of the world economic crisis imposed a necessary brake. Special emphasis was placed on cultural programmes, with generous subsidies for theatre, cinema, museums, and libraries, and also for scientific research.

Probably the most important reform was the least glamorous: the decentralization that increased regional autonomy and reversed the age-old trend of concentrating political, economic, and administrative power in the national capital. By allowing the local pride of such historic regions as Provence, Normandy, Brittany, and Languedoc to reassert itself, France demonstrated that it was at last secure in its national identity — so secure French citizens even began carrying European passports. As a founder member of the European Community, France looked to a wider, continental challenge in the 1990s.

The vanity of political leaders—left, right, or centre— makes them ideal fashion models.

HISTORICAL LANDMARKS

Prehistory

28,000 B.C.	Cro-Magnon man in Dordogne
2000	Celts invade France from east

Gaul

600	Phocaean Greeks found Marseille
125-121	Romans establish colony of Provincia (Provence)
59–50	Julius Caesar conquers Gaul
486 A.D.	"Barbarians" end Roman control
496	Clovis, King of Franks, converts to Christianity to rule Gaul

Middle Ages

732	Arabs halted by Charles Martel at Poitiers.
768-814	Charlemagne king of Franks
987	Hugues Capet first king of France
1066	Duke William of Normandy conquers England
1096	French lead First Crusade
1209	Pope orders wars against "heretics" in southwest
1337-1453	Hundred Years' War
1431	Joan of Arc executed

Ancien Régime

1515-47	François I marks ascendancy of absolutist monarchy
1572	St Bartholomew's Day massacre of Protestants in Wars of Religion
1598	Henri IV protects Protestants with Edict of Nantes
1624-42	Cardinal Richelieu governs for Louis XIII
1642-61	Cardinal Mazarin takes over
1648	France seizes Alsace
1661-1715	Louis XIV moves court to Versailles
1685	Revocation of Edict of Nantes

Revolution and Napoleon

1789	Fall of Bastille (July 14); Declaration of the Rights of Man

1793	Louis XVI guillotined
1794	Robespierre guillotined
1804	Bonaparte crowns himself Emperor Napoleon
1805	Trafalgar lost, Austerlitz won
1812	Retreat from Moscow

Kings and Emperors Depart

1815	Napoleon defeated at Waterloo, Louis XVIII restored to throne
1830-48	"Bourgeois monarchy" of Louis-Philippe
1848	Liberal Revolution overthrows monarchy
1852	Napoleon III proclaimed emperor

Third Republic

1870-71	Franco-Prussian War. Germans seize Alsace-Lorraine. Napoleon III deposed
1914-18	World War I
1919	France regains Alsace-Lorraine
1936-37	Socialist-led Popular Front

War and Peace

1939-45	World War II. Germany occupies France, de Gaulle heads Resistance
1944	Allies invade Normandy (June 6)
1945-46	De Gaulle heads Fourth Republic's first government
1954	Mendès-France decolonizes Indochina and Tunisia
1962	France gives up Algeria
1968	Student rebels shake government
1981	Mitterrand elected Fifth Republic's first Socialist president
1992	Referendum for Maastricht Treaty: treaty approved by marginal majority
1994	The Chunnel, as the car and rail tunnel linking France and Britain is known, opens
1995	Conservative Paris mayor Jacques Chirac wins the presidency

WHERE TO GO

It's perhaps natural when planning a trip to France to think of it as a meal. If you're not travelling with the set menu of a package tour, but prefer to choose your destinations *à la carte*, you may at first be daunted by the sheer variety. To make the geography (if not the choice) simpler, we've divided the country up into just five regions: Paris and its vicinity (known to the French as the Ile-de-France); the Northeast (Picardy, Champagne, Lorraine, Alsace, Burgundy, and the Jura); the Northwest (Normandy, Brittany, and the Loire Valley); the Southeast (the Alps, Provence, the Côte d'Azur, and Corsica); and the Southwest (Périgord, the Atlantic coast, and the Pyrénées).

Since we aim at a representative rather than encyclopaedic survey of the country, our selection of places within those regions is by no means exhaustive. Experienced visitors to France may feel a few of their own favourite corners of the country have been given short shrift, even though they may find others they have never

Get away from the maddening crowds on a winding Jura mountain road.

heard about, but newcomers will have more than enough to choose from.

Depending on how much time you have available, you may want to combine at least two or three of the regions in order to get a sense of the great diversity of French life: the big city and the wine country, the mountains and the Atlantic or Mediterranean coasts.

The itinerary for a first visit to France is bound to include Paris. Ideally, divide your stay in two — sightseeing in the capital at the beginning, before you grow lazy at a seaside resort or in some sunny village in the hills, then shopping in Paris at the end, so you won't have to cart your purchases around with you for the rest of the trip. For a relaxing vacation, for example, you might want to combine Paris and the Ile-de-France with Normandy and Brittany. And for stark contrasts — of climate, countryside, and temperament — combine the capital with Provence or Corsica.

However, the mix shouldn't just be geographic. The cultural monuments of France, its cathedrals, museums, and palaces, deserve your attention, but they'll be much easier to digest and appreciate if you alternate them with plenty of time at the beach or on country walks. And if you feel like being idle, France does not lack places where it's a simple joy to do absolutely nothing at all. You'll also find that museum-going can be more fun if you vary your cultural diet with some of the more off-beat collections devoted to such diverse topics as comic-strips, toys, balloons, bread, graffiti, and fire engines.

Many people do not have the option of going to France outside the main holiday periods — Easter, July, and August. But if it's at all possible, plan your visit for the spring, autumn, or even the winter, when the big sightseeing destinations are blessedly easier to visit. The island church of Mont-Saint-Michel, on the Normandy coast, can be pure magic in the mists of December.

A tip for visiting the big museums in peak seasons: go at dinner time on a late-closing day. At least the French feel they have got something more important to do then.

GETTING AROUND

Even if you're the kind of traveller who likes to improvise and be adventurous, don't turn your nose up at the tourist offices. Tourism being a major factor in the country's balance of payments, the organization for foreign visitors in France is extremely efficient. For general information, the *office de tourisme*, both in your own country and in the regional capitals throughout France, is worth a visit.

Even the smallest towns, with maybe only one monument, vineyard, or pile of prehistoric fossils to boast of, invariably have a *syndicat d'initiative*. These friendly local tourist offices offer free maps and brochures, and advice about sporting and cultural events and camping facilities. With advance notice, the ones in the bigger towns can often provide an English-language guide for local sightseeing tours.

The Handy Travel Tips section at the back of this book (page 221) contains detailed practical guidance on the technicalities of travel in France, but here are some general thoughts to help you plan your trip.

First of all, *how* are you going to travel? The excellent system of roads and public transport (now reinforced by the Channel tunnel) makes the combination of car and train an attractive proposition. Take the train for long journeys, and rent a car at your destination to explore the back country. Several special rail cards include reduced rates for car rentals and even bicycle rentals.

Not By Bread Alone

Museum opening hours vary from season to season and year to year, so check the current situation with the local tourist office. You can be sure that most museums are closed on Tuesday, a day dictated by the French need to reconcile food and culture. It enables butchers, bakers, and grocers, whose day off is usually Monday, to start their week with a little fine art, while the next day museum guardians can get their meat, bread, and potatoes.

With the high-speed TGV *(Train à Grande Vitesse)* from Paris, you can be in Dijon for a visit to the Burgundy vineyards in an hour and a half, Lyon in two hours, then on to Avignon for your Provençal adventure in under four. Services also operate down the west coast to Rennes, Bordeaux, and the Pyrénées . The one frequently mentioned disappointment of French trains is the relatively uninspired dining-car service. Don't despair; make up your own picnic hamper from the local market before you get aboard — cold meats, salad, Camembert, grapes, *baguette,* and wine can add a terrific sparkle to the countryside flashing past the window.

For drivers in a hurry, the network of toll motorways (expressways) is first class, linking up most of the major cities and still expanding. Otherwise, it's more fun to explore the country along the good-quality secondary roads. If you're afraid of getting lost, follow the green arrows indicating the route of *Bison futé* (Wily Buffalo — a Red Indian invented by the Ministry of Transport), which proposes alternative itineraries in order to avoid traffic jams.

French drivers are adventurous and even aggressive, less spectacular than, say, the Italians, but not unskillful. Patient driving is always a good idea, but timidity will get you into an unholy mess in the Paris rush hour. In fact, it's wisest to drive as little as possible inside the cities. The *métro* (subway) is the fastest way around Paris, but the buses, both in the capital and the other big towns, are best for taking in the sights. Unless you feel really safe in French metropolitan traffic, keep your cycling — you can rent a bike at the railway station — for the villages and country roads. Even so, Paris

There is always room for conversation — even at a bistro's tiniest table.

43

recently created miles of cycling lanes that crisscross the entire city, making bicycling much safer (and more popular).

If you have plenty of time at your disposal, you might want to consider renting a sail-it-yourself barge or cabin cruiser and coast sleepily along the Canal de Bourgogne from Dijon, or the tributaries of the Loire, or the Canal du Midi from Toulouse down to the sea at Sète. It's great fun helping the keepers open the locks. With a couple of bikes on board, you can always stop along the way to explore inland. Larger hotelboats for up to 20 people, plus crew, are organized for gourmet cruises from one gastronomic port of call to another.

Try to vary the kind of places where you stay. Depending on your budget, it's worth going all out for at least one night for the exquisite comfort and service of a great hotel, either what the French call a *palace*, which usually refers to an old-fashioned luxury hotel, or a converted château, abbey, or mill house. On holiday, you owe it to yourself to be treated occasionally like a monarch. If you'd prefer to avoid these, then try hotels labelled *Logis de France* — good traditional hotels, usually with features typical of the region.

Some of the métro entrances are delightful masterpieces of Art-Nouveau design.

Too many modern hotels tend to be highly efficient and comfortable, but totally characterless. Even if you're able to afford a *palace* every night, don't miss out on the great charm of a simple country inn *(auberge)*. More frugal, but with the appetizing bonus of good country cooking, are the *gîtes ruraux* — often a converted farmhouse where the farmer's wife cooks your meal. These are ideal when hiking.

However and wherever you travel in France, one last piece of advice: even if you can't speak French properly, it's well worth learning just a few words. You've probably heard horrendous stories about how impatient the French can be with people who don't speak their language. In fact, it's usually a case of the foreigner not making even the slightest attempt to say *Bonjour, S'il vous plaît,* or *Merci beaucoup* to help break the ice.

It can be very disconcerting for an ordinary Frenchman to be confronted with a torrent of incomprehensible English (imagine someone in Houston or Huddersfield attempting to cope with a Frenchman who can't speak English). Despite their reputation, the French are a very courteous people, calling each other *Madame* or *Monsieur* and always saying an appropriate *Bonjour* or *Au revoir* when entering or leaving a shop or café. It may well be the inadvertent absence of such courtesies that raises the hackles of that touchy fellow who barks at you. But at least he doesn't bite. With the right smile, an *Excusez-moi, Monsieur* can melt even the coldest Gallic heart.

Being Berlitz, we'll try to help you with some of the simplest phrases (at the back of the book). The rest is up to you and your own desire to play the French game. *Amusez-vous bien!*

PARIS AND VICINITY

Anyone seeking a rapid sense of the country must start in Paris and its immediate surroundings. With France's heavily centralized civilization, Paris, more than most national capitals, dictates the country's tastes and style of life. All ambitious French people "go up" to

Paris to make their fortune, and so people from every region of France — with every local cuisine to feed them — are represented in the metropolis. Indeed, the Parisian's traditional contempt for the provinces is matched only by his fierce loyalty to the distant home of his ancestors, most often just one generation removed.

Before Paris became the national capital, it was the home of the medieval dukes of the region that is still known as the Ile-de-France — which, by gradually asserting itself over other duchies such as Burgundy and Normandy, imposed its name on the whole country. The Paris basin is a real treasury of national monuments. Roughly bounded by four rivers — the Seine, Oise, Aisne, and Marne — the Ile-de-France was the birthplace of the first great Gothic cathedrals, such as Saint-Denis, Senlis, Chartres, and Beauvais. It was the cradle of the French monarchy; its surrounding greenery and dense forests also provided good sites for later kings and nobles to build their chateaux, away from the troublesome mob of Paris, at Fon-tainebleau, Chantilly, and, of course, Versailles.

All the interesting sights around the capital are an easy day trip by car or local train, enabling you to keep your Paris hotel if you wish (but you'd probably find the local country inns a lot cheaper).

PARIS

The city and the people of Paris share a boundless self-confidence that exudes from every stone in its monuments and museums, bistrots, and boutiques, from every chestnut tree along its avenues and boulevards, from every street-urchin, mannequin, butcher, and baker, from every irate motorist and every charming maître d'hôtel.

About 20% of the entire population of France lives in the greater Paris area.

You readily forgive the bombast of some of the monumental architecture when you see what makes this the City of Light. Stand on the Pont Royal in late afternoon and look

From Bog to Bonaparte

The fishing village of the Celtic Parisii on an island in the Seine (today's Ile de la Cité) was conquered in 52 B.C. by the Romans, who called it Lutetia (Marshland).

Although Hugues Capet, first king of France (see page 20), made it his capital in 987, Paris did not become the permanent seat of royal government for another 600 years. Crusader Philippe Auguste took time off to build the Louvre as a fortress in 1190.

It was Henri IV who made Paris a truly royal capital. He built the splendid place des Vosges and place Dauphine, beautified the river banks, and completed the grand Pont-Neuf. Fashionable Paris evolved in the 17th century with the first elegant houses of the Faubourg Saint-Honoré and the Cours-la-Reine built for Marie de Médicis as precursor to the Champs-Elysées. Cardinal Richelieu enhanced its intellectual standing by creating the Académie Française, while bequeathing his magnificent home, the Palais-Royal.

After the humiliations of the Fronde revolts (see page 25), Louis XIV abandoned Paris for Versailles, but the town's cultural life reasserted itself under his successors. Cafés sprang up around the Palais-Royal as centres of the intellectual ferment preceding the Revolution.

From Bonaparte to Beaubourg

To celebrate his battles, Napoleon built the Arc de Triomphe and Place Vendôme, but he himself felt his most important achievements were those of a mayor rather than a conqueror — water purification, food markets (les Halles), slaughterhouses (la Villette), a new police force, and streamlined municipal administration. Under his nephew, Napoleon III, troublesome working-class neighbourhoods were razed to make way for wide boulevards and avenues, giving Paris its modern airy look — and a clear line of fire for the artillery in case of revolt.

If the Eiffel Tower was a fetish of the triumphant 19th century, modern Paris has proved no less daring. The Centre Pompidou, better known as Beaubourg, was the first big brash symbol of today's modernism. Then the Louvre sprouted a sparkling glass pyramid; the stainless-steel Géode mesmerized la Villette; and la Défense was framed by a titanic arch. Paris, bold as ever, was still thinking big.

down the Seine to the glass-panelled Grand Palais, bathed in the pink-and-blue glow of the river. That unique light brings a phosphorescence to the most commonplace little square or side street. To make sure the message is clear, Paris offers golden night-time illumination of its major historical buildings. To celebrate Bastille Day (July 14) or the 1944 Liberation (August 25), blue, white, and red laser beams are bounced off the Eiffel Tower, Arc de Triomphe, and Hôtel de Ville.

Despite the inevitable erosion of social change and urban renovation, the jargon of Paris's topography still evokes not just places but a state of mind. The Right Bank conjures up an image of solid bourgeois respectability. Historically the stronghold of merchants and royalty, today it still remains the home of commerce and government. Faubourg Saint-Honoré offers the luxury of jewellery shops and *haute couture,* and the more imperial than republican authority of the president's palace, while the Champs-Elysées claims the first-run cinemas, airline companies, and car showrooms.

The Left Bank has, in contrast, always presented a bohemian and intellectual image, dating back to the founding of the university and monasteries; and today, the Sorbonne, the Académie Française, the

Whether walked along or boated upon, the Seine guarantees grand views of the city.

publishing houses, and the myriad bookshops continue to exercise an intellectual magnetism.

But an unceasing flow and interchange of citizenry from one bank to the other takes place across the bridges of the Seine — a narrower and so much more manageable river than, say, London's Thames or New York's Hudson.

Paris is one of the world's most densely populated capitals. Its non-stop street scene derives from the fact that nearly every one of its 20 *arrondissements,* or districts, has shops, offices, and apartments side by side and on top of each other. There's always someone out there moving around. Join them.

The Seine

The river is by far the best place to begin to take the measure of Paris. Its mixture of grandeur and intimacy is the very essence of the city.

Again and again the Seine provides a spectacular vantage point for the city's great landmarks. The Eiffel Tower, the Palais de Chaillot and Trocadéro Gardens, the Grand and Petit Palais, the Palais Bourbon, the Louvre, and Notre-Dame all take on an enchanting, dreamlike quality if you see them first when floating by in a boat. The **guided boat trip** is well worthwhile.

But the Seine is also a river to be walked along, despite the traffic on the *voies express* along its banks. You can take delightful strolls between the Pont Sully, at the eastern end of the Ile Saint-Louis, and the Pont de la Concorde. Stop to rest occasionally on a bench beneath the poplar and plane trees along the Seine, ideally early in the morning or late in the afternoon, when that pink Paris light is at its best.

The river's bridges are a major attraction — four of them especially worthy of your attention. The **Pont-Neuf** (*neuf* means "new") is in fact Paris's oldest standing bridge, completed by Henri IV in 1606. It was a favourite of street-singers, charlatans, amateur dentists, professional ladies, pickpockets, and above all *bouquinistes* selling their old books and pamphlets out of boxes. Established booksellers on the

Ile de la Cité were enraged and drove them off to the banks of the Seine, where they've been ever since.

The centrally situated **Pont Royal**, built for Louis XIV in 1685, commands some splendid panoramas, with the Louvre and the Tuileries Gardens immediately over on the Right Bank, the Musée d'Orsay on the Left, the Grand and Petit Palais downriver, and the Palais de l'Institut de France, home of the Académie Française, upstream.

The **Pont de la Concorde**, truly the bridge of the French Revolution, was erected between 1787 and 1790. Stones from the demolished Bastille prison were used for its support structure — galling for Royalists, since it had originally been named Pont Louis XVI.

Paris by Boat

The river cruises are accompanied by multilingual commentaries on all the landmarks. Times vary, but they usually go from around 10am to 10:30pm. If you love boats, take a daytime trip at the beginning of your stay and a romantic night-time cruise at the end to enjoy the illuminations.

Bateaux-Mouches

Bateaux-Mouches have open-air or covered seating according to the weather. The year-round standard 70-minute tour starts from the place de l'Alma, goes west to the Pont Mirabeau, then turns back upriver as far as the Pont Sully at the end of the Ile Saint-Louis. The special lunch (1pm) and dinner cruises (8:30pm, jacket and tie for men) last 1 hour 45 minutes and 2 hours 15 minutes respectively. Telephone 01.40.76.99.99.

Vedettes

The vedette or motorboat tours take 60 minutes.

Vedettes Paris-Tour Eiffel start by the Pont d'Iéna (Left Bank) and the quai de Montebello, going west to the Pont de Bir-Hakeim and east to the Pont Sully and back. Telephone (01) 44.11.33.44.

Vedettes du Pont-Neuf leave from the Pont-Neuf, square du Vert-Galant, to the Eiffel Tower and back around the islands. Telephone (01) 46.33.98.38.

On moonlit nights, lovers head for the **Pont Alexandre III**, undoubtedly the most kitschily romantic of all with its *Belle Epoque* lanterns and melodramatic statues of Fame and Pegasus. They really don't care to know that it was built to honour Tsar Alexander for some obscure military treaty.

Right Bank

Etoile–Concorde–les Halles

Start at the **Place de l'Etoile** (officially Place Charles-de-Gaulle, but nobody calls it that), preferably on top of the **Arc de Triomphe**. One reason for climbing up Napoleon's gigantic triumphal arch — 50 metres (164 feet) high and 45 metres (148 feet) wide — is to get a good view of the 12-pointed star formed by the 12 avenues radiating from the arch in a *tour de force* of geometric planning. The vast sloping mound of the *place* cannot be taken in properly at ground level.

Over the years the Arc de Triomphe has taken on a mythic quality, as succeeding régimes have invested it with the spirit of the nation. Napoleon himself saw only a life-size wooden and canvas model of the arch. Louis-Philippe inaugurated the final version in 1836, complete with bas-reliefs and statuary celebrating the victories of the Revolution and the Napoleonic Empire. The Etoile's monumental ensemble was completed for Napoleon III by Baron Haussmann.

Victor Hugo was given a positively pharaonic funeral ceremony at the Arc de Triomphe in 1885. The Unknown Soldier of World War I was buried here in 1920, and three years later the Eternal Flame was kindled. When Hitler came to Paris as conqueror in 1940, this was the first place he wanted to see. But General de Gaulle gained his revenge by starting his march of Liberation here in 1944.

Avenue Foch, which leads away from the Etoile to the Bois de Boulogne, is still the grandest of the city's residential avenues, although somewhat democratized these days by the *boules* players on its gravelled side paths.

The **Champs-Elysées** remains the town's, perhaps the world's, most glamorous avenue. It stretches in an absolutely straight line from the Arc de Triomphe to the Place de la Concorde, bordered by chestnut trees all the way. The first two-thirds, as you walk down the Champs-Elysées, are devoted to cinemas, shops, and café terraces. You'll find the best vantage points for people-watching between Avenue George V and Rue Lincoln on the "shady" side, and at the Rue du Colisée on the "sunny" side.

After the Rond-Point, there's a pleasant park — where a very popular stamp-collectors' market is held every Thursday — that will take you down to the **Place de la Concorde**. This gigantic square has had a hard time earning its pacific name. More than 1,000 people were guillotined here during the Revolution and the counter-revolutionary White Terror that followed. In 1934 it was the scene of bloody fascist rioting against the government. Ten years later it was the Germans' last hold in Paris. Today, with its floodlit fountains and elegant lamps, it is a nighttime romance and a daytime adventure — both for the pedestrian pausing to enjoy the vast opening of the Paris sky and for the driver daring to make his way around it.

Smack in the centre you'll see most ancient monument in Paris, the 23-metre- (75-foot-) tall pink-granite Obelisk of Luxor from the temple of Ramses II, dating back to 1300 B.C. and erected here in 1836. For a

The last vestige of the past at the new shopping centre of les Halles is the church of Saint-Eustache.

change, this was not something Napoleon plundered on his campaigns but a gift from Mohammed Ali, viceroy of Egypt.

After the bustle of the Champs-Elysées and Place de la Concorde, take refuge in the cool shade of the chestnut trees in the **Jardin des Tuileries**. Fragments of the royal palace destroyed in the 1871 Commune are still standing by the **Jeu de Paume** museum in the northwest corner. The gardens are now a favourite with children watching marionette shows, riding donkeys, or sailing and sinking their boats on the circular ponds.

At the eastern end of the Tuileries stands the pink **Arc de Triomphe du Carrousel**, roughly contemporary with its bigger brother at the Etoile, visible in a straight line beyond the Obelisk. This imposing vista was originally planned for Napoleon to see from his bedroom in the Louvre. Nowadays the line is continued — or, some say, marred — by the modern skyscrapers of la Défense looming on the horizon.

Leaving the Louvre museum for a separate visit (see page 71), cross the Rue de Rivoli to the **Palais-Royal**, built for Cardinal Richelieu as his Paris residence in 1639, and originally named Palais-Cardinal. This serene arcaded palace, with its garden of lindens and beeches and a pond where the young Louis XIV nearly drowned, has always been a colourful centre of more or less respectable activity.

In the days of Philippe d'Orléans, Regent of France during Louis XV's minority, it was the scene of notorious orgies. To meet the family's extravagant debts, ground-floor rooms were turned into boutiques (today still selling coins, medals, engravings, and antiques) and cafés that attracted fashionable society, together with some shady hangers-on (artists, charlatans, prostitutes, pickpockets) and intellectuals. On 13 July 1789, a young firebrand orator, Camille Desmoulins, stood on a table at the Palais-Royal's Café de Foy to make the call to arms that set off the French Revolution the next day. After Waterloo, Prussian General Blücher arrived to blow 1,500,000 francs in the course of a single night at one of its many rambunctious gambling dens.

East of the Palais-Royal, the old food markets of les Halles (now moved to the more hygienic and inevitably less colourful suburb of Rungis) have been replaced by gardens, new apartment buildings, and the **Forum des Halles**, a rather garish shopping centre. Around it, the lively neighbourhood of cafés, boutiques, and art galleries linking up with the Centre Pompidou (alias Beaubourg, see page 73) is very popular with the young crowd. The liveliest meeting-place is around the handsome Renaissance **Fontaine des Innocents**, once part of a cemetery.

On the north side of les Halles, another monument of the Renaissance period, although decidedly Gothic in silhouette, is the church of **Saint-Eustache**, remarkable for its beautiful stained-glass windows over the choir.

Vendôme–Opéra–Madeleine

The airy octagonal **Place Vendôme** still exudes the grandiose opulence of its original conception under Louis XIV; at that time only his financiers could afford the exorbitant rents. Three centuries later, not that much has changed — a score of international banks have their offices here, along with celebrated jewellers, the Ministry of Justice, and the Ritz Hotel.

The spiral of bronze bas-reliefs on the Vendôme column, commemorating Napoleon's victories and topped by a statue of the emperor himself, was cast from 1,250 cannons captured from the Austrians at Austerlitz.

Window-shop your way past the goldsmiths and furriers of the Rue de la Paix to the **Opéra Garnier**, the massive neo-Baroque monument to the gorgeous pretensions of Napoleon III's Second Empire. Completed in 1875, four years after his downfall, it is claimed that it is the world's largest theatre, though seating only 2,000 people.

The Boulevard des Capucines and the Boulevard des Italiens, known as the **grands boulevards**, meet at the Place de l'Opéra. They are perhaps less fashionable now than in their heyday at the end of the 19th century, but you can still recapture some of the atmosphere. On the Boulevard des Capucines, you retrace the footsteps of Renoir, Manet, and Pissarro taking their paintings to the former studios of the photographer Nadar, at number 35, for the first Impressionist exhibition, held there in 1874. Today the boulevards are where you will find some of the most popular cinemas — appropriately, since it was at the Grand Café in Boulevard des Capucines that the Lumière brothers staged the first public moving-picture show in 1895.

Regularly mistaken for the stock exchange, the Bank of France, or a theatre, the **Madeleine** doesn't look much like a church, but that's what it is. Napoleon wanted to turn it into a *Temple de la Gloire* for his Great Army, but his architect persuaded him to build the Arc de Triomphe instead. The restored monarchy opted for a church, as originally planned under Louis XV. The huge Greco-Roman edifice, consecrated only in 1842, was left without transept, aisles, bell-tower, or even a cross on the roof. Parisians like it most for the flower market at its base and the grand **view** from the top of the steps down the Rue Royale to the Place de la Concorde.

Down on the right is Maxim's restaurant, which began as an ice-cream parlour and is now a monument more venerable than the Madeleine. Cutting across the Rue Royale, the **Rue du Faubourg-Saint-Honoré** is the city's most luxurious shopping street. At

Sustaining its tradition of resident artists, Montmartre's Place du Tertre is virtually a gallery.

number 55, peek through the heavily guarded gates of the French president's Elysée Palace.

Montmartre

> **Underground fares in Paris are the same irrespective of the distance you travel.**

Long famous as the home of artists and bohemian crazies, who call it "la Butte" ("the Mound"), Montmartre is an essential piece of Paris mythology. It claims a fabled past as Mons Martyrum — where, after being decapitated, the town's first bishop, Saint Denis, picked up his head and walked away. Scholars insist it was really named Mons Mercurii, and was the site of a pagan Roman temple. Difficult to decide in a neighbourhood that includes the Sacré-Coeur and Pigalle.

Topographically, Montmartre is still the little country village of 400 years ago — narrow, winding, hilly streets and dead-ends. Leave the car behind and take the Porte de la Chapelle line on the *métro* from Concorde to Abbesses. Do *not* get off at Pigalle; however attractive you may find its lurid glitter at night, by day it might depress you into not visiting the rest of Montmartre.

From the Place des Abbesses, take Rue Ravignan to 13, Place Emile-Goudeau. This was the site of the **Bateau-Lavoir** studio, an unprepossessing glass-roofed loft reconstructed since a 1970 fire. Here, if in any one place, modern art was born: Picasso, Braque, and Juan Gris developed Cubism, while Modigliani painted his own mysteries and Apollinaire wrote his first surrealistic verses. Nearby, the illustrious predecessors of these "upstarts" — Renoir, Van Gogh, and Gauguin — lived and worked in the Rue Cortot, Rue de l'Abreuvoir, and Rue Saint-Rustique (site of the restaurant A la Bonne Franquette, where Van Gogh painted his famous *La Guinguette*). Coming a long way down in the artistic scale, street painters still throng the **Place du Tertre**, Montmartre's historic village square, where marriages were announced and criminals hanged.

On the Rue Saint-Vincent, at the corner of Rue des Saules, look out for Paris's own vineyard, the Clos de Montmartre, whose wine reputedly "makes you jump like a goat."

At the other end of the Rue Saint-Vincent, you will come around the back of the **Sacré-Cœur** basilica. You have probably spotted it a hundred times during the day, so its back view will make a welcome change. This weird 19th-century Romano-Byzantine church has a somewhat dubious reputation. Aesthetes scorn its over-ornate exterior and extravagant interior mosaics; working-class people of the neighbourhood resent the way it was put up as a symbol

Crowds flock to Sacré-Cœur, mainly for the view of Paris from the dome or the terrace below.

of penitence for the insurrection of the 1871 Commune and defeat in the war against the Prussians. The miraculously white façade derives from its special Château-Landon stone that whitens and hardens with age. For many, the most attractive feature is the view of the city you get from the dome or from the terrace below.

Marais

The Marais district, north of the two islands in the river, has bravely withstood the onslaught of modern construction to provide a remarkably authentic record of the development of Paris from the days of Henri IV, at the end of the 16th century, up to the Revolution. Built on land reclaimed from the marshes, as the name suggests, some of Europe's most elegant Renaissance houses *(hôtels)* now serve as museums and libraries.

Take the *métro* to Rambuteau and start at the corner of the Rue des Archives and **Rue des Francs-Bourgeois**, named after the poor people who were allowed to live here tax-free during the 14th century. France's National Archives are kept here in an 18th-century mansion, the **Hôtel de Soubise**. Across a vast horseshoe-shaped courtyard, you rediscover the exquisite Rococo décor of Louis XV's epoch in the apartments of the Prince and Princess of Soubise. Up on the first floor is the **Musée de l'Histoire de France**, where you can see the only known portrait of Joan of Arc painted in her lifetime and Louis XVI's diary, with its famous entry noting *"Rien"* ("Nothing") for 14 July 1789.

A garden (not always open to the public) connects the Hôtel de Soubise with its twin, the **Hôtel de Rohan**, on Rue Vieille-du-Temple. Look out for Robert le Lorrain's fine sculpted horses of Apollo over the old stables in the second courtyard. Two other noteworthy mansions to look out for on the Rue des Francs-Bourgeois are the **Hôtel Lamoignon**, at the corner of Rue Pavée, and the **Hôtel Carnavalet**, home of the illustrious 17th-century lady of letters Madame de Sévigné, today the **Musée historique de la Ville de Paris**.

At the end of Rue des Francs-Bourgeois is what many consider to be the city's most handsome residential square, the **Place des Vosges**. Henri IV had it built in 1605 on the site of a horse-market. The square achieves a classical harmony with subtle diversity of detail in the gables, windows, and archways of its stone and red-brick façades. Its gardens, once a favourite spot for aristocratic duels, now serve as a pleasant children's playground. The best time to see the square as a whole is in winter, when the lovely chestnut trees are bare and don't obscure the façades. Victor Hugo used to live at number 6, which is now a **museum** of his manuscripts, artifacts, and drawings.

Finish your visit to the Marais with a walk through the old **Jewish quarter** (or *shtetl*, as Paris Jews call it) around the Rue des Rosiers. Jews have lived there continuously, apart from recurrent persecutions, since 1230, and Rue Ferdinand-Duval was known as Rue des Juifs (Jews' Street) until 1900. The other main street of the *shtetl*, the Rue des Ecouffes (a medieval slang word for money lender), completes the lively shopping district. Jews from North Africa are gradually replacing the Ashkenazi of Eastern Europe, who themselves took over from the original Sephardim. Delicatessens and *falafel* shops keep the district nicely "ecumenical."

Cimetière du Père-Lachaise

Such is the city's perpetual homage to the great of its past that cemeteries enjoy a special, not at all lugubrious, place in Parisian life. In a haven of calm (the grounds are beautifully kept), the avenues of tombs provide a fascinating walk through history. The largest of Paris's "cities of the dead," Père-Lachaise has a population estimated at 1,350,000 buried here since its foundation in 1804.

A little map available at the entrance will help you to locate the tombs of the famous, which include Rossini and Chopin, La Fontaine and Molière, Sarah Bernhardt and Oscar Wilde.

The Islands

Ile de la Cité

Shaped like a boat, with the square du Vert-Galant as its prow, the Ile de la Cité is in effect the cradle of the city of Paris, as it was the original dwelling place of the fishermen

The cradle of Paris — the Ile de la Cité is rich in religious and political history.

of early Lutetia. In the middle of the 19th century, it fell victim to the overambitious urban planning of Baron Haussmann. The much praised but often insensitive prefect of Paris swept away most of the medieval and 17th-century structures, leaving only the Place Dauphine and the Rue Chanoinesse as testimony to the island's rich residential life.

The baron was also seriously thinking of replacing the triangular **Place Dauphine's** gracious gabled and arcaded red-brick architecture with neo-Grecian colonnades — but fortunately he was forced out of office for juggling his books before the wreckers could move in. The *place* was built in 1607 by Henri IV, whose equestrian statue is to be seen on the nearby Pont-Neuf. Today its sidewalk cafés shaded by plane trees enjoy an intimacy that's worlds away from the big city.

The massive **Palais de Justice**, housing the law courts of modern Paris, holds echoes of the nation's earliest kings, who dwelt there, and of the aristocrats and Revolutionary leaders, who in turn were imprisoned there before execution.

It also conceals a superb Gothic masterpiece, the **Sainte-Chapelle**. The delicate walls of 13th-century stained glass (Paris's oldest) and harmonious proportions confer an ethereal quality upon the chapel, in startling contrast to the ponderous palace surrounding it. It was completed in 1248 by the sainted King Louis IX to house precious relics, such as Christ's crown of thorns. The 15 **stained-glass windows** depict 1,134 scenes from the Bible.

Between 1789 and 1815 the chapel served variously as a flour warehouse, a clubhouse for high-ranking dandies, and finally as an archive for Bonaparte's Consulate. That saved the chapel from projected destruction, because the bureaucrats couldn't think where else to put their mountains of paperwork. These days they find space in the endless corridors of offices around the courtrooms of the Palais and the *police judiciaire,* haunt of Inspector Maigret of the famous detective novels of Georges Simenon. The great *Salle des pas perdus* is worth a visit for a glimpse of the lawyers, plaintiffs, witnesses, court reporters, and hangers-on waiting nervously for the wheels of French justice to grind into action.

But their anxiety is nothing in comparison to the trepidation of those condemned to bide their time in the prison of the **Concierg-erie** during the Revolutionary Terror (1793–1794). Named after the royally appointed *concierge* in charge of common-law criminals, this dreaded "antechamber of the guillotine" welcomed Marie-Antoinette and Robespierre, Madame du Barry and Saint-Just, Danton and 2,500 others. Take the guided tour of the Galerie des Prisonniers. The Salle des Girondins displays a guillotine blade, the crucifix to which Marie-Antoinette prayed before execution, and the lock of Robespierre's cell. Look out on the Cour des Femmes, where husbands, lovers, wives, and mistresses were allowed one last tryst before the tumbrels came.

The site of the great cathedral of **Notre-Dame de Paris** has had a religious significance for at least 2,000 years. In Roman times a temple to Jupiter stood here, followed in the fourth century by the

---

Lucrative Sacrilege

After 1789, the Sainte-Chapelle remained intact, unlike many other churches. The destruction it narrowly avoided would not have been, as is too often believed, at the hands of violent, God-hating Revolutionaries. It would have been undertaken by peace-loving, profit-minded entrepreneurs who made a fortune during and long after the Revolution by dismantling churches and monasteries to build factories and houses from their masonry. Such, for instance, was the fate of the great abbeys of Jumièges in Normandy (see page 122) and Cluny in southern Burgundy (pages 113).

Undeniably, Revolutionary crowds did plunder the church's treasury, venting their spleen on a church that had for centuries taxed and exploited them, more for the clerics' personal benefit than for the spiritual welfare of their flock. The aesthetic considerations of later generations did not count for much during a revolution, either for the have-nots or for the haves.

first Christian church, Saint-Etienne. A second church, dedicated to Our Lady, joined it 200 years later. Both were left derelict by Norman invaders until Bishop Maurice de Sully authorized construction of the cathedral to replace them in 1163. The main part of Notre-Dame took 167 years to complete and, in its transition from Romanesque to Gothic, it has been called a perfect expression of medieval architecture. Few remain unimpressed by its majestic towers, spire, and breathtaking flying buttresses.

Despite its huge size, the cathedral achieves a remarkable balance in its proportions and harmony in its façade. The superb central **rose window**, encircling a statue of the Madonna and Child, depicts the Redemption after the Fall. Look for the **Galerie des Rois** across the top of the three doorways. The 28 statues representing the kings of Judah and Israel have been remodelled after the drawings of Viollet-le-Duc; the original ones were pulled down during the Revolution, since they were thought to be the kings of France. (The 21 heads discovered in 1977 are now displayed in the Musée de Cluny; see page 76.) Inside, the marvellous lighting is due in part to two more outsize rose windows dominating the transept. To the right of the entrance to the choir there is a lovely statue of the **Virgin and Child**.

As with many other Gothic masterpieces, the name of the first architect is unknown, but the renowned Pierre de Montreuil is credited with much of the 13th-century construction. During the 18th century, more damage was done by the "improvements" of redecorators of the *Ancien Régime* than by Revolutionary iconoclasts. For the present structure, we must be grateful to the great restorer-architect Eugène Viollet-le-Duc, who worked centimetre by centimetre over the whole edifice from 1845 to 1863. He was working in response to the public outcry started by Victor Hugo's novel, *Notre-Dame de Paris.*

The only original bell remaining is the South Tower's famous *bourdon,* whose much admired purity of tone was achieved by melting down its bronze and mixing it with gold and silver donated by

There's something disturbing about the sardonic smiles of the gargoyles up on Notre-Dame.

Louis XIV's aristocracy. Nowadays, the bells are operated not by a hunchback but by an electric bell-ringing system installed in 1953.

Ile Saint-Louis

Very much a world apart, the Ile Saint-Louis is an enchanted self-contained island of gracious living, long popular with the more affluent gentry and celebrities of Paris. In modern times, President Georges Pompidou lived here (on the quai de Béthune), much preferring it to the ponderous Elysée Palace. In the 17th-century **Hôtel Lambert**, on the corner of Rue Saint-Louis-en-l'Ile, Voltaire carried on a tempestuous affair with the lady of the house, the Marquise du Châtelet.

The island's fine church, **Saint-Louis-en-l'Ile**, is as elegant as the mansions — bright and airy with a golden light illuminating an attractive collection of Dutch, Flemish, and Italian 16th- and 17th-century art and some superb tapestries from the 12th century.

One of the most notable mansions is **Hôtel Lauzun** (17, quai d'Anjou), built in the 1650s by the great architect of Versailles, Louis Le Vau. Its highly ornamental interiors provided a perfect setting for the fantasies of the Club des Haschischins founded by Charles Baudelaire and Théophile Gautier.

Today, one of the island's greatest attractions is to buy an ice cream cone from the local merchant and stroll along the poplar-shaded streets to the western end of quai d'Orléans. There, you have a wonderful **view** of the apse of Notre-Dame

Left Bank

Latin Quarter

What's the origin of the name? Perfectly simple: from the 13th century, when the city's first university moved from the cloisters of Notre-Dame to the Left Bank, the young came to the *quartier* to learn Latin.

In those days *l'université* meant merely a collection of people — students who met on a street corner, or in a public square or courtyard, to hear a teacher lecture from a bench, or from an upstairs window or balcony. These days there are overcrowded classrooms, but

---

Right Moves

The neighbourhoods of the Left Bank trace from east to west the inexorable career of a successful Parisian intellectual — heart on the left, wallet on the right. The forces of protest and outright revolt have traditionally been nurtured in the *Quartier latin*, before subsiding into the lifelong scepticism voiced in the cafés of Saint-Germain-des-Prés. The rebels graduate from the university and move, if they prosper, west to the more genteel Faubourg Saint-Germain, closer to their publishers. If they hit the jackpot — a bestseller, their own law practice, even a ministry — they can move on to the more spacious apartments around the Champ-de-Mars, with a view of the Eiffel Tower for the kids. Without crossing the river to the notoriously snobbish 16th arrondissement, they can enjoy the same comforts and claim that they're still on the Left Bank.

the tradition of lively open-air discussion continues, often over an endlessly nursed coffee or glass of wine in one of the sidewalk cafés on the Boulevard Saint-Michel, in the streets around the faculty buildings, or in the ever-present cinema queues.

Begin with the **Place Saint-Michel**, where Paris students come to buy their textbooks and stationery, and the young of other countries come to sniff the Latin Quarter's mystique (and other more heady stuff) around the bombastic Second Empire fountain. Plunge into

An artist pedals his works around the old quarter.

the narrow streets of the Saint-Séverin quarter — to the east, Rue de la Huchette, Rue de la Harpe, and Rue Saint-Séverin — into a medieval world updated by the varied exotica of Turkish pastry shops, smoky Greek barbecues, and stuffy little cinemas. A moment's meditation in the exquisite 13th- to 15th-century Flamboyant Gothic church of Saint-Séverin, where Dante is said to have prayed, and you are ready to confront the Latin Quarter's citadel, the **Sorbonne**.

Founded in 1253 as a college for poor theological students by Robert de Sorbon, Louis IX's chaplain, it took shape as an embodiment of the university under the tutelage of Cardinal Richelieu. In the *grand amphithéâtre,* which seats 2,700, you can see the cardinal's statue, along with those of Descartes, Pascal, and Lavoisier.

As you contemplate Puvis de Chavannes' monumental painting on the back wall, allegorizing Poetry, Philosophy, History, Geology, and other academic disciplines, try to imagine 4,000 students packed into the hall in May 1968, arguing whether to have the whole thing plastered over. The student revolt against overcrowding, antiquated teaching, and stifling bureaucracy, seen as symbols of a dehumanized social system, made the Sorbonne a focal point of the movement. When the police invaded its precincts — which for centuries had guaranteed student immunity — the rebellion erupted into the streets.

Around the corner is the huge, domed, neoclassical **Panthéon**. It was originally intended as a church for Louis XV, but is now a secular mausoleum of some of the nation's greatest heroes. In the crypt are interred the remains of Voltaire and Rousseau, Hugo and Zola, assassinated Socialist leader Jean Jaurès, and Louis Braille, the inventor of the alphabet for the blind. The most recent hero to be so honoured was the World War II Resistance fighter, Jean Moulin.

Time for a break in the **Jardin du Luxembourg**. If you want to picnic in the park (sorry, not on the grass), make a detour first to the old street market behind the Panthéon on the **Rue Mouffetard**, old hunting-ground of Rabelais and Rabelaisians ever since. Despite their 17th-century origins, the Luxembourg Gardens avoid the rigid geometry of the Tuileries and Versailles. The horse chestnuts, beeches, and plane trees, the orangery and ornamental pond were a major inspiration for the bucolic paintings of Watteau.

Montparnasse

In the twenties, Montparnasse took over from Montmartre as the stomping ground of the capital's artistic colony, or at least of its avant-garde. American expatriates such as Hemingway, Fitzgerald, Gertrude Stein, John Dos Passos, and Theodore Dreiser also contributed to the free-living mystique.

While other quarters are known for their palaces and churches, Montparnasse (named after a 17th-century gravel mound since removed) has cafés and bars for its landmarks, most of them along the **Boulevard du Montparnasse**. The Closerie des Lilas, a centre for the French Symbolist poets at the turn of the century, served as a meeting-place for Lenin and Trotsky before World War I and for Hemingway and his pals after the war; the Select, the first all-night bar to open in Montparnasse, in 1925, quickly became a Henry Miller hang-out and continues resolutely to resist efforts to spruce it up; la Coupole, favourite of Sartre and Simone de Beauvoir, is still going strong, as much a living theatre as a restaurant; breakfast was consumed at the Dôme, for a change of air; and the Rotonde, favoured by Picasso, Vlaminck, and Modigliani, is back as a restaurant after a spell as a cinema. Around the corner, on Boulevard Raspail, is a splendid Rodin bronze of Balzac. Habitués just pretend not to see the monstrous 58-floor Tour Maine-Montparnasse office block by the railway station.

Saint-Germain-des-Prés

Saint-Germain-des-Prés is *the* literary quarter par excellence — home of major publishing houses, bookshops, and literary cafés, and the Académie Française. But it's also a charming neighbourhood for day-long people-watching and antiques-hunting or gallery-hopping.

The cafés around **Place Saint-Germain-des-Prés** act as the "village centre." On the north side is the Café Bonaparte, and on the west the famous les Deux Magots. Both provide ringside seats for the lively street theatre of mimes and musicians, who pass around the hat, and the neighbourhood eccentrics, who provide entertainment for free.

The Café de Flore up the boulevard has more intellectual aspirations, and a somewhat confusing ideological history. During the Dreyfus Affair it served as a base for the extreme right-wing Action Française; in 1914 for the Surrealists Apollinaire and André Salmon, who liked to provoke brawls; and, in the fifties, for Sartre's more peaceful left-wing existentialists, who never got enough sleep to find the energy to fight.

The **church** of Saint-Germain-des-Prés is an attractive mixture of Romanesque and Gothic, with an 11th-century clocktower. To the north of the church, the Rue Bonaparte takes you to the prestigious **Ecole des Beaux-Arts**. Incorporated in its structure are fragments of medieval and Renaissance architecture and sculpture. On the Rue des Beaux-Arts is the hotel (now simply but expensively called l'Hôtel) where Oscar Wilde died in 1900. He complained about the "horrible magenta flowers" of the wallpaper in his room, saying "one of us has to go." Now both have.

The **Institut de France**, handsome home of the august Académie Française, is on the quai Conti by the Pont des Arts. It was built by Louis Le Vau in 1668 to harmonize with the Louvre across the river. The academy was founded by Cardinal Richelieu to be the supreme arbiter of the French language.

Periodically decried as a bunch of prestigious old fuddy-duddies, the academy's 40 lifetime members are chosen in hotly contested elections to update its French dictionary, but are distinguished mostly for their acceptance speeches and fulsome obituaries. Guides to the Institut unfailingly point out the east pavilion, site of the 14th-century Tour de Nesle. They say Queen Jeanne de Bourgogne used to watch from there for likely young lovers whom she summoned for the night and then had thrown into the Seine.

☛ *Invalides–Eiffel Tower*

The massively monumental **Hôtel des Invalides** was built by Louis XIV as France's first national hospital for soldiers. Today it houses the **Musée de l'Armée** and is also the supreme celebration of the Emperor Napoleon, his body having been brought here from the island of Saint Helena in 1840.

Set in the crypt directly beneath the Invalides' soaring golden dome, **Napoleon's tomb** is awesomely elaborate. His body, dressed in the green uniform of the Chasseurs de la Garde, is encased in *six* coffins, one inside the other Chinese-box fashion. The innermost coffin is of iron, the next of mahogany, then two of lead, one of ebony, and the outer one of oak. The monument of red porphyry from Finland rests on a pedestal of green granite, encircled by 12 colossal Victory pillars sculpted by Pradier. Also in the crypt are the remains of Napoleon's son, brought to France from Vienna by Adolf Hitler in 1940.

The military complex continues with the Ecole Militaire and the spacious gardens of the **Champ-de-Mars**, once the site of military exercises and parades and the series of World's Fairs held between 1867 and 1937.

There are monuments that you can ignore and those you have to look at twice, and then there is the **Eiffel Tower**. Monuments usually celebrate heroes, or commemorate victories, or honour kings or saints; but the Eiffel Tower is a monument for its own sake, a proud gesture to the world, a witty structure that makes aesthetics irrelevant. Its construction for the World's Fair of 1889 was an astounding engineering achievement — 15,000 pieces of metal joined together by 2,500,000 rivets, soaring 300 metres (984 feet) into the air but standing on a base that is only 130 metres (1,400 feet) square.

Like many other World's Fair exhibits, the tower was slated for destruction in 1910. But nobody had the heart to go through with it, although there was no shortage of people who hated it.

The Eiffel Tower — visible from all over Paris, and recognized throughout the world.

Maupassant, for example, signed a manifesto against "this vertiginously ridiculous tower," and Verlaine rerouted his journey around Paris in order to avoid seeing it. Nowadays, everybody seems to love it. It has a splendid new inner illumination at night, a popular *brasserie* on the first platform, an elegant gourmet restaurant on the second, and a view from the top stretching more than 60 km (37 miles) on a pollution-free day.

Bois de Boulogne

These 900 hectares (2,224 acres) of parkland on the western edge of the city constitute one of Baron Haussmann's happier achievements. He transformed the old Rouvray forest, left completely wild until 1852, into the closest thing Paris has to a London-style park, with roads and paths for cycling and rambles, horse trails, boating lakes, restaurants and cafés with open-air dancing — and, in addition, the grand race course at Longchamp.

One of the main attractions is the **Parc de Bagatelle**, a walled garden with the city's most beautiful display of flowers. For the children, the **Jardin d'Acclimatation** offers a miniature railway, Punch

Schoolchildren using the "buddy-system" as they explore Bois de Boulogne.

I.M. Pei's pyramid provides a striking Louvre entrance.

and Judy show, house of distorting mirrors, pony rides, and a miniature farm of pigs, goats, and chickens.

Museums

The Louvre

The Louvre museum is so huge that people are sometimes frightened to go in at all. But you do not have to be an art fanatic to realize that to come to Paris without setting foot inside this great and truly beautiful palace would be a crime. No other museum has such a comprehensive collection of painting and sculpture. If you plan your visit right, it can be an exhilarating pleasure.

First of all, get up very early on a sunny day and walk across the gardens of the Place du Carrousel. Admire Maillol's nubile sculptures, which adorn the gardens, then sit on a bench to take in the sheer immensity of this former home of France's kings that is now a monumental showcase of so many of the world's great art treasures.

At the east end is the Cour Carrée, covering the original fortress built by Philippe Auguste in 1190 to protect Paris from river attack while he was away on a crusade. Stretching out from the Cour Carrée (of which you should see Perrault's marvellous colonnade on the east façade) are the additions of François I, Henri IV, Catherine de Médicis, Louis XIV, Napoleon I, and Napoleon III. Former president François Mitterrand's great glass pyramid in the Cour Napoléon completes eight centuries of construction.

This latest addition is designed by American architect I.M. Pei in order to provide a spectacular modern entrance, together with underground bookshops and cafés, at the centre of corridors leading to the various wings of the museum. Part of the palace's medieval foundations, disclosed during renovation, can also be seen.

François I, the Louvre's first major art collector, acquired four Raphaels, three Leonardo da Vincis, and one Titian (a portrait of the king himself). By 1793, when the leaders of the Revolution declared the palace a national museum, there were 650 works of art in the collection; there are now, it is estimated, some 173,000. So don't be depressed if you don't have time to see everything!

If you're planning several visits, you might like to concentrate on just one section at a time — the Italian, the French, the Spanish, the Flemish and Dutch, for example, but not forgetting the important sections devoted to ancient Egyptian, Greek, and Roman antiquities.

For an overall view of the museum's collections, we've attempted a small selection of highlights:

Egyptian: lion-headed goddess *Sekhmet* (1400 B.C.) and the colossal *Amenophis IV* (1370 B.C.).

Greek: the winged *Victory of Samothrace* and the beautifully proportioned *Venus de Milo.*

Italian: the sculpture of *Two Slaves* by Michelangelo; Leonardo da Vinci's fabled *Mona Lisa (La Joconde),* and his sublime *Virgin of the Rocks;* Titian's voluptuous *Woman at Her Toilet* and sombre *Entombment of Christ;* the poignant *Old Man and His Grandson* of Ghirlandaio.

French: Poussin's bittersweet *Arcadian Shepherds;* Watteau's hypnotically melancholy *Gilles* and graceful *Embarkation for*

Cythera; Delacroix's *Liberty Guiding the People;* and Courbet's penetrating study of provincial bourgeois life, *Funeral at Ornans.*

Dutch and Flemish: Rembrandt's cheerful *Self-Portrait with a Toque,* his beloved *Hendrickje Stoffels,* also portrayed nude in *Bathsheba Bathing;* Van Dyck's gracious, dignified *Charles I* of England; among the scores of Rubens, his tenderly personal *Helena Fourment;* Jordaens' *Four Evangelists* as diligent Dutchmen.

German: a gripping *Self-Portrait* by Dürer; Holbein's *Erasmus.*

Spanish: the uncompromising Velázquez portrait of ugly *Queen Marianna of Austria;* El Greco's powerfully mystic *Christ on the Cross;* Ribera's gruesomely good-humoured *The Club Foot.*

English: Gainsborough's exquisite *Conversation in a Park;* and Turner's atmospheric *Landscape with River and Bay.*

Beaubourg

The official name of one of Europe's most important cultural centres is Centre d'art et de culture Georges-Pompidou, or Centre Pompidou (after the French president whose pet project it was). But Parisians seem to have an aversion to naming major monuments after political leaders, so in all probability this bright and dynamic monster will continue to be known simply as Beaubourg, after the 13th-century neighbourhood that surrounds it. A combination of public library, modern-art museum, *cinémathèque,* children's workshop, industrial-design centre, experimental music laboratory, and open-air circus, it is the most popular show in town.

After an initial reaction similar to the delight and rage originally provoked by the Eiffel Tower, people have grown accustomed to the construction's resemblance to a multicoloured oil refinery. This comparison is readily accepted by the Centre Pompidou's architects, Italians Renzo Piano and Gianfranco Franchi and Englishman Richard Rogers, who deliberately left the building's service systems visible and colour-coded: red for the transportation, green for the water pipes, blue for the air-conditioning ducts, and yellow for the electrical system.

One of Beaubourg's simplest pleasures is just going up the escalators in the long glass tubes that run up the side of the building, watching the stunning view of Paris rooftops unfold. Or mingle with the cosmopolitan crowd outside watching the performers, artists, and fire-eaters at work.

Other Major Museums

Though physically part of the Louvre, the **Musée des Arts décoratifs** is a separate museum with its own entrance at 107, Rue de Rivoli. The rich permanent collection includes tapestries, furniture, and porcelain, but look out for the fascinating temporary exhibitions that are held here, featuring great styles and eras of design history such as Jugendstil, Bauhaus, and the American 1950s. Next door is the **Musée des Arts de la mode**, devoted to high fashion, the decorative art of which Paris is still the world capital.

Across the river, the 19th-century Orsay railway station has been transformed into the **Musée d'Orsay**. This exciting new museum embraces France's tremendous creativity from 1848 to 1914 in the domains of painting, sculpture, architecture and industrial design, advertising, newspapers, book publishing, photography, and the early years of the cinema. It also displays the collection of Impressionists and their followers transferred from the Jeu de Paume museum, which is now used for temporary exhibitions (see page 53).

On the river side of the Tuileries, the **Orangerie** is best known for its ground-floor rooms decorated with Monet's beautiful *Nymphéas* murals, offering a moment of repose after a hard day's sightseeing. But you should also take a look upstairs at the excellent Walter-Guillaume collection of works by Cézanne, Renoir, Utrillo, Douanier Rousseau, and Picasso.

Another quite recent addition to the roster of Paris museums is the long-awaited **Musée Picasso** at 5, Rue de Thorigny, in the Marais (*métro* Saint-Paul). From the private collections of Picasso's heirs, the museum has received more than 200 paintings and 158 sculptures, in addition to hundreds of drawings, engravings, ceramics, and models for theatre décors and costumes. Also on display is Picasso's personal collection of masterworks by fellow artists Braque, Matisse, Miró, Degas, Renoir, and Rousseau. Splendidly housed in the Hôtel Salé, a beautifully restored 17th-century mansion, the museum offers an extremely moving portrait of the man, his family, his mistresses, and friends, with letters, manuscripts, photo albums, notebooks, his French Communist Party membership card, bullfight tickets, and some holiday postcards.

Converted from the old Orsay railway station, the Musée d'Orsay is a must-see.

After years of renovation, the **Musée Jacquemar-André** reopened to the public in 1996. Housed in the elegant residence of a famous 19th-century collector, at 158 Boulevard Haussmann, the museum displays one of France's finest gatherings of Italian Renaissance art, in much the same spirit as New York's Frick Collection or London's Wallace Collection.

La Villette — in the northeast corner of the city (*métro* Porte de la Villette) — has been converted from the world's biggest slaughterhouse into a futuristic complex of cultural and scientific activities.

Refusing to call itself a museum, La Villette's **Cité des sciences et de l'industrie** puts the accent on public participation in all phases of space technology, computers, astronomy, and marine biology. The unabashed functionalism of its architecture carries the Beaubourg principle to a logical conclusion. Its most attractive symbol is the shining stainless steel **Géode** sphere containing a revolutionary cinema with a hemispheric screen 36 metres (118 feet) in diameter. There's also a giant rock-concert hall, **le Zénith**, situated alongside an avant-garde musical counterpart to the scientific "city," the **Cité de la musique**.

In the Palais de Chaillot (Trocadéro), the **Musée de l'Homme** is devoted to man's prehistory, and the fascinating **Musée du Cinéma** has reconstructed sets and studios, historic posters, original scripts, costumes of Garbo and Catherine Deneuve, John Wayne's hat and Rudolf Valentino's jellaba.

Then there are also: the **Musée de Cluny** (6, Place Paul-Painlevé, *métro* Maubert-Mutualité), for the great *Lady with the Unicorn* tapestry and also for sculpture of Paris's Roman and Gothic past; **Musée Guimet** (6, Place d'Iéna), a superb collection of Indian, Japanese, and Chinese art; **Musée de l'Affiche** (18, Rue de Paradis), for advertising posters of the past and present.

Many museums are devoted to the work of just one artist, the most fascinating of these being **Musée Rodin** (at 77, Rue de Varenne), with its lovely sculpture garden and useful children's play area. Others well worth visiting include the home of **Balzac** (at 47, Rue Raynouard) and **Delacroix's** studio (at 6, Rue de Furstenberg).

Fountains and Fireworks

Beginning at 3:30 pm on three Sundays a month, from May to September, the *grandes eaux* of the Apollo, Neptune, and Dragon fountains are turned on. The spectacular display recaptures some of the splendour of festivities at the court of the Sun King. There are also several special nighttime floodlit shows with fireworks. Details (and reservations for the firework displays) can be obtained from the Versailles Office de Tourisme, 7, rue des Réservoirs, tel. 01.39.50.36.22.

ILE-DE-FRANCE
Versailles

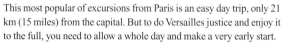

This most popular of excursions from Paris is an easy day trip, only 21 km (15 miles) from the capital. But to do Versailles justice and enjoy it to the full, you need to allow a whole day and make a very early start.

Organized bus tours start at the Tuileries Gardens, on the Rue de Rivoli side. However, the palace and gardens are so enormous that you may prefer to see them at your own pace, leaving out what your head and feet can't take.

With a little planning, you can transform an otherwise tiring day into a delightful treat. Try the following agenda: early start at a Paris street market to buy a picnic (better than the Versailles tourist traps); morning tour of the palace; stroll through the palace gardens to lunch beside the Grand Canal; siesta and tea in the gardens of the

---

Statistics of Grandeur

Not just a whim of megalomania, building Versailles was Louis XIV's cold political decision to force his hitherto obstreperous nobles into submission by impoverishing them with permanent attendance at his court. Designed to lodge 3,000 courtiers and servants, the palace took 50 years to build, spanning the whole of his reign. It was still incomplete at his death.

Louis Le Vau and Jules Hardouin-Mansart were the architects, while Charles Le Brun directed the interior design and monumental sculpture, and André Le Nôtre laid out the gardens. Of the 36,000-strong work force (plus 6,000 horses), 227 men died on the job.

The 115 hectares (280 acres) of gardens and parkland are only a tenth of what had to be tended for the Sun King, including 150,000 flower plants that were changed 15 times a year.

And it all cost 65 million livres (French pounds). Exorbitant, says any self-respecting anti-royalist — but to put it into perspective, it's been calculated as the equivalent of what republican France spends on just one aircraft carrier and was in any case a spit in the ocean compared with the 3,000 million that Louis XIV spent on his wars.

Petit Trianon; finally, wander back across the palace gardens for a last sunset view of the great château.

The Palace

If you don't already have a clear idea of what kind of man Louis XIV was, take a long, hard look at his palace. Never did a piece of architecture more exactly express the personality of its builder than the Château de Versailles does — extravagant, pompous, dazzling, formidable, glorious, and vain.

Louis XIII had hoped to make his favourite hunting lodge a modest retirement home. But his son turned Versailles into a self-centred universe that was far from modest, proclaiming his own grandeur in a vast, sprawling edifice of stone and brick, marble, gilt, and crystal.

The palace has been splendidly restored since World War I with the help of private contributions, most notably from John D. Rockefeller. Wherever the original furnishings and decoration were missing, superb appropriate equivalents have been installed.

As you make your way through the gilded gates and cross the vast Cour des Ministres where the state secretaries worked, past the imperious statue of Himself to the main entrance on the right of the Cour Royale, you realize it wasn't Mussolini who invented the Long Walk to intimidate his underlings seeking an audience.

Inside, the self-guided tour is instantly more reassuring. You begin at the intimate little **Royal Chapel**, a gem of High Baroque that has a harmonious décor of white marble with gilded altar and balustrades. You get the king's-eye view looking down into the nave where the courtiers worshipped.

In the rooms of the **Grands Appartements**, named after the gods and goddesses whom Louis felt to be his appropriate companions, the king entertained his courtiers three times a week: Monday, Wednesday, and Thursday.

The **Salon de Diane** was a billiard room — not many people could beat Fast Louis. The table's gone, but Bernini has left a superb bust of the champion at 27. The ceiling painting of the Sun King in his chariot and pictorial references to Alexander the Great and Augustus Caesar make it abundantly clear the **Salon d'Apollon** was Louis XIV's throne room.

But by far the most astonishing of these royal apartments is the glittering **Galerie des Glaces** (Hall of Mirrors), 73 metres (240 feet) long, built to catch every ray of the setting sun in the 17 tall arched panels of mirrors. This was the palace's grandest reception hall, where the king gave his wildest parties and received his most important foreign envoys. Le Brun's paintings depict Louis XIV's wars in Holland and his more peaceful achievements at home.

In the **Queen's Bedroom**, 19 royal children were born, many of them — as was the custom — with members of the public looking on.

On a separate guided tour, you can visit the marvellous **Royal Opera** of Louis XV, and the king's private apartments. The **King's Bedroom**, with two portraits by Van Dyck, is set at the exact centre of the sun's path from east to west. The court was encouraged to come every day to witness the monarch's rising from bed and moment of retirement. Louis XIV died here in 1715 of gangrene of the leg.

The Gardens

If English and Japanese gardens attempt, in their different ways, to enhance nature by "tidying it up" while imitating a "natural" landscape, the French garden, of which Versailles is the supreme expression, quite deliberately imposes a formal pattern.

Resuming a tradition of classical Rome, André Le Nôtre used the paths and avenues of trees and statuary to divide flowerbeds, ponds, and fountain basins into intricate geometric patterns. Pause for a moment at the palace's western terrace alongside the Galerie des Glaces for a first view of his harmonious, subtly asymmetrical arrangement of the grounds.

As you make your way through the gardens, look back occasionally at the changing perspectives of the palace. Directly beyond the western terrace is the Axe du Soleil (Path of the Sun) leading down to the **Bassin d'Apollon** (Louis XIV's solar obsession is quite unavoidable). Adorned with sculptures of Greek mythology, this and the great **Bassin de Neptune** and **Bassin du Dragon** in the northeast corner served as centrepieces for royal garden parties.

Beyond the Bassin d'Apollon is the **Grand Canal**, on which the King kept his Venetian gondolas. Today, small boats are available for you to row yourself.

To the northwest of the château, the **Grand Trianon** palace, surrounded by pleasantly unpompous gardens, was the home of Louis XIV's mistress, Madame de Maintenon, where the aging king increasingly took refuge.

The picturesque **Petit Trianon**, where Marie-Antoinette tried to hide from that nasty Revolution, has the allure of a doll's house in comparison with the rest of Versailles. Its gardens, with ponds, mounds, and shady woods, are English in style; a relaxing change from the formality of the château. The childlike playfulness of the doomed queen's hideaway is reinforced by her **Hameau**, a hamlet of thatched cottages where she and her retinue pretended to be milkmaids and farm boys.

Stained-glass detail — one of the countless intricacies of Chartres cathedral.

Chartres

One of the most moving experiences that you will encounter on a journey across France is to drive through the wheat fields of the fertile Beauce plain, some 50 km (30 miles) south of Paris, and see, looming suddenly on the horizon, the silhouette of **Chartres cathedral**.

This unquestionable masterpiece of French civilization marks the transition in the 12th century from the solid, sober Romanesque style of the Church's beginnings to the more airy, assertive Gothic of its ascendancy. Apart from a few decapitated statues, it came miraculously unscathed through the Wars of Religion and the Revolution.

As you face the harmoniously asymmetrical western façade, the southern tower, the **Clocher Vieux**, is a supreme expression of Romanesque simplicity, whereas the taller northern tower, the **Clocher Neuf**, is already lighter, with its slender, more ornate steeple.

On the central porch, the **Portail Royal**, note the stately, deliberately elongated sculptures of Old Testament figures — in contrast to the freer, more vigorous statuary that adorns the church's northern and southern porches.

Inside, the supreme glory of the cathedral is its 173 **stained-glass windows**. Their unique "Chartres blue" and deep red bring an ethereal light into the nave, especially when the late-afternoon sun is shining through the western rose window depicting the Last Judgment. Among the oldest and most famous of the windows, on the southern side of the choir, is an enthroned Mary with Jesus on her lap, **Notre-Dame de la Belle Verrière**. The church is dedicated to Mary, representing her 175 times in the various sculptures and windows.

In the paving of the centre aisle of the nave you'll notice a large circular **labyrinth**. Medieval worshippers traced its path, from the circumference to the centre, as part of a mystic spiritual exercise.

Back outside, from the Episcopal Garden *(Jardin de l'Evêché)*, at the rear of the cathedral, a stairway takes you down to the **old town**. Its streets of attractive 16th- and 17th-century houses, built along the banks of the Eure river, afford a pretty view of the cathedral.

Fontainebleau

The great forest just south of Paris was favourite hunting country for both François I and Henri IV, and their **palace** is an elegant monument to their Renaissance tastes. Napoleon cherished it as a place for reflection, and it was at Fontainebleau that he abdicated in 1814 to go into a first exile on the Isle of Elba.

Allegorical paintings in the **Galerie de François Ier** bear testimony to the king's preoccupation with war and death, and also to the sanctity of kingship. **Napoleon's apartments** have recently been refurbished with the furnishings of his empire, and a new Napoleonic museum has been installed in the Louis XV wing.

But save most of your time and energy for exploring the majestic **Forest of Fontainebleau** — 25,000 hectares (over 60,000 acres) of oak, beech, silver birch, pine, chestnut, and hornbeam (*charme*).

Apart from the delightful walks and indeed lengthy hikes over well-marked paths, a great attraction is the miniature mountain range of sheer rockfaces and cliffs, much appreciated by apprentice climbers for trying out their equipment and technique before tackling the Alps. The most popular are the rugged Gorges de Franchard, due west of the palace — whereas the Gorges d'Apremont (near the little town of **Barbizon**, famed as a haunt of 19th-century landscape painters) tend to be less crowded.

Skewered

One day in April, 1671, Louis XIV visited Chantilly with 5,000 — yes, 5,000 — friends for a three-day stay. The Condé family's brilliant but highly sensitive master chef, Vatel, went berserk earning his title of *Contrôleur général de la Bouche de Monsieur le Prince* (General Supervisor of the Prince's Mouth). Bad enough on the first night when three tables had to go without their roast. When the fresh fish failed to arrive the next day, Vatel went up to his room and ran himself through with his sword.

A royal treat at Fontainebleau, even if not quite the kind of carriage that François I used.

Chantilly

Fifty km (30 miles) to the north of Paris, Chantilly is celebrated for its château, its elegant racecourse and stables — and, not least, for the *crème chantilly* (whipped cream) served at the château gates on hot waffles.

The **château**, which belonged to the powerful Condé dynasty in the 17th century, consists of a not ugly but somewhat bastard reconstruction of the great edifice destroyed in the Revolution — known as the Grand Château — joined to the charming, authentic Renaissance building called the Petit Château.

The main body of the château houses the **Musée Condé**, a superb collection of Italian, French, and Dutch masters, including works by Raphael, Veronese, Fra Angelico, Poussin, and Watteau, and portraits by Clouet, Van Dyck, and Teniers. One of the charms of the collection is that the paintings are hung not in any classical order but according to the personal whim of their last owner, the Duke of Aumale.

The palace grounds are a pleasant place for a walk, especially the English Garden behind the Petit Château. Louis XIV was very envious of the Grand Canal, ponds, and waterfalls designed by André Le Nôtre and insisted the master gardener do even better at Versailles. You may prefer the more intimate scale of Chantilly.

In June, the **Hippodrome**, west of the château, is host to the prestigious Prix du Jockey Club horse race. But all year round, you can visit the monumental 18th-century **Grandes-Ecuries** (stables), now a horse museum — with live horses contentedly munching hay next to wooden statues.

Senlis

For your first taste of unspoiled village life, just a quick 50 km (30-mile) drive north from Paris, visit the charming little town of Senlis, with its imposing Gothic **cathedral** and handsome 15th- and 16th-century houses, still partly encircled by Gallo-Roman ramparts. The finely sculpted porch on the cathedral's western façade inspired the design for Chartres cathedral and also for Paris's Notre-Dame.

Compiègne

Some 80 km (50 miles) up the autoroute du Nord from Paris, Compiègne is another classical Ile-de-France royal hunting forest and palace. In addition to being Marie-Antoinette's last home, the **palace** was a favourite of Napoleon III and his wife Eugénie, whose extravagant memorabilia constitute the **Musée du Second-Empire**.

Also in the palace is a fascinating **Musée de la Voiture**. It displays all kinds of vehicles, from the coach that carried Napoleon to and from Moscow in 1812 to a splendid 4-horsepower Renault car from 1904 and other turn-of-the-century classics.

The **Forest of Compiègne** offers plenty of good walking; or, if you prefer to ride, you can hire a horse at the village of Saint-Jean-aux-Bois. The forest is famous for its **Clairière de l'Armistice,** where, in Marshal Foch's private railway carriage, the Germans signed the Armistice that marked their defeat in 1918. Twenty-two years later, Hitler obliged the French to sign their capitulation in the same place.

NORTHEAST

The invaders pouring over the northern and eastern frontiers these days tend to be peaceful — tourists from Britain, the Netherlands, Belgium, and Germany. But the plains and plateaux of Flanders and Picardy, Alsace, and Lorraine have historically been the arenas of bloody war.

During the Hundred Years' War, England knew its days of glory on the Picardy fields of Crécy and Azincourt (Agincourt). For Louis XIV's wars against the Netherlands, the military architect Vauban built a line of fortifications in the frontier towns, at Calais, Dunkerque, Douai, Valenciennes, and — still visible — the great citadel at Lille.

In more recent times, Flanders and the river valleys of the Somme and Marne were the major battlefields of World War I. Alsace and Lorraine suffered humiliating conquest at Wissembourg and Metz in 1870 and then again in 1940, but witnessed the resurrection of the French Army at the Liberation.

The windswept countryside is dotted with poignant memorials and military cemeteries. The villages have a hardy charm, and the larger towns, Arras and Amiens to the north, Nancy and Strasbourg to the east, exude great civic pride. Linking north and east, the fields of Champagne and its royal city of Reims have also known their wars, but today prefer, for our greater joy, to bask in bubbly.

Deeper into the interior, Burgundy is a more solidly implanted heartland. Most famous today for its vineyards, it was historically the stronghold of the dukes of Dijon, alongside the ecclesiastical empires of the Cluny and Cistercian monasteries and their great Romanesque churches.

To the east, the Jura mountains of Franche-Comté offer visitors invigorating hikes through dense forests and along the rivers of the valley landscapes celebrated in the paintings of Gustave Courbet.

PICARDY

If you're coming into France from the English Channel or across the Belgian border, and you have time, don't just rush straight down the *autoroute* to Paris. Picardy has plenty of interesting stops and even some worthwhile short detours for a more leisurely journey.

Saint-Omer

Prosperous from the textile industry since the Middle Ages, the town emerged from bombardment in two world wars with a gentle serenity unusual for the austere north.

Once a cathedral, the 13th-century **Basilique Notre-Dame** dominates the town with an imposing grandeur. Note the fine stone sculptures of the Virgin and a Last Judgment over the south porch. Inside, the marble and alabaster treasures evoke the wealth of the diocese in the 16th and 17th centuries, particularly the elaborate chapel screens and, in the northern arm of the transept, an intricate astronomical clock. Nearby, the 13th-century sculpted figures of the *Grand Dieu de Thérouanne* are strangely foreshortened — as they were originally intended to be seen from below (on another church).

The **Hôtel Sandelin** museum is well worth a visit, both for the splendid 18th-century mansion, with its Louis XV furnishings, and for its rich collections of porcelain from all over the world. The Saint-Omer decorative glazed earthenware *(faïence)* is a major feature, and the Delft collection is outstanding, not only for its celebrated blue ware but also for some exquisite polychrome pieces.

Tobacco fanatics and non-smokers alike will love the museum's display of more than 2,000 terra-cotta pipes. The enamelled bowls depict demons and dogs, Napoleon and Jesus, and quite a few naughty scatological and erotic scenes.

Le Touquet

In order to attract a clientèle from the capital, this seaside resort added the name Paris-Plage. It might more aptly have called itself Knightsbridge-Plage, being a pure creation of London's smart set at the end of the 19th century, when swimming became all the rage. Today it's something of a nicely faded museum piece, but the sailing and windsurfing are good, and the riding, golf, and tennis in Le Touquet are splendid. In the lovely **forest**, you'll find elegant Tudor-style timbered villas that it's more diplomatic to call "Anglo-Norman."

Arras

This is the place celebrated among British schoolchildren for the tapestry through which Hamlet stabbed poor old Polonius. The town, just off the *autoroute* from Calais, has two of the most beautiful city squares in France. The classical Flemish style of the 17th- and 18th-century arcades and of the gabled façades of the **Grande Place** and the **Place des Héros** invites comparison with the great squares of Brussels and Bruges.

Amiens

The majestic **cathedral** of Picardy's capital is without doubt an authentic masterpiece of French Gothic architecture. Its construction was almost completed in a mere 44 years in the middle of the 13th century; as a result it was possible to maintain a homogeneous architectural style. Miraculously the cathedral's noble silhouette escaped unharmed from the heavy air raids of World War II.

Its glory is the oak carving of the 110 **choir stalls**, the work of great 16th-century cabinet-makers whose names — Jean Turpin, Alexandre de Heudebourg, Arnould Boulin — deserve mention alongside their more celebrated contemporaries of the Italian Renaissance. Dramatically depicting more than 400 scenes from the Old and New testaments, 3,650 figures present a magnificent pageant of the customs and costume of the people of François I. Among the panels of Cain and Abel, Abraham and Isaac, Jesus and Mary, all very Flemish figures, are carvings of a Picardy baker, dairymaid, fruitmonger, and laundress.

The **Musée de Picardie** (48, Rue de la République) has a good collection of paintings, most notably a couple of Van Goyen landscapes, El Greco's *Portrait of a Man*, a witty self-portrait of Quentin

Joy from Trouble with Bubbles

Ever since Roman times, the wine growers of Champagne knew they had a good product. But until the end of the 17th century, they had a problem with bubbles, which they had the devil of a time getting rid of. Then a monk named Dom Pérignon, cellar master at the abbey of Hautvillers, decided he liked this bubbly stuff and found a way of stabilizing it by blending it with other wines and adding an exact dose of sugar. Mere technique — the *méthode champenoise* — is not enough, however, to make real Champagne.

There are only 23,000 hectares (57,000 acres) of true Champagne vineyards — 1.5% of the national total — and their grapes alone, red and white, are authorized to go into a Champagne bottle. The white chardonnay grapes growing south of Epernay on the Côte des blancs, bring the light, fresh note; the pinot noir on the Montagne de Reims add body; and the pinot meunier west of Epernay add a dash of fruitiness. You'll find these grapes all over the wine-growing world, but only the Champagne region has that special chalky soil, not only for the vineyards, but also for the vaults of the cellars.

The wine growers harvest their grapes in October and bring them to the underground galleries of the major producers for pressing and a first fermentation that turns the sugar into alcohol. By the New Year, a clear wine, usually 75% red and 25% white grapes, is ready for the all-important cuvée, the cellar master's secret blend with up to 30 other wines that gives each label its distinctive taste. Natural yeasts and a small amount of cane sugar are added prior to bottling and a second, slower fermentation, which lasts about three months. The wine is then left to age. Every day the bottles are turned alternately one-eighth to the left or right, to remove the deposits that attach to the sides. This takes at least a year — or three for a vintage, *millésime,* after an outstanding harvest, when older wines are not needed for the cuvée. From time to time the bottles are carefully shaken to bring the deposit up to the top. This is removed by freezing, before the addition of *liqueur de dosage* — a mixture of cane sugar in vintage Champagne, which determines the degree of "dryness" — extra sec, demi sec, or brut.

Topped with a fresh new cork, wire muzzle, and shiny little seal, that, at last, ladies and gentlemen, is Champagne. Cheers!

de La Tour, and François Boucher's erotic pink nymphs.

CHAMPAGNE

In the great French lexicon of good living, no word is more loaded with magic than Champagne. Magic in the miraculous conjunction of geology, topography, and climate that has produced the world's most celebrated wine.

In this northernmost of France's wine-producing regions, which enjoys a bright mellow summer and mild winter, the Champagne country around Reims and Epernay has ideal south-facing slopes to exploit every last ray of sun, together with just the right chalky soil to store and release the requisite heat and humidity among the vines.

Of Reims cathedral's sculptures, the Smiling Angel is famous as a symbol of the town's hospitality.

Add the ingenuity of the cellar masters who concoct the magic potion, and you have the makings of a very good party. The great manufacturers will be glad to give you a glimpse of how they do it. You'll also have ample opportunity to sample their products.

Reims

If Champagne is the wine of kings, then Reims is the town that consecrated the divine right of kingship. It was here, at the end of the fifth century, that Saint Rémi is believed to have baptized the pagan

Clovis, and here again that Hugues Capet was anointed and crowned first king of France in 987. It was a major achievement of Joan of Arc to have Charles VII crowned at Reims cathedral in 1429. Charles X, last of the Bourbons, sought the same divine legitimacy in 1825 with a Reims coronation.

The magnificently proportioned 13th-century **cathedral** was badly damaged by fire in World War I, but it has been well restored and it remains one of the country's greatest Gothic edifices. Try to see its lovely buff stone façade in the late afternoon sun, armed with a pair of binoculars to study the rich sculpture of the Gallery of Kings high above the windows.

In the interior, the most noteworthy of the surviving 13th-century **stained-glass windows** are the rose window above the western entrance, illustrating the life of the Virgin Mary, and the one devoted to the Creation in the north arm of the transept. Directly beyond the altar is the **Chagall chapel**, in which the Russian artist connects his Jewish origins to the Christian religion with a window depicting Abraham and Jesus.

The originals of the cathedral's major sculptures are on display next door in the museum of the archbishop's residence, the **Palais du Tau**. The most famous pieces are the Smiling Angel, symbol of Reims hospitality, and the allegorical figure of the Synagogue, blindfolded because it was felt that the Jews were too stubborn to behold the truth of Christianity.

For an hour's tour of the city's **Champagne cellars**, you can get details at the Office de tourisme, 2, Rue Guillaume de Machault, Reims, telephone: 03.26.77.45.25. The cellars are in fact 250 km (155 miles) of galleries quarried out of the city's chalk foundations back in the days of Roman Gaul. Practically all the major Champagne labels offer tours. Piper-Heidsieck has a little train; Ruinart, the oldest, is organized on three levels; Taittinger is partly installed in the crypt of a demolished abbey, and Mumm is one of the few to give free samples at the end of visits.

Epernay

The town's advantage over Reims is that you can combine a visit to its cellars — Moët & Chandon or Mercier — with a drive southward along the great **Côte des blancs** vineyards that produce the white chardonnay grapes. The prettiest view of the vines and the Marne Valley is just 10 km (6 miles) down the D 10 at **Cramant**.

Also out of town, you can see a reconstitution of Dom Pérignon's famous 17th-century cellar and laboratory in the abbey museum of **Hautvillers**, just 6 km (4 miles) north of Epernay.

LORRAINE

A region of strategic importance guarding the eastern approaches to Paris, Lorraine has long been a pawn in France's perennial conflicts with Germany. Amid the resulting devastations of war and the more-recent depression of the region's declining coal, iron, and steel industries, the historic town of Nancy stands out as a gleaming survivor. Its golden 18th-century architecture makes it a rewarding stopover on any journey between Paris and Alsace.

Nancy

Head straight for **Place Stanislas**. Surrounded by elegant classical mansions and gilded wrought-iron grilles with ornamental gateways, which frame the marble fountains of Neptune and Amphitrite, the square is one of the most harmonious urban spaces in Europe.

Visit the **hôtel de ville** (in the largest of the mansions) for its fine staircase — designed by the same Jean Lamour who created the wrought-iron grilles — but above all for the marvellous view it offers of the square. In the centre stands a statue of the man responsible, King Stanislas Leszczyński of Poland.

Deposed by the Russians in 1736, Stanislas had the good fortune to be Louis XV's father-in-law and was given the Duchy of Lorraine as compensation. He expressed his gratitude by devoting the rest of his life to refurbishing a town devastated by the Thirty Years' War of the previous century.

The square's grand, spacious effect is completed to the north by an **arc de triomphe** (dedicated to Louis XV) at the entrance to the long **Place de la Carrière** — also graced by 18th-century mansions and Jean Lamour's iron grilles.

At the end of the *place* — in the Grande Rue — a splendid Renaissance doorway is all that remains to remind us of the former glory of the old ducal palace. Inside the palace, the **Musée historique lorrain** offers a fascinating glimpse of Nancy before Stanislas. Jacques Callot's horrifying engravings of the Thirty Years' War have their antidotes in the more serene paintings of Georges de La Tour.

Stroll back to the Place Stanislas through the **Pépinière** gardens. In the northwest corner you can see Rodin's statue of the great 18th-century landscape painter who is most widely known by his pseudonym, Claude Lorrain (or, in Britain, Lorraine), although his name was originally Claude Gellée.

The **Musée des Beaux-Arts**, at 3 Place Stanislas, has a good collection of European art — notably Tintoretto, Ruysdael, Van Goyen, Ribera, and Rubens, with the French represented by Delacroix, Courbet, Bonnard, and Manet.

ALSACE

One of the reasons why the Germans and the French have always fought for possession of this province is very simply that it's such a good place to live. Rich farmland, vineyards, and dense forest, with the solidly protective Vosges mountain range on one side and the great Rhine river on the other, combine to make Alsace a nicely self-contained region.

The turmoils of history have left a dialect and an architecture of unmistakably Germanic origin, a political tradition indelibly marked by the French Revolution, and a cuisine that subtly mixes the two

Alsace or Elsaß?

The French base their historical claim on the lands of their Gallic ancestors for whom, with Julius Caesar's blessing, Germany began on the other side of the Rhine. The Germans claim the territory as an inheritance of the German-controlled Holy Roman Empire after the death of Charlemagne.

Nominally under the Germans throughout the Middle Ages, Alsace was submerged among hundreds of petty German principalities until it became a vital buffer zone in the Franco-German rivalry.

After the Thirty Years' War, Alsace was more than happy to accept French protection — consecrated by Louis XIV's formal acquisition of Strasbourg in 1681. The Revolution of 1789 was decisive in injecting the French language and customs into Alsatian life. The *Marseillaise* was composed in Strasbourg in 1792 for the French Army of the Rhine (later it was adopted by the volunteers of Marseille). Alsace provided some of Napoleon's most distinguished generals — Kléber, Kellermann, and Rapp.

When the Germans seized Alsace in the war of 1870, thousands of Alsatians preferred exile in Algeria, or elsewhere in France. But the province of Elsaß prospered under Kaiser Wilhelm, and not everybody was delighted in 1918 by the welcome back to France's chaotic Third Republic.

The Third Reich helped most of the skeptics change their minds. Under the Nazis, the French language was outlawed. Names had to be changed (from Charles to Karl, Jean to Hans), French-style wreaths were forbidden in cemeteries, *baguettes* and *berets* —"this ridiculous headgear, totally un-Germanic" were banned. Alsace was supposed to disappear as a distinct cultural entity and become part of an administrative district of Oberrheingau.

Today no province waves the French flag more fervently than Alsace. But Alsatian workers don't hesitate to commute across the border into Germany for higher salaries; and the two- and three-star restaurants of Ammerschwihr, Strasbourg, and Illhaeusern are overflowing with German customers.

nations. The people seem to feel neither more German nor more French, just Alsatian — the best of both worlds.

This seems highly appropriate for a region that houses the European Parliament in its capital city, Strasbourg. Make your base here or in Colmar for excursions into the surrounding wine country and its spotless medieval villages.

Strasbourg

The city has emerged handsome, if not unscathed, from its troubled past. Many Gothic and Renaissance buildings have been lovingly restored. The *Weinstuben* (wine bars) of its old neighbourhoods are hospitable gathering places for university students whose predecessors include Goethe and Bonaparte.

It's a good town for walking the narrow streets, or for taking a **boat cruise** on the river Ill, which divides into two branches to loop the historic centre. Launches start from the Pont Sainte-Madeleine behind the Château des Rohan.

The celebrated asymmetrical silhouette of the magnificent Gothic **cathedral**, with its single tower and steeple rising on the northern side of its façade, gives your tour of the city an inspiring start.

When Goethe arrived in Strasbourg for the first time, he just dropped his bag at his hostel, Zum Geist, and rushed off to visit the cathedral. The stout-limbed can follow his example, and start by climbing the 300-odd stairs to the platform just below the steeple for a fine **view** over the city.

Combining the architectural style of Ile-de-France Gothic with Rhenish German sculpture, the cathedral is an apt symbol of Alsatian culture. The original designer, Erwin von Steinbach, began the pink Vosges sandstone façade in 1277, but only got as far as the splendid **Gallery of Apostles** over the central rose window.

Goethe marvelled at the asymmetrical silhouette of Strasbourg's imposing Gothic cathedral.

*Strasbourg's Petite France is a haven
of peace in the modern city.*

Ulrich von Ensingen — the master builder of the great cathedral
of Ulm — began construction of the octagon of the north tower in
1399. The graceful openwork spire was added in the 15th century by
Johannes Hültz of Cologne. The French Revolutionaries threatened
to tear the steeple down because it offended their principle of equality, but were reassured when one of the townsmen coiffed the spire
with a patriotic red-white-and-blue bonnet. All traces of an ugly
19th-century attempt to "balance" it with a second tower have been
removed.

The Revolutionaries couldn't be dissuaded from destroying most
of the cathedral's statues, although 67 were saved (many of the originals are now housed in the Musée de l'Oeuvre Notre-Dame next
door). The central porch is still intact, depicting Jesus's entry into
Jerusalem, the Crucifixion, and other scenes from the Bible.

Inside stands a formidable Flamboyant Gothic **pulpit**, built for
the preacher Geiler von Kaysersberg to match his terrifying fulmi-
nations against the Protestant Reformation. Among the cathedral's
admirable 12th- to 14th-century **stained-glass windows** in the
nave and northern aisle there are portraits of medieval German emperors.

The great popular attraction, situated in the southern arm of the transept, approached through the Portail de l'Horloge, is the 19th-century **astronomical clock** in which Death and all kinds of other jolly little figures parade around the dial to announce 12 noon. For some reason this happens at 12:30 P.M., but in the summer get there at noon anyway, or you won't see a thing. Then after everyone's gone, stay on to see the marvellous 13th-century sculpted **Angel's Pillar** *(Pilier des Anges)* in peace.

A sound-and-light *(Son et Lumière)* show is held at the cathedral in summertime, both in German and in French, recounting 2,000 years of the city's history.

On the Place de la Cathédrale, at the beginning of the Rue Mercière, stands the 13th-century **Pharmacie du Cerf** (Stag Pharmacy), older than the cathedral and reputedly the oldest pharmacy in France. The other venerable house in the square, now a restaurant, is the **Maison Kammerzell**. The ground floor dates from 1467, and the beautifully sculpted wooden façade of the superstructure from 1589.

Guardian of the city's medieval and Renaissance treasures, the **Musée de l'Oeuvre Notre-Dame** is itself made up of a superb group of 14th-, 16th-, and 17th-century houses around a secluded Gothic garden on the Place du Château, south of the cathedral. Besides sheltering the most vulnerable of the cathedral's statuary and some stained-glass windows from the earlier 12th-century Romanesque building, the museum has a fine collection of Alsatian medieval painting by Konrad Witz, Martin Schongauer, and Hans Baldung Grien.

In the midst of the predominantly Germanic old city centre, the **Château des Rohan**, the classical 18th-century residence that was the home of Strasbourg's princes and cardinals, makes an emphatically French statement.

The furniture collection of the château's delightful **Musée des Arts décoratifs** offers interesting comparisons between Parisian and Alsatian aristocratic and bourgeois tastes of the 17th and 18th centuries. But the museum's pride and joy is its great ceramics collection, displaying beside Europe's finest porcelain and faïence the astonishing Rococo craftsmanship of the Strasbourg Hannong family, most remarkably a huge tureen in the form of a turkey. If you didn't get enough of the astronomical clock in the cathedral, you can have a close-up view here of figures from the original 14th-century model.

The château also houses Strasbourg's **Musée des Beaux-Arts**, noteworthy for its Giotto Crucifixion, Raphael's *La Fornarina,* and the remarkable sombre realism of Watteau's *L'Ecureuse de cuivre*.

Behind the château, cross the Pont Sainte-Madeleine over the Ill and stroll along the quai des Bateliers, past the remnants of old Strasbourg, to the bizarre 14th-century **Place du Corbeau** near the bridge of the same name.

Continue along the quai Saint-Nicolas to the **Musée alsacien** at number 23, a group of 16th- and 17th-century houses appropriate to the colourful collections of Alsatian folklore. Children love the ancient toys and dolls. Instruments of worship and ritual illustrate the religious life of the province's important Jewish community.

Make your way westward to the Pont Saint-Martin for a first view of the city's most enchanting quarter, the old tannery district known as **la petite France**. At a point where the Ill divides into four canals, the tanners shared the waterways with the millers and fishermen. Sturdy gabled houses line the Rue des Dentelles and the quaintly named Rue du Bain-aux-Plantes.

The timbered façades and the immaculate balconies brightly festooned with geraniums are an attractive reminder of Strasbourg's German past. On an uncrowded day, treat yourself to an expensive meal at one of the delightful waterside restaurants.

The **Barrage Vauban** — remains of the fortifications Vauban built for Louis XIV — spans the Ill to the west. Its roof affords a splendid panoramic **view** across the canals and La Petite France to that soaring silhouette of the cathedral. At sunset, it makes the perfect finish to a day's walk. But many like to start out from here, with an early morning view of the ensemble, and then reverse the order of the walk we have proposed, reserving the cathedral for a triumphant climax.

Route du Vin

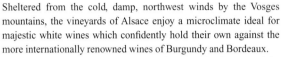

Sheltered from the cold, damp, northwest winds by the Vosges mountains, the vineyards of Alsace enjoy a microclimate ideal for majestic white wines which confidently hold their own against the more internationally renowned wines of Burgundy and Bordeaux.

The vineyards hug the gentle slopes between the Vosges and the Rhine Valley along a single narrow 120-km (75-mile) strip that stretches from Marlenheim, just west of Strasbourg, down to Thann, outside Mulhouse. The winding "wine route" is well signposted; its charming medieval and 16th-century villages and castles — such as Haut-Koenigsbourg and Kaysersberg — make it the prettiest vineyard tour in the country, best of all during the October wine harvest. Tasting and purchases are possible at many of the properties. Ask at the local *syndicat d'initiative* or Colmar's Maison du vin d'Alsace for information about the vineyard tours organized from Obernai and Turckheim, among others.

A walk around the lovely limeshaded ramparts of **Obernai** will convince you of the perennial prosperity of its wine growers and farmers. Among the elegant, spotless timbered houses of the 16th-century Place du Marché, note the fine **Halle aux blés** (Corn Market) and **hôtel de ville**, as well as the handsome Renaissance **Puits aux six seaux** (Six Pails Well) situated between the town hall and the parish church.

Equally famous for its Riesling wines and its Renaissance houses, **Riquewihr** is almost too picturesque to be believed and so is often overcrowded during the tourist season. Cars must be left at the southern end of the town. If you're lucky enough to arrive in Riquewihr on a quiet day, have a good look at the stately **Maison Liebrich** (1535) and at the **Maison Preiss-Zimmer** (1686), on the main street (Rue du Général-de-Gaulle).

Just before you reach the main gate and town symbol, the 13th-century **Dolder**, turn off to the right and take a peep at the little **ghetto** in the wooden-galleried Cour des Juifs. And for people who enjoy inspecting ancient instruments of terror and torture, there's a medieval chamber of horrors in the **Tour des Voleurs** (Thieves' Tower).

Nestling at the foot of its ruined castle, the pretty medieval town of **Kaysersberg** is widely known as the birthplace of the Nobel Peace Prize winner Dr. Albert Schweitzer (1875–1965). His parents' house has become the **Centre Culturel Schweitzer** (124, Rue du Général-de-Gaulle), devoted to the life of the humanitarian, who was also a great performer of Bach's organ works.

The parish church, the **Eglise Sainte-Croix**, is worth a visit for its splendid 16th-century **altarpiece** by Jean Bongartz of Colmar. It is a polychrome sculpted wooden triptych of 18 panels, which portray in moving detail the last days of Jesus. A 10-minute walk up the wooded hill to the **castle tower** gives you a delightful view of the town and the surrounding valley of the Weiss river.

To escape from the madding crowd, seek out the unspoiled little town of **Turckheim** — the absolute epitome of the shiny, bright Alsatian village. Its 16th- and 17th-century charm is preserved within a triangular rampart.

☞ Colmar

Some people make a pilgrimage to Colmar with the sole purpose of visiting the great Musée d'Unterlinden. But the town itself, with its miraculously preserved old city centre, has much else to offer. It also makes a quieter alternative to Strasbourg as a base for touring the vineyards of Alsace.

Converted from a 13th-century convent of Dominican nuns, the **Musée d'Unterlinden** provides a perfect setting in which to view one of the world's undisputed masterpieces of religious art, Matthias Grünewald's awe-inspiring **Issenheim altarpiece**, displayed in the chapel. Created for the Issenheim convent of Saint Anthony between

1512 and 1516, the altarpiece originally folded out in three panels, which are now mounted for exhibition in separate sections.

To appreciate the full climactic impact of the whole work, view it in reverse order, starting at the far end with the stately sculpted polychrome wooden panel of Saints Augustine, Anthony, and Jerome, carved by Niklaus Hagenauer. The first of Grünewald's painted panels depicts on one side the conversion and temptation of Anthony and, on the other, the birth of Jesus and a chorus of angels. The second panel is devoted to the Annunciation and Resurrection and, on the reverse side, what is perhaps the most pain-filled and exalted Crucifixion ever realized. Grünewald's illuminated colour and uncompromising realism achieve an almost terrifying emotional intensity.

Once you have recovered your composure, be sure to see the superb altarpiece of Martin Schongauer, Hans Holbein's portrait of a woman, and, a proud new acquisition, Lucas Cranach's exquisite *Mélancolie.* The modern collection of Braque, Bonnard, and Picasso offers an intriguing counterpoint.

In the old town centre — which is closed to traffic — keep an eye open for the many handsome gabled houses of the Renaissance period: the **Ancienne Douane** (Old Customs House, Grand-Rue); **Maison des Arcades** (Grand-Rue); **Maison Pfister** (Rue des Marchands); and **Maison des Têtes** (Rue des Têtes).

As soon as a town has a couple of canals with quaint bridges over them, likely as not the neighbourhood will be called Little Venice. Colmar is no exception. Its **petite Venise** is south of the Old Town. From the Saint-Pierre bridge, you have a lovely view of its flowery river banks, weeping willows, and timbered houses, with the tower of Saint Martin's church in the distance, none of it remotely Venetian but still very pretty. The district on the opposite bank of the river was once a fortified enclave, inhabited mainly by market gardeners who used to sell their wares from barges on the river. Today it still holds on to its original, colourful name of *Krutenau* (Vegetable Waterway).

Because it was recently vandalized, the **Eglise des Dominicains** is now open only during the summer months, when it exhibits its great treasure (stolen and recently recovered), Martin Schongauer's beautiful altarpainting *Vierge au buisson de roses* (Madonna in the Rose Bower). Take a look, too, at the remarkable 14th- and 15th-century **stained-glass windows**.

Colmar is also the birthplace of Auguste Bartholdi, designer of the Statue of Liberty. His 17th-century house (30, Rue des Marchands) is now the **Musée Bartholdi**, displaying his models and drawings. His statue of Napoleon's general Jean Rapp, another local boy, can be seen on the Place Rapp.

BURGUNDY

The Burgundy area boasts a marvellous variety of attractions: the wines, of course, and the fine gastronomy that goes with them; lazy days on the Canal de Bourgogne, drifting past green meadows; the grand ducal palace of Dijon, and Dijon's museums.

While the Ile-de-France is the cradle of the great Gothic cathedrals, the major jewels of French Romanesque architecture are to be found in Burgundy, from Vézelay to Autun and south to the noble ruins of Cluny. The special joys of Burgundy are in the tiny villages, some of which we'll tell you about, but more that you'll be delighted to discover for yourself. Their manor farms and millhouses, exquisite parish churches, and open-air stone laundries *(lavoirs)* down by the stream are the rural soul of France.

If you are driving down from Paris, you'll get the best out of Burgundy by leaving the *autoroute* at either the Courtenay or the Auxerre exit and touring the rest of the way on the perfectly good — and above all beautiful — secondary roads. The TGV goes through to Montbard, Dijon, and Beaune.

Auxerre makes a good stop for your first excursions into the Burgundy interior, particularly if you want to stock up for a picnic. It is the main distribution point for the famous Chablis white wines, but

Luckily for bikers, Burgundy's vineyards are not very hilly.

you may prefer to drive out to the vineyards in delightful undulating country east of the *autoroute.*

Vallée du Serein

This is just one out of a score of leisurely backroad excursions you can make through northern Burgundy's meandering green valleys. Either cutting across from Tonnerre or starting out from the village of Chablis, follow the course of the little Serein river (a tributary of the Yonne) towards Avallon.

Notice as you go the huge farmhouses, veritable fortresses, characteristically roofed with *laves,* flat volcanic-stone tiles, which add to the landscape a marvellous patina of colour and texture. The finely arched front doors are often at the top of a sturdy staircase over the street-level cellar. You can spot, set in the stone walls, little sculpted heads of angels or demons, floral motifs, or the scallop shell (*coquille Saint-Jacques*) marking the route of medieval pilgrims to Spain.

Noyers is a fortified medieval village with 16 towers in its ramparts. Many of its timbered and gabled houses date back to the 14th and 15th centuries, particularly on the Place de l'Hôtel-de-Ville and the Rue du Poids-du-Roy. From the little Renaissance church, there's a pretty view over the winding river.

At **L'Isle-sur-Serein**, the river divides momentarily to encircle the tranquil little town and the ruins of its 15th-century château.

Leave the river briefly to loop east around Talcy, with its Romanesque church, and the 13th-century château of Thizy, before ending the excursion at **Montréal**. This medieval town boasts a Gothic church with a Renaissance interior; note the carved oak choir stalls and Nottingham alabaster altarpiece.

The Good, the Bad, and the Ugly

From 1363 to 1477, the dukes of Burgundy amassed great wealth and power, to the envy of most of the kings of Europe, but what they really liked was fancy nicknames.

Philippe le Hardi (the Bold) won his when, at the age of 14, he slapped an English soldier in the face for insulting the king of France, Philippe's father. He was equally slap-happy with the enormous dowry he got from his wife, Marguerite de Flandres, bringing the greatest Flemish artists to his court, covering himself in gold, silver, jewels, and ostrich feathers, and, 20 years before his death, ordering the most magnificent tomb in France. He died broke and his sons had to hock the family silver to pay for the funeral.

Jean sans Peur, notoriously ugly but Fearless, earned his name by slaughtering Turks, but it's more difficult to explain what, from a French point of view, was so Good about Philippe le Bon, who sold Joan of Arc to the English for 10,000 pieces of gold.

The last of the four great dukes got the name he deserved. He sought to consolidate the veritable empire that the family estates had become by invading Lorraine to link up Burgundy and Franche-Comté with possessions in Luxemburg, Picardy, Flanders, and Holland. Proclaiming himself a latter-day Alexander the Great, he lost everything at the Siege of Nancy and went down in history as Charles le Téméraire — the Foolhardy.

Abbaye de Fontenay

This venerable Cistercian abbey, about 6 km (4 miles) east of the TGV station at Montbard, turns its back on the world, standing behind high walls in a lovely valley at the edge of a forest. The building has been rescued from its humiliating 19th-century conversion into a paper-mill, and the cloisters present once more the calm and simplicity that were the ideals of Saint Bernard de Clairvaux, the abbey's 12th-century founder.

As you go through the gate decorated with the arms of the Cistercian order, you'll notice a niche for a guard dog below the staircase. On the right is an austere hostel and chapel for the few pilgrims that passed this way, and beyond it the forge of the hard-working Cistercians. To the left of the entrance are the monks' bakery and an imposing pigeon loft.

Paid for by Bishop Everard of Norwich, for whom Fontenay was a refuge from the hostility of Henry II of England, the **abbey church** has a sober, unadorned beauty — no belltower, as there were no distant faithful to be called to worship, but harmonious proportions in the interior, and fine acoustics because Saint Bernard was a great lover of music. A serene statue of the Virgin Mary (13th century) stands in the north arm of the transept.

Vézelay

An exquisite centre of spirituality in a beautiful rustic setting, Vézelay is the home of one of the major churches on the pilgrim route from Germany and the Netherlands to Santiago de Compostela in Spain. Nowadays it is the target of a new breed of pilgrims — the tourists who flock here in search of the quintessential Burgundy. If you're travelling at the height of the tourist season, this is one of those places where it is vital to make a really early start in order to get in ahead of the crowd.

To recapture something of the experience of the medieval pilgrim, having parked your car — or alighted from the bus — down at the Place du Champ-de-Foire, pass through the turreted Porte Neuve and follow the **Promenade des Fossés**, which takes you along the ancient ramparts lined with walnut trees.

At the Porte Sainte-Croix, there is a magnificent view over the Cure river valley and the path that leads to the place where, in 1146, Saint Bernard exhorted King Louis VII to lead the French on the Second Crusade. This was also to be the starting point of the Third Crusade in 1190, when England's Richard the Lion-Hearted joined forces with Philippe Auguste.

Vézelay's **Basilique Sainte-Madeleine**, originally under the obedience of Cluny and repository of the relics of Mary Magdalen, remains a masterly achievement of French Romanesque architecture, in spite of the damage inflicted by natural disasters, wars, and revolution. The restorations of Viollet-le-Duc have maintained the church's majestic harmony.

The narthex, or entrance hall to the nave, is crowned by a magnificent sculpted **tympanum** of Jesus enthroned after the Resurrection, preaching his message to the Apostles. On the central supporting pillar is a statue of John the Baptist — beheaded not by Herod but by iconoclastic Huguenot vandals.

The nave is a wonder of light and lofty proportions, enhanced by the luminous beige stone and the splendid ribbed vaulting. In contrast to the exalted quality of the tympanum's sculpture, the robust carvings of the **capitals** in the nave are lively and down-to-earth, making a clearly popular appeal to the throngs of visiting pilgrims.

The themes depicted on the capitals are from the Bible and the legends of the saints. Beside David and Goliath, Daniel in the lions' den, and the building of Noah's ark, one curious sculpture shows Saint Eugenia, tonsured and disguised as a monk, opening her robe to convince a sceptical friar that she's a woman. Although the basilica is dedicated to Mary Magdalen, surprisingly she doesn't figure among the sculptures.

On the tree-shaded **terrace** beyond the basilica, relax on one of the benches and enjoy the splendid view looking out over the forested plateau of the Morvan. Then explore the old houses, wells, and courtyards in the town's narrow lanes leading back down to the Place du Champ-de-Foire.

Autun

At the other end of the densely wooded Morvan plateau, Autun's 12th-century **Cathédrale Saint-Lazare** makes a natural point of comparison with Vézelay's Basilique Sainte-Madeleine. While the Autun **tympanum** may lack the elevated spiritual impact of its counterpart at Vézelay, its rich carving of Jesus presiding at the Last Judgment is full of vitality.

On the left, you see the happy few being welcomed by Saint Peter. Immediately to the right of Jesus is the weighing of the souls, with Saint Michael

The bizarre monsters sculpted at Autun cathedral were supposed to scare believers away from sin.

trying to stop Satan from cheating. On the far right, a cauldron is boiling a few of the unlucky ones.

Below Jesus' feet is a Latin inscription which suggests that the tympanum was the work of one man, Gislebertus (Gilbert). It says: "Gislebertus did this. May such terror terrify those in thrall to earthly error, for the horror of these images tells what awaits them."

Gilbert is also believed to have carved the superb **capitals** topping the pillars of the nave and aisles. Some of the more fragile pieces are exhibited in an upstairs **chapter room**, worth a visit for a close-up view of his magnificent workmanship. The sculpture places a graphic emphasis on the ugliness of sin (the hanging of Judas, the devil tempting Jesus) and the simple beauty of virtue (such as the Flight into Egypt or Mary Magdalen).

At the nearby **Musée Rolin** you can view a fine collection of Burgundian and Flemish painting and sculpture. The museum is partly housed in the elegant 15th-century mansion that belonged to Nicolas Rolin, a wealthy dignitary and the benefactor of the famous Hôtel-Dieu at Beaune (see page 113).

☞ Dijon

Dijon is Burgundy's stately capital. It's the ideal gateway for a tour of the vineyards to the south or a drive around the pretty Val-Suzon to the north. It's also a good starting point for barge cruises on the Canal de Bourgogne (see page 44).

Not the least of the city's attractions is the shopping centre around the Place Darcy and Rue de la Liberté, where you can hunt for such regional delicacies as the famous mustards, *pain d'épices* (gingerbread), and *cassis*, the blackcurrant liqueur that turns an or-

---

Keep It Simple, Brother

Son of an aristocratic family near Dijon, Bernard de Clairvaux was determined to counter the pomp and opulence displayed by the powerful Cluny monastery with a return to the austerity of the earliest Benedictine monks.

"Why," he wrote to a fellow abbot, "all this excessive height in the churches, disproportionate length and superfluous width, why the sumptuous ornament and curious painting to catch the eye, distract the spirit and disturb meditation?"

While Cluny's preoccupation with worship left no time for manual or intellectual labour, Bernard's Cistercian monks led a rigorous life of scholarship, hard work, and frugal diet. Today, the monastery at Clairvaux at the northern edge of Burgundy, of which Bernard was abbot, observes another form of frugality — it has been converted into a prison.

---

dinary white wine into a deliciously refreshing *kir*. For wines other
than your immediate picnic needs, you're better off waiting for your
tour of the vineyards or the wider selection available at Beaune.

To evoke the town's past glories, you must head for the semi-
circular Place de la Libération (formerly the Place Royale), designed
by Jules Hardouin-Mansart, architect of the Château de Versailles.
The elegant 17th- and 18th-century façades of the **Palais des Ducs**
conceal the underlying Renaissance structures of the dukes' heyday,
but many of their treasures remain to be seen in the interior, as part
of the **Musée des Beaux-Arts**.

You get a notion of the magnificence of Burgundian court life by
starting your visit with the **ducal kitchens**, built in 1435. Imagine
the banquets prepared in the six enormous walk-in cooking hearths,
blackened now by a couple of centuries of smoke, that arch over in a
soaring Gothic vault to the central ventilation.

The ground-floor rooms of the museum have a model of the old
palace and a collection of Burgundian sculpture from the 15th century to the present day. In the upstairs picture galleries, the dukes'
close links with the Flemish masters of their day are amply illustrat-
ed by works such as the fine *Nativité* of the anonymous Maître de
Flémalle and Dierick Bouts's *Tête de Christ*. The collection also includes important paintings by Rubens, Frans Hals, Veronese, Konrad Witz, and Martin Schongauer.

But the museum's greatest treasures are undoubtedly the dukes'
tombs in the **Salle des gardes** — brought here from the Charter-
house of Champmol, which was destroyed during the Revolution. It
took the sculptors Jean de Marville, Claus Sluter, and Claus de
Werve 26 years (from 1385 to 1411) to complete the intricate marble
and alabaster sculptures for the extravagant **mausoleum of Philippe
le Hardi**. On the sides of the tomb bearing the recumbent statue of
the duke are carved 41 marvellously expressive figures of mourners
cloaked in monastic capes, variously praying, meditating, and
lamenting. The double sepulchre of Jean sans Peur and his wife,

Marguerite de Bavière, is also lavishly sculpted, although more stylized. Near the ducal tombs is Rogier van der Weyden's portrait of
the third great duke, Philippe le Bon, with the Golden Fleece — the
emblem of the chivalrous order that he founded in 1429.

To the north of the palace, along the Rue de la Chouette and the
Rue Verrerie, you'll find some attractive late-Gothic and Renaissance houses, with picturesque inner courtyards, that have been
transformed into antique shops. In the Rue des Forges, note the
Hôtel Chambellan (at number 34) and the **Hôtel Aubriot** (at number 40), home of the Provost of Paris who built the accursed
Bastille prison.

Côte d'Or

The kingdom of wine, the power of legend: for some people, this
destination is *the* reason for coming to France. Delightful as the
vineyards of Burgundy may be, the landscape and villages of certain
other *routes des vins* may be considered prettier — those of Alsace,
for instance. And other wine growers, such as those around Bordeaux, may perhaps have more handsome châteaux. But none can

*There's a fortune in these fingers — workers carefully
check the grapes at the Clos de Vougeot vineyards.*

*The rich decoration of the old Hôtel-Dieu hospital
testifies to Beaune's historic prosperity.*

compose a true connoisseur's poem like the one that follows, just by reciting a few names on the map.

First verse, consisting solely of red wines, is the *Côte de Nuits*: Gevrey-Chambertin, Chambolle-Musigny, Vougeot, Vosne-Romanée, Nuits-Saint-Georges. In the second verse, the *Côte de Beaune,* the whites follow the reds: Aloxe-Corton, Beaune, Pommard, Volnay, Meursault, Puligny-Montrachet, Chassagne-Montrachet, Santenay. These two verses together make up the *Côte d'Or,* the most expensive and delicious poem in the world.

From Dijon down to Santenay, the Côte d'Or is just 60 km (37 miles) long. Nothing to do with "coast," *côte* here means "hillside." As you drive south from Dijon, be sure to get off the main road, the N 74, on to the parallel D 122, signposted as the *Route des grands*

crus (route of the great vintages). You then eventually rejoin the N 74 at Clos de Vougeot.

You may keep seeing a sign at the edge of vineyards: *"Grappillage interdit,"* which means just what it says — "Don't steal the grapes," referring more particularly to those you might think were free for all, the ones left hanging at the end of the harvest. Don't even think of it; the Burgundians are keen hunters! Many of the famous vineyards are open to visitors, but tasting is strictly for serious customers that manifest a clear intention of buying.

The shell of its ancient abbey is all that's left of Cluny's mighty monastic empire.

The village of **Gevrey-Chambertin** makes a good first stop. The medieval château shelters the wine harvest in its great cellars. But the best cellars open to the public are those in the château at **Clos de Vougeot**, owned by the Cistercian monks until the Revolution and now the property of the Chevaliers du Tastevin (fraternity of wine tasters). The splendid old vats and winepresses are themselves worth the visit, and the guides will tell you more than you ever wanted to know about wine.

For the beginner — and for most others, too — **Beaune** is the place to buy. It's the centre of the industry, and practically all the great wines are represented here. You won't get a better bargain at the vineyard unless you know the owner. A little **Musée du Vin**

(Rue d'Enfer) tells the history of wine-making, with all its paraphernalia, from Roman times to the present day.

Beaune's best-known building, the **Hôtel-Dieu,** is a beautifully preserved 15th-century hospital (recently converted to an old peoples' home) founded by Chancellor Nicolas Rolin. Be sure to see the masterpiece of Flemish art commissioned by Rolin for the hospital chapel, Rogier van der Weyden's altarpiece of the Last Judgment. It is now on display in the museum, along with tapestries that adorned the walls of the unheated hospital wards to keep the patients warm.

Cluny

The abbey that today stands in ruin at the southern tip of Burgundy ruled its medieval world the way Louis XIV's Versailles dominated 17th-century France. Imagine the Sun King's palace reduced to rubble, with a few isolated but noble structures left standing to bear the weight of the vanished splendour, and you can appreciate something of the exquisite melancholy that rises from the stones of Cluny.

The gigantic 12th-century **Abbatiale Saint-Pierre-et-Saint-Paul** was the largest church in Christendom until the completion of Saint Peter's in Rome in the 17th century. Only the right arm of one of the two transepts and the octagonal belltower, the **Clocher de**

Not with a Bang, But a Whimper

Founded in 910, Cluny organized the first crusades and masterminded the pilgrimages to Santiago de Compostela. Its abbots were emperors. At the beginning of the 12th century, it ruled more than 1,450 monastic institutions, with 10,000 monks, beyond French borders to Spain, Italy, Germany, and Britain. The abbey's destruction began in 1798, not by revolutionary iconoclasts hell-bent on revenge for centuries of exploitation, but by a merchant from nearby Mâcon. He bought the abbey for 2,000,000 francs and systematically dismantled it over a period of 25 years — in order to build a set of national riding stables.

l'Eau-Bénite, remain. But even this truncated edifice imposes its grandeur, and Cluny's excellent young guides (English-speaking in summer) help us conceive the rest. There used to be five naves, two transepts, five belltowers, and 225 choir stalls.

The elegant classical 18th-century **cloisters** make a poignant contrast with the Romanesque church. The 13th-century **granary**, beside an even older flour mill, has been turned into an admirable **museum** for the abbey's sculpted capitals displayed on reconstructed pillars.

To see some of Cluny's impact on the surrounding countryside, visit a few of the villages whose Romanesque churches were built by Cluny's architects and craftsmen: among them, Saint-Vincent-des-Prés, Taizé, Berzé-la-Ville, and Malay, each a little gem.

JURA

The Jura mountains cover several eastern *départements* making up the region of Franche-Comté. The area relies on the geography of its

The Loue river inspired Gustave Courbet.

Modern art adorns the Arc-et-Senans saltworks.

rampart-like mountains and dense pine forests to keep it remote and, even today, blessedly unspoiled for nature-lovers.

Besançon

A convenient base for excursions, the capital of the Franche-Comté region has an attractive town centre around the pedestrian zone of the **Grande-Rue**.

The city's **Musée des Beaux-Arts** (in the Place de la Révolution) claims to be the oldest in France (1694). Of the Italian paintings, Bellini's *L'Ivresse de Noé* (The Drunkenness of Noah) and Giordano's *Philosophe cynique* are outstanding. Look, too, for Cranach's *Lucrèce* and *Le Repos de Diane*, and fine French works by Ingres, Courbet, and Bonnard.

Arc-et-Senans

The 18th-century **Saline Royale** (Royal Saltworks), now abandoned, is surely one of the most elegant factories in the world. It was in fact the nucleus of a utopian city conceived by Claude-Nicolas Ledoux, who had the outlandish idea of making working conditions for the salt-labourers pleasant. In green surroundings, the buildings of the saltworks are set in a semicircle around administrative offices, each with easy access to the other and all in simple classical style.

There is a **museum** devoted to Ledoux's plans, models, and avant-garde theories; and seminars are held here on urban and industrial planning for the future.

Vallée de la Loue

A favourite excursion in the Jura is to trace the Loue river and its tributary, the Lison, back to their cascading **sources** through the landscapes that inspired so many of the paintings of Gustave Courbet.

His home town was **Ornans**. Stand on the Grand Pont for the celebrated view of the strange old timbered houses, reflected in the calm waters of the river that runs through the middle of the town. Close by the bridge is the **Musée Courbet**, in the house where the artist lived, with the old walking stick depicted in his famous painting *Bonjour monsieur Courbet*.

Les Reculées

These intriguing horseshoe-shaped valleys nestle like narrow amphitheatres against abrupt rocky cliffs, making rewarding destinations for a pleasant day's hike.

One of the best is the **Cirque de Baume**, between Lons-le-Saunier and Baume-les-Messieurs. Southeast of Arbois, the **Reculée des Planches** takes you to the fairy-tale waterfalls of the Cuisance and ends at the dramatic **Cirque du Fer à Cheval**. By then you'll be more than ready to sample some heady Arbois wine — try the *vin jaune* with a chunk of Comté cheese.

NORTHWEST

The sea played an important role in the history of the northwest corner of France. The Scandinavians came in their longships, landing on the Normandy coast and penetrating as far as Angers and Tours in the

Loire Valley. Brittany has ever been a seafaring province, populated by Celts fleeing from the Anglo-Saxons across the Channel. Today, Normandy offers a patchwork landscape of rich green hedgerowed farmland, and a rich dairy cuisine to go with it; lazy days at the elegant old seaside resorts; the timeless wonder of the Mont-Saint-Michel; the monumental reminders of medieval Norman warriors at Bayeux and the latter-day liberators of World War II on the D-Day beaches.

Getting the Ants Out of Their Pants

It took a long time to stop the Normans (Norsemen, or North-men) from moving around. The Scandinavian seamen made their first isolated incursions into France while exploring the northern Atlantic in the second and third centuries. But they found nothing to hold their attention until prosperous Christians along the Seine Valley began building monasteries and churches with treasures of gold, silver, and jewels.

In 820, the Norsemen staged their first major invasion in their dragon-headed longships, subsequently plundering their way up the river to Paris. Masters of guerrilla warfare and ambush, they had horses aboard for lightning raids into the interior. Chartres was one of their prime targets. To cut his losses, the French king Charles le Simple had the simple idea in 911 of giving these madcaps some land to settle down on: the Duchy of Normandy.

Duke Rollo and his men made their capital at Rouen. They converted to Christianity and happily set about organizing towns and farms and trade, just like any other civilized people. Those who couldn't take to the sedentary life went off on Crusades to the Holy Land, to devote their bloodthirsty pillaging and pirating to a good cause.

Conquest and exploration, often amazingly far from home, were always a useful safety valve for the Normans' natural aggressive energies: England and Sicily in the 11th century, Sierra Leone in 1364, Brazil in 1503, Canada in 1506, Florida in 1563. Chicagoans to this day honour the passage of a great sailor from Rouen: the financial district of the Middle West's "Wall Street" bears the name of La Salle, who passed that way on his exploration of Lake Michigan and the Mississippi River in 1682.

Brittany's is a wilder, less civilized countryside, with a jagged coastline to match. Its oysters and mussels are as fresh as the sea breezes, and its people as weather-beaten as their granite houses. But nestling in the hollows of the windswept heaths are havens of pious calm among the parish closes, and you'll discover plenty of peaceful sandy beaches in sheltered coves along the otherwise buffeted Brittany coastline.

From its aristocratic past, the Loire Valley has preserved not only its countless châteaux. The good life is there in abundance for anyone with the leisure to enjoy it. Its wines make an excellent accompaniment for game from the forests of Sologne or for the freshwater fish of the Loire's tributaries.

NORMANDY

The region divides into an eastern half, Haute-Normandie, along the Seine Valley, similar in scenery to the Ile-de-France; and the more rugged Basse-Normandie to the west, more akin to neighbouring Brittany. Vast expanses of land are cultivated for agribusiness; the more traditional orchards and lush meadowland cattle pastures produce the famous strong cider and pungent cheeses.

No farmer is as cheerful as the prosperous Normandy breed.

The settled, tranquil existence of the solid bourgeoisie of Rouen or Caen and the even more solid farmers round about makes you wonder whether the tumultuous history of their murdering, raping, pillaging ancestors isn't all a jolly myth.

Dieppe

France's oldest seaside resort and the closest beach to Paris is a popular gateway to Normandy for those crossing the English Channel from Newhaven. To stretch your legs before starting out on the road, cross the drawbridge from the ferry port to the **port de pêche** (fishing port). At the early morning market, the phlegmatic Dieppois fishermen are as lively as they ever get.

The **Musée de Dieppe**, in a 15th-century château in the Rue de Chastes, has a good collection of model ships and some fine scrimshaws, carvings in ivory, dating from the 18th century when elephant tusks were a major import from Africa and Asia.

The courageous but abortive Canadian raid on Dieppe in World War II is commemorated in the **Musée de la guerre et du raid du 19 août 1942**, 2 km (about 1 mile) west of town on the D 75 road (route de Pourville).

Rouen

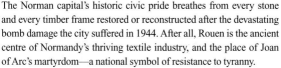

The Norman capital's historic civic pride breathes from every stone and every timber frame restored or reconstructed after the devastating bomb damage the city suffered in 1944. After all, Rouen is the ancient centre of Normandy's thriving textile industry, and the place of Joan of Arc's martyrdom—a national symbol of resistance to tyranny.

Hugging a loop in the Seine, the town did draw at least one advantage from the war — the factories on the left bank were destroyed, leaving room for a modern residential area. The industries were rebuilt on the outskirts. On the right bank, the charming medieval and Renaissance centre around the cathedral has been renovated and is now reserved for pedestrians.

Start your walk, not at the cathedral, but at the western end of the historic district, on the **Place du Vieux-Marché**. The old and new Rouen come together around the bright and airy market halls and the attractive modern **Eglise Sainte-Jeanne-d'Arc**. Nearby is a monument to mark the spot where Joan was burned at the stake in 1431. Some stones have been excavated from the rostrum of her judges. Inside the church there are some fine 16th-century **stained-glass windows**, salvaged from an older church bombed in 1944.

Leading eastward from the market is Rouen's most famous street, the **Rue du Gros-Horloge** — now as always the city's bustling commercial centre. Its timber-framed houses of the 15th, 16th, and 17th centuries are marvellous examples of sturdy Norman architecture, achieving a very pleasing irregularity in the way the plaster is set in oblique forms between the solid oak posts and collar beams supporting the balconies. The elegant Renaissance arched clocktower of the **Gros Horloge** is Rouen's emblem, its Eiffel Tower. The ornamental gilded clock face has only one hand, for the hours.

Beside the clock is a 14th-century belfry which still rings its bell at 9:00 P.M., time of the old curfew. Take the spiral staircase to the roof for a lovely **view** of the city and its circle of hills around the Seine Valley.

East of the Gros Horloge stands the great **cathedral**, made famous in modern times by Monet's many Impressionist studies of its façade. The asymmetry of the two towers embracing the delicate tracery of the slender spires creates a highly original silhouette among France's best-loved cathedrals.

The façade offers a remarkably harmonious anthology of Gothic architecture. The north tower, the **Tour Saint-Romain**, has the sober simplicity of the cathedral's early Gothic beginnings in the 12th century, while the architecture of the taller, more elaborate south tower, the **Tour de Beurre**, is Flamboyant Gothic of the 15th century. According to local belief, this "Butter Tower" was paid for by Catholic burghers in return for the privilege of being allowed to eat Normandy butter during Lent. The austerely sculpted porches flanking the main entrance are from the early period, and the more ornamental elongated central porch and the gabled upper windows were added in the 15th and 16th centuries. The main spire is neo-Gothic of the 19th century.

The rather severe interior of the cathedral contrasts with its elaborate exterior, but the impact of the double-storeyed nave is lightened by the tall arches of the choir. In the Chapelle de la Vierge (beyond the choir) is the monumental Renaissance **Tomb of the Cardinals of Amboise**, with superbly sculpted allegories of the cardinal virtues. On the south side of the choir is the more modest tomb of the most heroic of medieval English kings, portrayed recumbent above the inscription in Latin: "Here is buried the heart of King Richard of England, known as the Lion-Hearted."

Behind the cathedral, cross over the Rue de la République to the 15th-century **Eglise Saint-Maclou**, the richest example of Flamboyant Gothic in the country. Note the masterful Renaissance carving of the oak doors on the central and north portals. In the interior, the same exuberant artistry can be admired in the sculpted wood **organ frame** and the stone tracery of the **spiral staircase**.

Turn north on **Rue Damiette**, graced by some of the town's handsomest old houses. The street leads to the elegant 14th-

Rouen's charming historic district includes the streets that lead to Saint-Ouen.

century Gothic abbey church, the **Abbatiale Saint-Ouen**, best observed from the little park east of the chancel.

The last great monument of the old town, in the Rue aux Juifs, is the grand **Palais de Justice**, a jewel of Renaissance and Flamboyant Gothic architecture built on the site of the medieval ghetto. Recent excavations uncovered a 12th-century **synagogue** (visits by arrangement with the Office de tourisme, Place de la Cathédrale).

This prosperous city has a well-endowed **Musée des Beaux-Arts** (square Verdrel), with works by Velázquez, Caravaggio, Perugino, Veronese, and Rubens. French painters include Delacroix and François Clouet — as well as Géricault, who was born in Rouen.

☞ Jumièges

The D 982 leading westward from Rouen is the start of the **Route des Abbayes**, which meanders through woodland and meadows around the medieval Norman abbeys — most of them enjoying their heyday under William the Conqueror — at Saint-Martin-de-Boscherville, Jumièges, Saint-Wandrille, Le Bec-Hellouin, and Caen, culminating in their masterpiece, Mont-Saint-Michel.

Riding off into the sunset on Normandy's tranquil beaches.

Among them, the stately ruins of the **abbey** of Jumièges occupy a special, inevitably romantic place. The white-granite shells of its two churches, the Romanesque Notre-Dame and the smaller-scale Gothic Saint-Pierre, with trees and grass growing in and around the nave and chancel, have survived their intended end with moving dignity.

Duke William returned from his conquest of England to attend the consecration of Notre-Dame in 1067. Seven centuries later, the Benedictine monastery was disbanded by the Revolution, and the buildings were blown up with explosives by a local wood merchant who had bought them cut-price at an auction. But the sturdy edifices resisted total destruction and are still dominated by Notre-Dame's two soaring square towers, minus their original spires.

Honfleur

Situated on the Seine estuary, this port has witnessed the beginning of nearly all of Normandy's seafaring adventures — and is still a mecca for sailing enthusiasts. Towering over the sheltered yachting harbour of the **Vieux Bassin**, the houses with their slate and timber façades gleam in the sun or, even more striking, glisten in a thunderstorm.

The old shipbuilders' quarter, along the **Rue Haute**, is well worth exploring. It runs westward from the Lieutenance, the 16th-century remains of the royal governor's house at the harbour mouth.

Deauville

Blending charming old-fashioned elegance with convenient modern comforts, the most prosperous of Normandy's seaside resorts is also the most expensive. But even if your budget doesn't extend to one of those seafront *palaces*, as the French call their luxury hotels, stop off on the wooden promenade (the celebrated **planches**) for some of the most amusing people-watching in France. This is where a company director takes his secretary for a weekend business conference and runs into his wife with the chairman of the board. The white sandy **beach** with its colourful canvas sun shelters

Gentility at Cabourg.

is a delight and the swimming perfectly good — but, amazingly, few people turn away from the spectacle on the *planches* long enough to go into the water.

Horse-lovers come for the summer racing, flat and steeple, and for the prestigious yearling sale. What they win on the racing, they lose at the casino. The tennis and golf are first class. Yachtsmen should bear in mind a Deauville proverb: if you can see the port of Le Havre, it will rain in the afternoon, and if you can't, it's already raining.

Côte Fleurie

Between the estuaries of the Touques and Dives rivers, 20 km (12 miles) of sandy beaches, handsome villas, and picturesquely weather-beaten old hotels possess a nostalgic appeal for devotees of Napoleon III's Second Empire and the *Belle Epoque* of the 1900s.

The oldest of this coast's resorts, **Trouville,** is now a slightly down-market Deauville, but just as lively. It has an excellent beach — where people seem less reluctant to go swimming — and bistrots on the port serving much better seafood.

The charm of **Houlgate** is in the trees and flowers of its gardens and its sandy beach. Take the long walk at low tide east to the cliffs of the **Vaches Noires** (Black Cows).

Cabourg is the most stately of the old Channel resorts. Take tea at least at its splendid **Grand Hôtel**, a true national shrine in which Marcel Proust wrote part of his *A la recherche du temps perdu*. It is the custom to fall asleep over a leather-bound copy in your deckchair.

Across the river is the little town of **Dives-sur-Mer**, where — as residents like to remind English visitors — William embarked in 1066. To rub it in, there's a Rue d'Hastings and a list of the Conqueror's companions on a wall of the parish church.

Pays d'Auge

A delightful excursion inland from either end of the Côte Fleurie will take you to the essence of the popular image of Normandy, with its fruit-laden orchards, rolling valleys, and massive timbered manor houses, the land where the apples are turned into cider and Calvados and the dairies churn out pungent, creamy Camembert, Livarot, and Pont-l'Evêque.

You can buy some of the best Camembert — labelled VCN, *Véritable Camembert de Normandie* — at the Monday-morning market in

Blissful serenity on Trouville beach.

Vimoutiers, 55 km (34 miles) south of Deauville. But local tourist offices will gladly guide you to farms where you can sample the regional cheeses and buy them on the spot — more fun than in the unexceptional towns of Camembert, Pont-l'Evêque, and Livarot themselves. Drivers should be wary of the cider — it can pack almost as much punch as the Calvados.

Caen

Little is now left of Caen's historic centre, but its good hotels and excellent seafood restaurants make it, with Bayeux, a useful starting-point for visits to the D-Day beaches. Caen was the first major objective of the D-Day landings. It took two months to capture and was devastated by Allied bombs and the shells of the retreating Germans.

Fortunately, the noble silhouette of the **Abbaye aux Hommes** has survived (best seen from the Place Louis-Guillouard). Its church, the **Eglise Saint-Etienne**, harmoniously combines Romanesque towers and nave with Gothic steeples, choir, and chancel. It was begun in the momentous year of 1066, and William the Conqueror made its first abbot his archbishop of Canterbury. The elegant 18th-century monastery buildings have become Caen's town hall.

The remains of William's solid 11th-century castle now house an excellent collection of European painting in the town's **Musée des Beaux-Arts**. Highlights include Poussin's *Mort d'Adonis*, Tiepolo's *Ecce Homo*, Veronese's *Tentation de saint Antoine*, and Rubens' *Abraham et Melchisédech*.

Camembert — one of France's famous cheeses.

The nearby **Musée de Normandie** makes a handsome introduction to regional folklore.

Bayeux

Proudly the first French town to be liberated in World War II (on the day after D-Day), Bayeux was blessedly preserved from destruction. Its Gothic cathedral dominates a charming **old town** *(vieille ville)* of medieval and Renaissance houses on Rue Saint-Martin, Rue Saint-Malo, and Rue Bourbesneur.

But the town's most cherished treasure is the magnificent **Bayeux Tapestry** (or more accurately, embroidery), which was created for Bayeux Cathedral in 1077 to tell the story of Duke William's conquest of England. It is lovingly mounted in the Centre Guillaume-le-Conquérant, in the Rue de Nesmond, and is accompanied by a fascinating film (in an English and French version) that explains the work's historical background.

Courage is a prerequisite for bathers who brave Normandy's cold waters.

No dreary piece of obscure medieval decoration, the beautifully coloured tapestry gives a vivid and often humorous picture of life at William's court, with insights into medieval cooking, lovemaking, and the careful preparations for war. These and the climactic Battle of Hastings are depicted with all the exciting action and violence of a modern adventure film, with a cast of 626 characters, 202 horses, 55 dogs, and 505 other animals.

Adding insult to injury, it was a group of defeated Anglo-Saxon artisans who had to do the wool-on-linen embroidery, 70 metres (230 feet) long and 50 centimetres (20 inches) high, under the supervision of William's half-brother, Odon de Conteville, Bishop of Bayeux.

D-Day Beaches

Before 6 June 1944 the peaceful stretch of coast west of Cabourg, from Ouistreham to the Cotentin peninsula, was known simply as the Côte du Calvados, a flat, undramatic shoreline, broken by a few unspectacular chalk cliffs and sand dunes. And then, at 6:30 A.M. on D-Day, came the first of a fleet of 4,266 vessels to turn the beaches into beachheads with their now illustrious code names of **Sword**, **Juno, Gold, Omaha,** and **Utah**.

Today, with the flames and dust of battle long gone, the coast has retrieved its calm. At a site that's so charged with the emotion of death and war, the atmosphere of rather bleak serenity is in itself as evocative as the few remaining hulks of the Allies' rusty tanks and boats, the Germans' concrete bunkers and blockhouses, some simple monuments on the sites of the action, and the miles of crosses at the military cemeteries.

To see where the British and Canadians, with the support of the Free French forces, attacked on the eastern half of the beaches, start out at the port town of **Ouistreham-Riva-Bella**. A museum, in the Place Alfred-Thomas, details the combined Anglo-French operation to capture this stretch of **Sword Beach**, with uniforms and weapons used during the action, including a pocket submarine and Goliath tank.

Drive west along the D 514 to **Bernières** and **Courseulles** (where the Canadians staged their **Juno Beach** landings, marked by monuments on the beaches), and then the Canadians' cemetery 4 km (2½ miles) to the south at Reviers.

 At **Arromanches**, you can see the most fascinating monument to British ingenuity in the Allied landings — the remains of the artificial **Mulberry Harbour**. The floating steel-and-concrete jetties and pontoons, hauled across the English Channel, were the only way of unloading tanks and heavy artillery on a coastline (**Gold Beach**) without natural harbours. The **Musée du Débarquement** on the seafront includes an exciting film explaining the whole heroic action.

The Americans' **Omaha** and **Utah** beaches, from Colleville to La Madeleine, are now official map references, a cartographer's tribute to the theatre of the fiercest fighting in the D-Day landings. The windswept, desolate coastline frequently recalls the stormy conditions that prevented the Americans from setting up their own Mulberry Harbour to land their equipment. More eloquent than any museum are the 9,386 white marble crosses of the **American military cemetery** on a cliff overlooking Omaha Beach at Colleville-Saint-Laurent.

The Utah Beach museum and monument are 5 km inland from La Madeleine, near Sainte-Marie-du-Mont. The Caen, Bayeux and local tourist offices can direct you to the 27 Allied and German military cemeteries in the region.

Mont-Saint-Michel

There's no way of getting round the claim of its most fervent admirers: the island sanctuary at the border between Normandy and

---

First Look

A detailed visit of Mont-Saint-Michel is certainly worthwhile, but it's that perspective from a distance that's the most moving. For those coming from Caen, stop in Avranches for a panorama of the bay from the Jardin des Plantes or drive out to the coast road (D 911) between Saint-Jean-Le-Thomas and Carolles. Best of all, if you're prepared to splash out and get high above the madding crowd, fly over the abbey on the special excursions organized from Avranches airport. But if you have no time for any of these, do at least get off the main highway, N 176, when approaching the mount and take the D 43 coast road via Courtils for that all-important first view.

Brittany is truly a *Merveille de l'Occident* — a "Wonder of the Western World." That first glimpse of the towering, steepled abbey rising from the sea on its rock is a moment invested with ineffable mystery. Whatever your faith or lack of it, sooner or later a visit to this formidable and exquisite fortress of the Christian Church is imperative.

Sooner or later, because the time when you visit can make a great difference. If you want to recapture something of the atmosphere of the medieval pilgrimages, when thousands of the faithful used to swarm across the island, loading up with souvenirs and fake relics and fighting their brethren for a meal or a bed, join the new secular pilgrims in the summer months, arriving by the busload rather than mule. But if your mood is more contemplative, go in the early

Surrounded by perilous seas, Mont-Saint-Michel symbolizes the Archangel's stand against Satan.

spring, autumn, or even winter, when you can wander around the abbey and its village like a monk.

The bay around the mount's granite outcrop has been steadily silting up in recent years, so that it's an island only during the spring tides. These are most dramatic during the spring and autumn equinox, when the sea comes in at a rate of nearly 50 metres (164 feet) a minute over a distance of 15 km (9 miles). This proved highly dangerous to the pilgrims, who approached the abbey across the sands (the causeway joining the island to the mainland was not built until 1874).

On what was once a Celtic burial ground (originally named Mont-Tombe), the bishop of the nearby town of Avranches began by building an oratory in the eighth century — at the prompting, he claimed, of the Archangel Michael. Then in 1017 Benedictine monks started work on the flat-roofed abbey you can see in the Bayeux Tapestry, propped up on a platform with blocks of brown granite brought from the Channel islands of Chausey, 40 km (25 miles) away.

By the 14th century, the abbey was surrounded by a fortified village. The pilgrims flocked here throughout the Hundred Years' War, paying tolls to the English, who controlled the surrounding territory — though they never succeeded in breaking through the mount's defences. After a period of steady decline, the monastery was dismantled

Getting It in the Eye

The story told in the tapestry from the Norman point of view may come as a bit of a shock to the average patriotic British schoolchild. English King Harold is shown as a treacherous weakling who cheated noble, generous William out of the throne promised him by king Edward the Confessor.

Some scenes to watch out for: a unique view of Mont-Saint-Michel without, of course, its later Gothic additions (panel 17); a bad omen, Halley's comet (April 1066) flies over the newly crowned Harold (panels 32-33); Battle of Hastings, William raises his visor to reassure his men that he's still alive (panels 53-55); Harold Rex Interfectus Est - Harold gets it in the eye (panel 57).

even before the Revolution. It was saved from total destruction only to end up, ignominiously, as a state prison.

Beginning on the upper terrace with a splendid view of the bay, the hour-long guided tour (conducted in English, French, or German) takes you through three levels of abbey buildings: the church, cloister, and refectory at the top; the Salle des Chevaliers (Knights' Hall) and Salle des Hôtes (Guests' Hall) in the middle; and the storeroom and almonry underneath.

The **abbey church** combines a sturdy Romanesque nave with a markedly lighter and more airy Flamboyant Gothic chancel. The choir and chancel do not stand on the island's granite core but on a platform formed by three crypts, with the massive columns of the **Crypte des Gros Piliers** doing most of the work.

In a magical space looking out over the sea, the beautifully sculpted columns of the **cloister** create a perfect framework of grace and delicacy for a moment's meditation. With the cloister, the monks' ethereally lit **refectory**, the grand **Knights' Hall,** and the elegant **Guests' Hall** together make up the masterpiece of 13th-century Gothic architecture that earned the abbey its name of *la Merveille*.

BRITTANY

The province of Brittany, as its natives never tire of telling you, is a country apart, proud of its regional culture, its robust seclusion. The people are remote on their Armorican Peninsula, the Far West of Europe, suspicious of the vacationing Parisian but unostentatiously hospitable to the foreign visitor.

Only a separate holiday can do the region more than scant justice. But on a first visit as part of a larger French tour, you can at least get a sense of Brittany's craggy coastline on the Côte d'Emeraude (Emerald Coast)

> Breton is the only Celtic language spoken on the European continent. The language has no official status and fewer than one million people speak it.

between Cancale and Cap Fréhel, then relax a while at one of the gentler seaside resorts, such as Dinard on the north coast or La Baule on the south, and have fun exploring the prehistoric menhir country around Carnac. In the interior, you can capture the essence of Breton piety in the calvaries of the Parish Closes *(enclos paroissiaux)* at Saint-Thégonnec and Guimiliau, and perhaps hike around the forests and rocky landscapes between Huelgoat and Roc Trévezel.

Get out your walking shoes to explore the craggy Brittany coast.

Côte d'Emeraude

As a change of pace after Mont-Saint-Michel, the Emerald Coast's 70 km (43 miles) of rugged cliffs and caves alternating with quiet beach resorts offer a delightful confrontation with nature plus plenty of sunny self-indulgence.

Start with the little port town of **Cancale**, a major centre of oyster-breeding since earliest Celtic times. Modern techniques now make the oysters good to eat all year round — not, as of old, just in the months with an "r." Look out over the oyster beds from the port's jetty, the **Jetée de la Fenêtre**.

Take the coast road, the D 201, to **Pointe du Grouin**, a cliff 40 metres (130 feet) high, with a spectacular view of the

The art of wearing Brittany headgear! It adds precarious height and makes it possible to bend an ear without bending the bonnet.

Chausey Islands to the north and itself a good example of Brittany's coastal wilderness.

Look eastward across the Bay of Mont-Saint-Michel for your final glimpse of the abbey, before heading west to **Saint-Malo**. This town is steeped in seafaring history; its sailors left their name as far afield as the Malouines, claimed by the British as the Falklands. Saint-Malo remains an important fishing port for cod and, more romantically, has an attractive harbour for yachts.

In World War II Saint-Malo was badly bombed as a last bastion of the Germans, but the old town, surrounded on three sides by the sea, has been tastefully restored. Its **ramparts**, built and rebuilt from the 12th to the 18th centuries, make a bracing walk, with the stretch between the Saint-Philippe bastion and the Tour Bidouane opening up a vista along the whole Emerald Coast. At low tide you can walk or wade out to the little island of Grand Bé, with its simple, unadorned tomb of the locally born Romantic writer Chateaubriand.

In the **Musée d'Histoire de la ville**, just across the lively Place Chateaubriand, the town's naval history is told through the lives of its great navigators and pirates, together with all the colourful paraphernalia of sailing.

Like many French seaside resorts, **Dinard** was a "discovery" of the British in the 19th century, long before French city slickers even dreamed of dipping a toe in the sea or lying on that gritty stuff called sand. The British, soon followed by Americans, appreciated the broad, sheltered beach, the particularly mild microclimate — palms, fig trees, tamarisk, and camellias all flourish here — and the easy access across the Channel.

In a still faintly Victorian atmosphere, Dinard has preserved all the best assets of a good resort: luxury villas and long, paved promenades, plush hotels, elegant boutiques, discothèques, casino, parks and gardens, and an Olympic-size public swimming pool.

The spectacle at **Cap Fréhel** is one of the most thrilling in Brittany. From cliffs 70 metres (230 feet) above the tumultuous sea, you look out across a wild defenceless promontory, a chaos of ruddy sandstone and slabs of black schist, huge waves breaking across the rocks of the Grande and Petite Fauconnière bird sanctuaries, scattered with colonies of cormorants and black-and-white guillemots. On a clear day, from the new **lighthouse** (145 stairs) you can see 100 km (62 miles) or more.

Parish Close Road

The *enclos paroissial* epitomizes the pious life of rural Brittany. This architectural ensemble encompasses church, cemetery, charnel house, and calvary, grouped in a square and entered via a triumphal arch.

In a morning's tour from Morlaix, about 160 km (100 miles) to the west of Dinard, you can take in three of the most important ones on a route signposted as the "Circuit des Trois Enclos."

Saint-Thégonnec represents the ultimate flowering of the art, its triumphal arch setting the

Guimiliau is adorned with varied and expressive — and sometimes shocking — retables (right) and sculptures (below).

tone for the majestic **calvary** of 1610. Among the 40-odd expressively sculpted figures dressed in the costume of Henri IV's time, notice the roped hands of the blindfolded Jesus and the angels collecting his blood; his tormentor, in breeches, is thought to be Henri IV himself. The **ossuary**, now a chapel, is late Renaissance in the very elaborate Breton manner — with Corinthian columns, lanterns, niches, and caryatids. The **church** has an even more elaborate Baroque pulpit.

At **Guimiliau**, more than 200 Old and New Testament figures are sculpted on its **calvary**. The elegant Renaissance style lends an unaccustomed sophistication to the nightmarish superstitions of medieval Brittany incorporated in the sculpture. Look for the servant girl hurtled into hell for flirting with the devil. The **church** has granite statues of Jesus and the Apostles adorning its porch. Inside, eight spiral columns support the mighty canopy of the 17th-century carved oak **baptistry**.

Although a lightning bolt toppled the tower of the **church of Lampaul-Guimiliau** in 1809, the church's interior remains impressive. The 16th-century polychrome rood beam spanning the nave is decorated with 12 prophetesses (on the chancel side) and scenes from the Passion.

Huelgoat

This pretty little town is mainly attractive as a base for excursions into the nature reserve of forests, rivers, and pools in the **Parc régional d'Armorique**. You can fish for perch and carp in the lake or for trout in the Rivière d'Argent (Silver River), or just glide around the lake among the swans. At the top end of the lake, you wander into dense forest through a fantastic chaos of rocks and grottos variously inhabited by the Devil, some more or less innocent virgin, and King Arthur himself.

Carnac

Like the wild countryside of the interior, the megalithic monuments of Brittany's **menhir country** on the south coast take you back into the legends and mists of time.

Brittany's megalithic menhirs remain a 5,000-year-old mystery.

Carnac is surrounded by fields with thousands of gigantic stones (menhirs) arranged in mysterious alignments and circles (cromlechs) set up some time between 5500 and 3500 B.C., at the rate of one stone a year. Scholars timidly suggest that the alignments are associated with cults of the sun or moon, and the cromlechs may be astronomical arrangements for predicting such phenomena as eclipses.

The alignments occupy three main fields a short walk north of town along the D 196. **Le Ménec**, the biggest, has 1,099 menhirs in 12 rows (plus 70 menhirs in a cromlech around part of the hamlet of Le Ménec). The field of **Kermario** has a dolmen (chamber built of flat slabs on pillars) and 1,029 menhirs in 10 rows. Among them is the Giant of Manio, a menhir over 6 metres (20 feet) high, shaped like a clenched fist. Most impressive is the **Kerlescan** alignment, 594 menhirs that form what local legend calls a frozen army. Once a year, the stones rise up in the middle of the night and march around.

The best time to see them all is early morning, looming out of the mist, or at sunset, throwing dramatic shadows.

La Baule

The best beach in Europe — at least that's the verdict of its regulars. Five km (three miles) of fine sand from Pornichet to Le Pouliguen stretch in a perfect half-moon, past chic sailing and beach clubs, along an **esplanade** of luxury hotels with a casino at the centre.

If you tire of the easy life on the beach front, take an excursion to the west of La Baule around the wilder coast of the peninsula past Batz-sur-Mer (pronounced *Bah*) to the pretty little fishing port and resort of Le Croisic.

LOIRE VALLEY

The Loire is the longest river in France — flowing an impressive 1,012 km (628 miles) from its source in the Vivarais mountains south of Saint-Etienne to its estuary west of Nantes — but the region of the most interesting châteaux, from Chambord to Angers, covers barely a fifth of that distance.

The route we propose for visitors driving down from Paris bypasses Orléans on the *autoroute,* exits at Blois, and, after a side trip to Chambord, heads west on the N 152 to Angers. Just reverse the route if you're coming from Brittany.

For centuries, the Loire river was a vital highway between the Atlantic and the heart of France, making Orléans a major distribution centre for exotic goods from the Orient. The gentry put their carriages on rafts and sailed to Brittany (it took six days from Orléans to Nantes). Commercial traffic declined during the 17th and 18th

---

Son et Lumière

It was the Loire Valley châteaux that started the craze for sound-and-light shows back in the 1950s. With their spectacular settings and rich historical background of romance and murder-most-foul, they are the ideal places for these English- and French-language dramatizations. Most of them run continuously throughout the summer months. The syndicat d'initiative at Blois (3, avenue du Docteur Jean-Laigret; tel. 02 54.74.06.49) can give you details of the programmes. The best are at Chambord, Blois, Chenonceau, and Azay-le-Rideau.

One of the many intricate views across the château courtyard in Blois.

centuries, revived briefly with the advent of the steamship in 1832, then succumbed to silting up and the onslaught of the railways. Today, the Loire is a sleepy waterway, running deep only with the autumn rains or post-winter thaw, and turning its sandbanks and mud flats into veritable islands during the summer.

Blois

Situated on a hill overlooking the Loire river, the town itself invites the visitor to linger a while in the narrow winding streets that lead from the cathedral to the château, pausing to admire the handsome old houses on the Place Saint-Louis and the Rue Porte-Chartraine.

The entrance to the **château** is through the brick-and-stone gateway of the late Gothic Louis XII wing, completed in 1503. Across the courtyard on the right-hand side is the château's most distinctive feature, the splendid **François I wing**. It was built only a dozen years after the Louis XII wing but, reflecting the contrast between the debonair Renaissance prince and his dour predecessor, is a world apart in elegance and panache.

The open loggias of its magnificently sculpted octagonal stone **staircase** dominate the façade. They served as a kind of grandstand for courtiers watching important personages arriving on state occasions. The little beasts carved on the balconies and elsewhere around the château are the royal family's personal emblems — including Louis XII's porcupine, François I's salamander, and Anne de Bretagne's ermine.

On the first floor of the château's François I wing, look out for the wood-panelled **cabinet** (study) of Catherine de Médicis, conniving queen mother and regent to three kings of France. Many of the 237 carved panels, each different, were believed to conceal poisons, as well as jewels and state papers. On the second floor, in 1588, her son Henri III used not poison but a dozen men armed with swords and daggers to do away with his archrival, Duke Henri de Guise.

Chambord

Upriver, east of Blois, in a huge densely wooded park surrounded by 32 km (20 miles) of high walls, the brilliant white **Château de Chambord** is the most extravagant of all the royal residences in the Loire Valley. To have easy access to the wild boar and deer (still to be seen from observation platforms on D 112 and D 33), François I built himself this glorified 440-room hunting lodge. Later kings abandoned it as too big and unheatable — despite 365 fireplaces.

There is an astounding fantasy if not harmony in the arcaded towers and terraces, alternating storeys of arched and rectangular windows,

The extravagant Château de Chambord boasts 365 chimneys, creating a fairy-tale roof line.

and the maze of turrets, stone lanterns, and chimneys. It's believed the central four-towered **donjon** — which makes a dream palace out of a classically feudal castle keep — may have been designed by Leonardo da Vinci, whom François brought to the Loire Valley in 1516. He certainly had the kind of mind that might have created the celebrated **double-ramped spiral staircase** in the donjon's centre, which enables people to go up and down without crossing each other.

Such aids to clandestinity were of vital importance for the jolly shenanigans that went on among François' suite of 2,000 courtiers — as you can imagine for yourself up on the balustraded **rooftop terrace** (which affords a fine **view** over the surrounding park). The nooks and crannies among the chimneys and turrets served as trysting alcoves for those who couldn't get one of the 440 rooms to themselves.

From Blois, follow the N 152 along the right bank of the Loire before crossing over to **Amboise** for a brief look at the remains of the château, largely dismantled under Napoleon. Leonardo da Vinci spent his last days in a small manor house nearby, the **Clos-Lucé**, now a museum illustrating his talents. A bust in the château gardens marks the site of his grave. Chenonceaux (unlike the château, the town is spelt with an "x") is on the south side of the Amboise forest.

There is a soothing symmetry to the gardens at Château Chenonceau.

Chenonceau

Raised on arches to span the Cher river, the château and its pretty gardens still evoke the romantic ghost of its beautiful chatelaine, Diane de Poitiers, mistress to Henri II. She no doubt owed her legendary health and complexion to regular washing and sensible eating — she swam nude in the river and grew her own artichokes in the gardens.

In the **apartments**, in addition to fine 16th-century Flemish tapestries and French, Italian, and Spanish furniture, you'll see Diane's neatly kept household accounts. No one knows whether Primaticcio's vivid contemporary portrait of her as Diana goddess of hunting does full justice to her beauty.

After Henri's death, his widow, Catherine de Médicis, took Chenonceau for herself and added the galleried floors of ballrooms and reception halls that complete the bridge across the river.

If the short walk from the main gate is too much for you, you can take an **electric train** in summer. There are **boat rides** on the river when the water is deep enough.

Loches

To the south of Chenonceaux, on the Indre river, the medieval village of Loches is as much an attraction as the château itself. The **church of Saint-Ours** is an utterly beguiling piece of Romanesque architecture: it has two steeples at either end of the nave, which is surmounted by two bizarre octagonal pyramids in place of a roof. In the interior, the **narthex**, or entrance hall, has some fine, although partially mutilated, sculptures. Over the nave, the two hollow pyramids appear to be designed in the style of chimneys for a castle kitchen.

Stroll along the Rue Saint-Ours and the Rue du Château, then wander around the **ramparts**. Particularly interesting is the 11th-century **donjon** (keep) that formed part of the town's southern defences. Two 15th-century additions served as prisons for royal enemies — most notoriously for the Duke of Milan, who was kept there in total darkness for eight years, only to drop dead on the day of his release, overcome by the blinding sunlight.

At the other end of the fortifications, the terrace of the **Logis royal** (Royal Lodge) affords a delightful view over the village and the Indre Valley. Architecturally, the lodge offers an interesting transition from sober Gothic to more decorative Renaissance. Inside is a little gem of Gothic art: Anne de Bretagne's private oratory, the niches of its stone walls finely carved with her ermine emblem and the symbolic cords of the Franciscan order.

Azay-le-Rideau

If French life still manages to evoke an image of grace and elegance, the **château** at Azay is its epitome. This treasure of late-Gothic architecture, with walls of dazzling white stone beneath grey slate roofs, casts a serene reflection into the waters of the Indre, 30 km (19 miles) southwest of Tours.

It was erected in the early 16th century by François I's treasurer, Gilles Berthelot — part of it on a Venetian-style foundation of timber piles close-driven into the bed of the river. Berthelot's wife,

An eloquent apocalypse tapestry in Angers is one of the Loire Valley's proudest possessions.

Philippe, supervised the design, and the delicacy of its forms, especially the slender conical turrets at each corner and the double-arched loggias of the **main staircase**, are the result. Notice inside how, with the château no longer serving the function of a fortress, the staircase innovated with straight flights and landings rather than the old spiral form that was designed to fend off invaders.

Madame Berthelot had the large vaulted **kitchen** built almost on a level with the river, so that an indoor well provided the closest thing to running water, and an unusually hygienic stone drain sent back the slops. You can see the kind of utensils and cake tins her cooks would have used—at least, until the king confiscated the castle because her husband was cooking the royal books.

Angers

The perfect base for exploring the Loire Valley from its western end, this bustling university town offers some first-class modern shopping in the pedestrian zone around the **Place du Ralliement**.

The ruins of the Eglise Toussaint (dating from the 13th-century) have been beautifully restored and incorporated into the town's **Musée des Beaux-Arts** (at 37, Rue Toussaint) to house a unique collection of sculptures by David d'Angers. This Who's Who of heroes revered in 19th-century France includes not only Balzac and Victor Hugo but also Gutenberg, Paganini, and George Washington (here in Angers you'll see a plaster bust, the bronze of which stands in the United States Congress).

In the imposing 12th- and 13th-century Gothic **Cathédrale Saint-Maurice**, look out for the excellent **stained-glass windows** covering 800 years of the noble art. If not the most beautiful, the **château** is certainly the most formidable in the Loire Valley, a real defensive fortress, its black ramparts still forbidding despite having had their towers decapitated on the orders of Henri III. The château's proudest possession is the great 14th-century **Apocalypse Tapestry** narrating the gospel of Saint John in moving detail. Seventy pieces of this remarkable work survive, out of an original hundred.

SOUTHEAST

Travelling through the southeast of France from the Alps, or down the Rhône Valley from Lyon through Provence to the Côte d'Azur (French Riviera), is like strolling on a sunny morning and taking a leisurely walk down to the beach for a dip in the sea or a lazy sun-bathe. It's one long exercise in self-indulgence.

In the Savoie Alps, the resorts around Mont Blanc (Western Europe's highest mountain) can be as exhilarating for their outdoor life during the summer as they are for their superb winter sports facilities (see pages 195 – 196) and unrivalled *après-ski* attractions. Though less energetic, life is equally refreshing down on the lovely lakes of Annecy and le Bourget.

The sun packs the sweetest of smells in the herbs of Provence.

The Rhône Valley region around Lyon is the epicentre of French gastronomy, so loosen your belt — and your purse-strings. But first work up a healthy appetite wandering around Lyon's charming back streets and alleyways.

In Provence, you take your jacket off and undo a few buttons and do some serious basking among the olive trees and vineyards. There are Roman theatres and amphitheatres to explore, the papal palace at Avignon and a feudal fortress at Les Baux. By which time you'll be ready to do nothing, in great style, in the fleshpots of the Côte d'Azur, or some desultory shopping and museum-seeing in the back country.

We also suggest a small selection of holiday resorts and excursions on Napoleon's wild and beautiful island of Corsica.

SAVOIE

The province of Savoie remained, despite occasional invasions, proudly independent of its more powerful neighbours, cannily playing off Italy and France against each other over the centuries until finally voting by plebiscite to throw in its lot with France in 1860.

Apart from a handful of enterprising smugglers, geologists, and botanists, the French steered clear of the Alps until the mountain-climbing craze was launched by the conquest of Mont Blanc in 1786. But it wasn't until 1924, with the first Winter Olympic Games at Chamonix, that skiing — at the time only cross-country — attracted international attention and a demand for ski resorts that are now famous.

Chamonix

The neighbourhood around the church has enough old-fashioned charm to retain something of the town's 19th-century pioneering atmosphere. For a fuller sense of what it was like when mountain-climbing and skiing were in their infancy, spend an hour or so in the **Musée alpin**, tracing the history of the region, its heroes, and their exploits, in photos and displays of equipment.

For your summer excursions by cable car and rack railway, don't forget to take a sweater, sunglasses, and binoculars — for the sudden change in altitude, brilliant sunlight, and fabulous panoramas. And go carefully until you're used to the rarefied atmosphere. The cable car *(téléphérique)* ride up to the **Aiguille du Midi** (3,800 metres/12,470 feet) is the most spectacular in the French Alps, offering a breathtaking view of **Mont Blanc's** snow-covered peak, altitude 4,807 metres

(15,770 feet), and the surrounding landscape. For some easy hiking, stop off at the lower station of Plan de l'Aiguille (2,310 metres/7,580 feet). The cable car up to **Le Brévent** (2,525 metres/8,284 feet), northwest of Chamonix, will give you a panoramic view of the whole north face of Mont Blanc and the Aiguille du Midi, too. For a close-up view of a glacier and formidable ice caves, take the cable car and rack railway up the Montenvers to the dazzling **Mer de Glace** (Sea of Ice).

Megève

This perennially fashionable resort is particularly popular for family skiing holidays. The slopes provide sufficient challenge without being breakneck, which makes them ideal for intermediate skiers and also enables instructors to pay special attention to children.

For summer visitors, in addition to superb facilities for tennis and swimming, the town's verdant setting of grassy alpine meadows and pine, spruce, and larch forest is perfect for hikes. A cable car takes you to **Mont d'Arbois** (1,833 metres/6,014 feet) for a great view of the Aravis peaks and Mont Blanc. Hikers then continue to **Mont Joly** (about 5 hours to and from the Mont d'Arbois cable-car station) for an even more spectacular view.

Annecy

This is one of the towns that define the quiet joy of provincial France. Cross the **Parc du Pâquier** to a waterfront observation platform for a first view of the lake and its backdrop of mountains. The lakeside promenade back towards town takes you over the Pont des Amours and west to the 15th-century Dominican **Eglise Saint-Maurice**.

In the middle of the Thiou river (whose source is the lake itself) stands the 12th-century prison, the **Palais de l'Isle**. Explore the **old town** and its 15th- and 16th-century houses along the Rue Perrière and Rue Sainte-Claire. The imposing **château** — former home of the Counts of Geneva — contains an interesting museum devoted to local archaeology and folklore and the natural history of the

Alps. The château's terrace is the best vantage point for pictures of the old town.

The cruises around **Lake Annecy** start from the Thiou river.  Some of them include a cable-car ride to the top of **Mont Veyrier** (1,291 metres/4,230 feet) and its spectacular panorama of the Alps, but all will give you a marvellous swan's-eye view of the jagged snowcapped peaks of the Dents de Lanfon and the rugged La Tournette to the east, and the gentler Entrevernes and Taillefer mountains to the west. If you drive, take the D 909 east to the Mont Veyrier cable car, continuing on to the pretty town of **Menthon-Saint-Bernard** and its medieval castle high above the lake. The D 42 takes you up to the **Col de la Forclaz** (1,157 metres/3,800 feet).

Aix-les-Bains

This spa town on the edge of the Lac du Bourget has for centuries offered cures for rheumatism and broken hearts. Ever since the fourth century Roman Emperor Gratianus took his natural hot bath here, people have been plunging into what they call the *bouillon* or "hot broth" at 42°C (107.6°F). In the 19th century, the Romantic poet Alphonse de Lamartine stopped off to fix his liver and a bout of melancholia with a

That pretty little Palais de l'Isle was once Annecy's prison.

lyric tribute, *Le Lac*, that had his fans weeping enough tears to flood the lovely chestnut trees and poplars on its banks.

The **Musée du Docteur-Faure** (Villa des Chimères, Boulevard des Côtes) exhibits some marvellous Rodin bronzes and water-colours, and works by Degas, Sisley, Corot, and Cézanne. But by and large, the great pleasure here is to do nothing at all: take the waters, siesta, stroll along the **Boulevard du Lac**, and siesta again.

The major attraction is the **lake cruise**, which starts out from the Grand Port. With its "harmonious waves…moan of the wind, sigh of the reeds, light perfume of the balmy air," the lake is truly as romantic and dreamy as Lamartine claimed. One of the cruise's destinations is the neo-Gothic **Abbaye de Hautecombe**, well worth a visit if you can attend a mass performed with the Gregorian chant.

RHONE VALLEY

From its source high in the Swiss Alps, the Rhône courses down to the Mediterranean, bending southwards at Lyon. It has always been France's vital central artery, serving as a channel for river, road, and rail traffic between the north and the south. Its valley was the main path of the Romans' invasion of Gaul, and the key to Lyon's commercial wealth in the Middle Ages.

Located at the crossroads between north and south, Lyon was the ideal choice as the Roman capital of Gaul. It has become the natural capital of French gastronomy: at the conjunction of Atlantic and Continental climates, the farmers get the best out of a subtle mixture of the cooler and damper north with the first hints of Mediterranean warmth and light. The regions around Lyon produce some of the best food in the country: poultry from Bresse; freshwater fish from the Savoie lakes; Charolais beef; pears, apples, and cherries from orchards to the north of town, and peaches and apricots from the ones to the south.

> Some local cooperatives produce very good wines. Much of it doesn't travel well and is therefore never exported.

The fruit industry started in earnest in the 1880s as a reaction to the dreaded phylloxera disease that struck the local vineyards. Today, the **Beaujolais country** thrives as never before, and wine-lovers on their way down to Lyon often make a detour through such sweet-sounding places as Juliénas, Chénas, Morgon, and Brouilly. Continuing south, opposite Tournon, they may want to pause in order to sample a celebrated *Côtes du Rhône* at Tain-l'Hermitage.

Lyon

Prosperous since the Middle Ages for its trade fairs, banking, and silk manufacture, Lyon still has a bouncy pride and taste for the good life.

Eating is a serious business in the gourmet mecca of Lyon, and often requires expert guidance.

Salade niçoise tastes even better than usual with a first pressing of oil from Castillon's olive groves.

In addition to the great shrines of *haute cuisine* in and around the city, appropriately sumptuous in décor and price, you should also seek out the little bars and cafés and the old-fashioned bistrots that the Lyonnais call *bouchons* (after the bunches of straw or foliage that served as a sign for the restaurant). But it's not easy to make your way around town to find them, since the city is built across the looping confluence of the Saône and Rhône rivers, with hills on either side and a peninsula in the middle. A street map is a must.

So head first for the tourist office on the huge **Place Bellecour**, in the middle of the peninsula between the two rivers. The square has a pretty flower market, and you know you're approaching the south of France when you see your first serious games of *boules* here.

Cross over the Pont Bonaparte to stroll around the fine Renaissance houses of Lyon's **old town** between the Saône river and the

Fourvière hill. Some of the best are along the Rue Saint-Georges, Rue Saint-Jean, and Rue Juiverie. In the Rue de Gadagne, in the handsome **Hôtel de Gadagne** you can see a museum of the history of Lyon and the marionettes of the town's celebrated Guignol theatre. If your French is up to it, you may enjoy the traditional folklore plays, parodies of opera, and contemporary satires performed at the Palais du Conservatoire (for details ask at the tourist office). To take in the full sweep of the city, ride the funicular railway from Gare Saint-Jean up the hill to the **observatory** at the Church of Notre-Dame-de-Fourvière.

The town's **Musée des Beaux-Arts**, finely housed in a 17th-century Benedictine abbey (20, Place des Terreaux), has a rich collection of European paintings, and sculpture. Among the most notable are three Rodin bronzes in its cloister, and works by Perugino, Veronese, El Greco, Rubens, Courbet, Manet, and Matisse.

PROVENCE

Though much of France is cool, green, and rational, it likes to think of itself as a Mediterranean country, warm, golden, and passionate. Blame it on the seductive charm of Provence. On those rare occasions when the Frenchman seeks to be loved, he seems to be trying to pass as a Provençal, a jovial, generous fellow with a colourful, pleasant-sounding, but not necessarily profound gift of the gab.

The monuments of the Roman Empire still stand proudly in Orange, Arles, and Nîmes, like the medieval strongholds in Les Baux and Avignon, but the most important pleasure of Provence remains the sensuality of its sun-soaked landscape. Squat little vineyards stretch to the foot of the rugged Alpilles, cypresses loom like signposts to the sea above the twisted olive trees and almond groves, while the aromatic umbrella pines provide natural shelter for a blissful nap.

As you drive through the scrubland they call *garrigue*, keep your window rolled well down to let in the fragrance of the lavender and

153

the wild rosemary, thyme, and savory to which local market gardeners add sage, tarragon, and marjoram for the famous *herbes de Provence*. Even the garlic and onions grown here have a sweet taste.

The accent is very definitely on unabashed indolence, but Provence bristles with cultural activity in the summer months, each town using its ancient amphitheatre, cathedral, or palace as a magnificent setting for festivals of music, theatre, and the other arts (see page 199).

The itinerary we propose deals in turn with the various layers of Provençal life: the "Roman" towns of Orange, Vaison, Nîmes, and Arles; the medieval bastions of Les Baux and Avignon; the ancient villages of the Lubéron mountains; and finally the cheerful streets of Aix-en-Provence.

Orange

The grandiose ancient monuments of this once-prosperous Roman trading centre on the road from Arles to Lyon strike a delightfully incongruous note in the peaceful Provençal backwater of today.

Since Orange is the gateway to Provence, make an appropriate entrance into town from the north, at the imposing three-arched **arc de triomphe**. Erected in A.D. 21, it stands on a traffic island across the old N 7, which here traces the route of the ancient Via Agrippa. The friezes on the northern side, depicting battle scenes, weaponry, and naval equipment, celebrate Julius Caesar's victories over the Gallic tribes of the region and the merchant fleet of the Greek colony in Marseille.

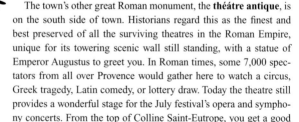

The town's other great Roman monument, the **théâtre antique**, is on the south side of town. Historians regard this as the finest and best preserved of all the surviving theatres in the Roman Empire, unique for its towering scenic wall still standing, with a statue of Emperor Augustus to greet you. In Roman times, some 7,000 spectators from all over Provence would gather here to watch a circus, Greek tragedy, Latin comedy, or lottery draw. Today the theatre still provides a wonderful stage for the July festival's opera and symphony concerts. From the top of Colline Saint-Eutrope, you get a good bird's-eye view of the theatre in relation to the triumphal arch and the Rhône Valley beyond.

Vaison-la-Romaine

A pretty excursion 30 km (19 miles) northeast of Orange along the D 975 takes you to the site of one of the most important towns of Roman Provence, excavated north of Vaison's attractive medieval quarters. To gain a better understanding of the layout of the ancient town, its streets, houses, shops, fountains, and theatre, visit the **museum** on the Puymin hill. It displays some superb marble sculptures of the second century A.D., most notably a Venus and the Emperor Hadrian and his wife Sabina.

Pont du Gard

Take the A 9 *autoroute* southwest from Orange till you come to the Fournès-Remoulins exit, then follow the D 981, to this gigantic 2,000-year-old **aqueduct**, without doubt the most impressive of all the Roman monuments preserved from ancient Gaul. It carried spring water from near Uzés to the town of Nîmes, over a distance of 35 km (22 miles).

Built of enormous granite blocks joined without mortar in three tiers of arches, 6 at the base, 11 at the middle level, and 35 at the top,

The Romans' Pont du Gard is a great feat of engineering, and also strikingly beautiful.

this highly functional construction is also remarkably beautiful, in total harmony with its landscape. The roof walkway is 275 metres (300 yards) long (vertigo victims abstain). You'll find the best view of the ensemble is from the river bank near the Château Saint-Privat, beyond the aqueduct.

Nîmes

The Emperor Augustus made a gift of this town to the veterans of his victorious battle against Antony and Cleopatra in Egypt, commemorated to this day in the Nîmes coat of arms with the chained crocodile of the Nile. The grand Roman **amphitheatre** *(arènes)* was built for gladiator battles; later it was used for combats between lions and Christians. Having served as a fortress for the invading Visigoths in the fifth century and as a communal residence for the poor in the Middle Ages, it has now resumed its tradition with summer bullfights.

The more pacific Greek-style temple known as the **Maison carrée**, an elegant monument dating from the first century B.C., is noted for the finely sculpted Corinthian capitals on its columns. After a varied history as town hall, residence, stable, and church, it was saved from plans devised by Louis XIV's minister Colbert to move it stone-by-stone to Versailles. Today it houses a small **museum** of Roman sculpture and mosaics.

The **Jardin de la Fontaine** — a pretty, tree-shaded 18th-century park on the slopes of Mont Cavalier at the northwest edge of the town — offers a refreshing respite from the summer heat and a good **view** of the surrounding mountains. The park is built around the spring of Nemausus, which gave the town its name; it includes a ruined temple attributed to the hunting goddess Diana, and a Roman tower of no known significance at all.

Arles

An important town in Roman Gaul, replacing Lyon as capital towards the end of the Empire, Arles boasts a powerful **amphitheatre** *(arènes)*, seating over 20,000 in the days of the gladiators. For the most spectacular view, climb up to the broad path that runs along the roof of the arches on its perimeter.

Less lucky than the one at Orange, the Roman **theatre** *(théâtre antique)* has been reduced to ruins over the centuries, as builders carted away masonry for their houses, churches, and town walls — but the remains, in a pleasant park, are quietly eloquent of its noble past.

In the **Eglise Saint-Trophime** (on Place de la République), you can see the Roman influence recurring in the triumphal-arch design of its splendid porch. This masterpiece of Provençal Romanesque sculpture depicts the Last Judgment in the tympanum above the doors, surrounded by statues of the saints. Nearby, the church cloister, **Cloître Saint-Trophime**, with its beautiful sculpted capitals on the pillars, is a haven of peace.

To the southeast of the town, cut off by a railway track, you'll find the melancholy remains of the **Alyscamps**, the famous Roman and medieval burial grounds that were a favourite subject of Van Gogh when he came to live in Arles in 1888.

La Camargue

At the delta of the Rhône, where its two arms spill into the Mediterranean, the Camargue has been reclaimed from the sea to form a national **nature reserve**, with modern resorts along the coast. The region is famous for its white horses, which you can hire to ride along the sandflats, and for the black bulls that race through the streets of Provençal towns to the bullfight. With permission from the Directeur de la

The Romanesque sculpture in the cloister of Saint-Trophime deserves detailed examination.

réserve, La Capelière, Arles, you can visit the nature reserve, popular with birdwatchers for its wild duck, herons, and pink flamingos.

☛ Les Baux-de-Provence

The astounding natural location of this medieval citadel, a single massive outcrop of rock cut adrift from the Alpilles mountains like a ship of war separated from its fleet, exerts a unique grip on the popular imagination. The invasion of the tourist buses in high season has made the little village surrounding the old fortress unbearably crowded. But a visit in early spring, autumn, or best of all, on a brilliant crisp winter's day can be a rare moment invested with all the magic of the Middle Ages.

The barons of Les Baux put the star of the Nativity on their coat of arms, claiming to be descendants of Balthazar, the lord of the treasury among the Three Wise Men. It was with that brazen pride that they ruled the 79 towns of medieval Provence, and their impregnable redoubt became a centre of courtly love prized by travelling troubadours.

Looking for the Ghost of Van Gogh

Van Gogh wrote in a letter from Arles: "Oh, the beautiful sun of midsummer! It beats upon my head, and I do not doubt that it makes one a little queer." It inspired his most fertile period, but also triggered the frenzy in which he cut off an ear and had himself committed to the asylum in nearby Saint-Rémy. A year later, he died after shooting himself. Today, the tourist office in the Boulevard des Lices provides a map tracing 30 of the sites he painted while in Arles. His house and favourite café have gone, bombed in 1944 — but beside the last stones of the Alyscamps and the *Jardin public* the sun is just as strong as ever, you can find fields round about filled with the sunflowers and olive trees Van Gogh loved to paint, and you can still imagine the painter tramping the road to Tarascon in the inadequate shade of the plane trees.

For centuries the barons defied the papal authority in Avignon and the kings of France, offering refuge to Protestants during the Wars of Religion, until Louis XIII ordered the destruction of the fortress in 1632 — and then made the residents pay the costs. However, the demolition of the citadel was a half-hearted job, as you can see when you stroll through the **Ville morte** (Dead City), the entrance of which is at the Musée lapidaire, in the Hôtel de la Tour-du-Brau. The ramparts, castle walls, and ruined chapels all reveal their own views over the sheer ravines to the surrounding mountains.

The jagged peaks of the Alpilles are the last gasp of the great Alpine chain that sweeps in a 1,200-km (750-mile) arc from Vienna. If you're tempted by a hike or bike ride around the valleys, drive then on into **Saint-Rémy-de-Provence**, where the *syndicat d'initiative* provides detailed itineraries and advice on renting a bicycle.

Avignon

The City of the Popes is today a proud cultural centre, home of one of Europe's greatest arts festivals, and all year round a lively and cheerful town of good cafés, art galleries, and fashionable shops. They no longer dance on the Pont d'Avignon, but there's plenty going on in the discothèques.

The opulence and luxury have disappeared from the **Palais des Papes**, but your visit will still give you an idea of the grandeur and above all the embattled situation of these maverick popes entrenched behind the ramparts of a feudal fortress. The entrance is on the west side, through the Porte des Champeaux, and the guided tour takes you across the Grande Cour (transformed into an open-air theatre for the summer festival) to the **Palais vieux**. Its forbidding design reflects the pious austerity of its builder, Benedict XII, quite out of keeping with the style of his high-living successors. East of Benedict's cloister is the **consistory**, where the pope met with his cardinals, today decorated with the superb **frescoes** of Simone Martini transferred from the porch of Notre-Dame des Doms cathedral. The process of raising the frescoes from the porch walls revealed Martini's original drawings, which are now displayed beside the finished paintings.

In Clement VI's more decorative **Palais nouveau**, Martini's disciple Giovannetti has painted frescoes of the Old Testament prophets on the ceiling of the Grand Audience Hall. Beyond the much-remodelled cathedral, north of the palace, is the pleasant garden of the **Rocher des Doms**, extending to the outer ramparts. From here you will get your best view of the **Pont d'Avignon** — more correctly called the Pont Saint-Bénézet — broken off halfway across the Rhône river. In fact, they used to dance *under* the bridge, on a little island.

The newly restored **Petit Palais**, at the northern end of the Place du Palais, displays, together with interesting Gothic sculpture and

Popes, Pro and Anti

Imagine the President of the United States deciding to leave Washington and build a new White House in the middle of Arizona. That's what it was like in 1309 when Pope Clement V moved his Holy See from the turmoils of Italy to Avignon. Seven popes, all French, made their home beside the Rhône. Like Rome, Avignon became a city of pomp and intrigue. It attracted great Italian artists, such as the poet Petrarch and Sienese painter Simone Martini, but was soon decried as "an unholy Babylon" of gaudy luxury and vicious riffraff. Not at all to the liking of the pious mystic, Catherine of Siena, who brought Pope Gregory XI back to Rome in 1377. But a year later, more power struggles caused the Great Schism — doctrinal problems were not uppermost in papal deliberations in those days. Rival popes, known as anti-popes, set up shop back in Avignon for another 40 years. The Schism ended and the infighting returned once and for all to Rome, but Avignon remained part of the papal lands in Provence until the French Revolution.

frescoes of the Avignon school, a fine collection of Italian painting from the 13th to 16th centuries, including major works by Taddeo Gaddi, Veneziano, Botticelli, and, the museum's masterpiece, Carpaccio's *Holy Conversation.*

The new **Foundation Angladon-Dubrujeaud** (5, Rue Laboureur) presents an exceptional private art collection kept secret until the museum's opening, in 1996. Here you'll find many 19th- and 20th-century masterpieces never before shown to the public, by the likes of Picasso, Cézanne, Van Gogh, Modigliani, Manet, and Degas. Centre of the bustling life of the modern town is the airy **Place de l'Horloge**, surround-ed by cafés and a pedestrian zone of smart shops along the Rue des Marchands. At the far end are the Place Jérusalem and an old synagogue.

For an interesting walk through the **old town**, start at the 14th-century **Eglise Saint-Didier**, with its excruciatingly painful altar sculpture of *Jesus Carrying the Cross* by the Dalmatian artist Francesco Laurana. The Rue du Roi-René will take you past some handsome 17th- and 18th-century houses; and on the pretty, cobblestoned **Rue des Teinturiers** you can see where the dyers used to work the paddlewheels for their Indian-style cloth in the little Sorgue river, emerging here from its underground course.

Avignon's July festival centres on the medieval Palais des Papes.

Lubéron and Vaucluse

Starting out from Cavaillon, home of France's, nay, the world's, most succulent cantaloupe melons, head east to the Lubéron mountains, the heart of the Provençal countryside and now a protected regional park. Whole valleys are carpeted with lavender, and the *garrigue* scrubland is ashimmer with every colour and fragrance of the sunny Mediterranean. The villages have been lovingly restored.

Perched on a spur of rock, the village of **Oppède-le-Vieux** has been rescued from its ruins by writers and artists seeking a residence off the beaten track. The most welcome visitor respects the peace of the writer and buys a canvas or two from the painter. **Ménerbes** is also up on a hill, with a medieval citadel that served as the Protestants' last redoubt in the 16th-century Wars of Religion. Behind the church on the outskirts of town you have a magnificent view over the mountains to the Vaucluse plateau and the distant peak of Mont Ventoux.

Bonnieux juts out over the Coulon Valley. From its terrace up on the hill behind the town hall, look northwest to the rust-coloured ravines surrounding **Roussillon**. In order to set off that startling red, the villagers of Roussillon paint their houses with every imaginable variation of ochre from the neighbouring quarries.

Its dramatic location, looking across to the Lubéron from the southern edge of the Vaucluse plateau, has made **Gordes** one of the most prosperous villages in the region, popular for its boutiques and little galleries. Its houses hug the hillside on steep, winding streets, leading to a 16th-century castle at the top. About 2 km (1 mile) southwest of Gordes is the strange little **Village Noir**, consisting of *bories*, old dry-stone cabins grouped around a baker's oven and serving as a museum of rural life in Provence.

 Aix-en-Provence

It was the first Roman town in Gaul (a citadel and spa founded in 125 B.C. as Aquae Sextiae), but nowadays there's nothing left of that.

Elegant, charming, and cheerful, Aix forces a grateful smile out of the most world-weary traveller.

The town's great treasure is a street. There are few more refreshing experiences than to arrive in Aix at the end of a long hot afternoon and walk along the majestic green arbour formed by the plane trees arching across the **cours Mirabeau** and its fountains. One side of the street is a quiet row of gracious buff-coloured 17th-century mansions, abandoned by their aristocratic owners to banks or pastry shops dispensing *calissons*, the celebrated local delicacy made from ground almonds, orange, and candied melon. The other side is a bustle of cinemas, boutiques, and cafés. A rendezvous on the terrace of the Café des Deux Garçons is one of the rare obligations that Provençal life imposes.

People still come to take the waters — the moss-covered fountain in the middle of the cours Mirabeau spurts water with a natural heat of 34°C (93.2°F). But the university keeps the spirit of the town young and cosmopolitan. You'll find fountains and little squares scattered all over the old town north of the cours Mirabeau (one of the most attractive of these squares is the tranquil **Place d'Albertas**).

The cathedral is less worthy of your attention than its exquisite little Romanesque **Cloître Saint-Sauveur**, a peaceful refuge for a quiet read. Chamber music and choral recitals are held there during Aix's summer music festival; the operas are performed behind the cloister, in the Palais de l'Ancien Archevêché.

Paul Cézanne spent the greater part of his life in Aix, and his studio (Atelier de Cézanne, 9, avenue Paul-Cézanne) has been preserved as a little **museum,** including his palette and other personal belongings. But the best way to evoke his memory is to make the pretty drive out to the subject of his most famous landscapes, the **Montagne Sainte-Victoire**, 14 km (9 miles) east of Aix on D 10.

COTE D'AZUR

When the British invented this playground in the 19th century, they called it the French Riviera, distinguishing it from the Italian one that begins round the corner at Ventimiglia. Nowadays, it's considered more chic to use its French name, the Côte d'Azur.

In summer it's overcrowded, but that's the fun of it. You can always head inland into the hills for a few moments' peace. It's the country's safest bet for good weather, for hot days and balmy nights. And apart from an occasional unsightly modern apartment block, the coastline outside the resorts still has considerable charm. The native umbrella pines share the landscape with the acacia, eucalyptus, and palm trees imported by the British for the inevitable gardens they built around their villas. For years they came only for the mild winter to cure their chilblains, going home for the summer when, in those days, the coast was infested by mosquitos.

Most of the beaches are great: the boys and girls are gorgeous, and the older set possess a Felliniesque charm that makes for some very entertaining people-watching. Nobody knows any more where the Côte d'Azur begins and ends. Purists restrict it to the stretch of coast from Cannes to Menton. That takes in only the original, more expensive resort towns: namely Juan-les-Pins, Antibes, Nice, and Monte-Carlo, with Menton dismissed as a pretty but too sleepy retirement community. In recent years, the tourist industry has extended the "Côte" westwards to include popular family-style resorts like Saint-Raphaël and Sainte-Maxime, and the special glamorous phenomenon of Saint Tropez. You really have to stretch your imagination to include Marseille too, but this tough and gritty metropolis is hard to overlook — particularly if you like *bouillabaisse*. The Marseillais insist it's the best, and it's not wise to argue with the

A painter is gaining a new perspective on Saint-Tropez's old port.

Marseillais. In fact, to keep them happy, we'll start with Marseille and work our way east.

Marseille

This noisiest and most boisterous of ports is not exactly a tourist attraction. But as France's oldest city, founded by Greek colonists 2,500 years ago, Marseille is not to be ignored. Its gabby citizens play the meanest game of *boule*; the politicians make their Boston, Chicago, or Liverpool counterparts look like choirboys; and endless police raids have still not succeeded in breaking the French Connection.

Soak up the city's heady atmosphere along the main thoroughfare, the **Canebière**, where sailors from all over the world have broken their hearts and their noses. The **Vieux Port** marks the spot where Phocaean-Greek merchants from Asia Minor docked to create their Western Mediterranean trading post. Today, it's a colourful harbour for yachts and motor launches. On the quai des Belges, you can take a cruise out to the **Château d'If**, the island prison that was the scene of Alexandre Dumas's *Count of Monte Cristo*.

Saint Tropez

The resort discovered by the film stars of the 1960s, and whose popularity has been perpetuated by fashion photographers, their models, and sundry groupies of the good life is still going strong. When it's deserted in wintertime Saint Tropez has an undeniably enchanting melancholy — but only for habitués who have known the summer madness.

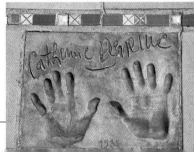

The handprints of Catherine Deneuve are just one step in the Cannes walk of fame.

The essence of Saint Tropez has always been the crazy parade of people along the **Vieux Port**, nipping in and out of boutiques with their ever more audacious fashions, on and off the flashy yachts and table-hopping through the cafés. Like the Deux Magots in Paris or the Deux Garçons in Aix, the **Sénéquier** might almost be consecrated by the Ministry of Culture as a national people-watching monument where, lounging in their scarlet canvas chairs, the pretty watch the beautiful, and others.

You may not find many masterpieces among the offerings of the harbourside artists, but the **Musée de l'Annonciade** (Place Charles-Grammont) has a quite outstanding collection of paintings from 1890 to 1940 — many of them studies of Saint Tropez itself. Housed in a handsomely renovated 16th-century chapel with wonderful natural Mediterranean light, they include important works by Bonnard, Van Dongen, Matisse, and Braque.

Away from the harbourside, the town keeps its Provençal character intact on **Place des Lices**, nicely shaded by plane trees for the morning market, a late-afternoon game of *boules,* or a sunset apéritif at the Café des Arts. For a fine view over the port, climb up to the 16th-century **citadel**, built to defend the town on a coast under constant attack from pirates. Drive out of town south along the D 93, signposted *Route des Plages*, to Tahiti or Pampelonne for the best **beaches**, which have fine sand shaded by lovely umbrella pines.

☛ Cannes

Pure piece of hedonism, this luxury resort offers a magnificent beach front, the most elegant of boutiques and jewellery shops, and the ultimate in grand hotels. An exquisite destiny for a sleepy little fishing village that was "made" by a nearby cholera epidemic in 1834. That's what stopped British law reformer Lord Brougham on his way to Italy. He fell in love with Cannes's climate, built himself a villa, and his aristocratic pals soon followed.

Overlooking the fine white-sand beaches, the **Croisette** is Cannes's grand palmtree-lined promenade; it runs from the Palm Beach casino past the great hotels to the old port and the gigantic new **Palais des Festivals**. This is the venue of the international film festival in May and the recorded music festival (MIDEM) in January. If you like a mob scene, both these festivals offer plenty of opportunities to gawk at the stars of show business, but don't expect to get in to any of the galas unless you have professional accreditation.

Up on the hill overlooking the port, **Le Suquet** preserves something of the old fishing village and gives you a fine view of the coast. This may whet your appetite for a boat cruise (from the port's Gare maritime) to the **Iles de Lérins**, where you can stroll through the eucalyptus and pine groves and beautiful flower gardens.

A few km (a couple of miles) east of Cannes are two towns renowned for their craftwork. At **Vallauris**, the ceramics and pottery industry was revived almost single-handedly by Picasso, who worked there after World War II. He also decorated its Romanesque chapel with murals entitled *La Guerre et la Paix* and left a bronze sculpture on the Place Paul-Isnard. **Biot** — certainly worth visiting for its well-preserved 16th-century centre — is known for heavy tinted glassware that has tiny Champagne-like bubbles.

Refreshing fountain for hot days in Saint-Paul-de-Vence.

Saint-Paul-de-Vence

This feudal fortified village is situated amidst colourful terraces of vines, bougainvillaea, and mimosa, with cypresses as their sentinels. To enjoy the view over the valley at leisure, take a drink on the terrace of the Colombe d'Or restaurant. If you stop for dinner, you'll be able to inspect the restaurant's famous collection of paintings by Matisse, Derain, and Utrillo. An even more impressive collection of modern art awaits you at the splendid **Fondation Maeght**, located on a grassy hill just outside the town. Here sculpture is the main attraction, with an imposing black stabile by Alexander Calder at the entrance, some monumental pieces by Miró in the gardens, and a matchless array of Giacometti statues in the beautiful courtyard.

Nice

An ancient Greek trading post, the town manages to combine the atmosphere of a resort with a gutsy, bustling city life. The tempting shops and first-class restaurants more than make up for the pebble beach. Instead of sprawling on sand, natives and visitors alike take the air on the grand **Promenade des Anglais**, financed by the town's English colony in 1822 to replace a wretched little footpath. Its most remarkable landmark is a masterpiece of *Belle Epoque* wedding-cake architecture, the pink-domed **Hôtel Negresco**. The promenade terminates with a spectacular display of flowers and fountains in the **Jardin Albert-Ier**.

The **vieille ville** is at its best at one of the early morning **fish market** held on Place Saint-François. Find out what's good that day for your evening meal. The **port** is worth a visit for a genteel waterside dinner or, more amusing, a drink at the rough-and-ready sailors' taverns.

For a good view over the port and the Baie des Anges, climb up to the little park on top of the hill still known as **Le Château**, even though its castle was destroyed nearly 300 years ago. The ruins you can see there now are the remains of the 11th-century cathedral.

Don't be fooled by the tranquil exterior of the Monte-Carlo Casino. Inside, stakes are high and many players only seem *calm.*

Les Corniches

The route from Nice to Monaco, along the precipices of the Maritime Alps' southern slopes, offers one of the most spectacular drives in the country. There are actually three winding roads, or *corniches*, all safe but exciting: the *Grande*, the high road, starting out from the avenue des Diables-Bleus in Nice; the *Moyenne*, the middle one, beginning at Place Max-Barel; and the *Inférieure*, along the coast from Boulevard Carnot, but practically always jammed with traffic.

The **Grande Corniche** follows the route of the ancient Roman road, Via Aurelia. Stop off at **Belvédère d'Eze** and **La Turbie** for great views of the coast, especially at night for the lights of Monaco. In La Turbie, climb up to the remains of a curious 2,000-year-old Roman mon-

Table For One

One evening back in the 1920s, James Gordon Bennett didn't like being kept waiting for his usual table at Monte-Carlo's Café Riche. So, the multimillionaire American newspaper publisher bought the café, fired the manager, and gave it to Ciro, his favorite waiter.

ument — the towering **Trophée des Alpes**, erected by Emperor Augustus to commemorate victories over the 44 Gallic tribes named in the inscription on the base.

The highlight of the **Moyenne Corniche**, the best road of the three, is the hilltop village of **Eze**. Hanging at a dizzying angle above the sea, it was once the fortress of Ligurian brigands. In summer it's a bit of a tourist trap, but take a look at the cacti and tropical flowers (plus ruins of a 14th-century castle) in the **Jardin exotique**. Its terrace affords the best view of the coast.

☞ Monaco

The cliché is the truth, a marvel deserving close examination: Monaco really is a millionaire's paradise. Ever since the roulette wheel and baccarat tables began bringing in enough money to do away with taxes in the 19th century, this tiny principality has attracted the cream of dethroned Eastern European monarchs, tired American moguls, and Nordic striplings resting their tennis elbow and athlete's foot.

Surrounded by **exotic gardens** to provide a little sweet-scented breathing space, gleaming skyscrapers have sprung up to pack all that wealth into the tiny area between the mountains and Mediterranean. North of the square-shaped port, **Monte-Carlo** is the centre of the principality's luxury. The world's most celebrated **casino** was designed by Charles Garnier, architect of the Paris Opera House, and has the same grandiose nonsense all over the façade, foyer, and gambling rooms. Don't miss the lovely nude nymphs smoking cigarillos on the ceiling of the Salon Rose.

Across the square, the **Hôtel de Paris** is another monument of unabashed ostentation. In the lobby, gamblers in search of luck have stroked Louis XIV's bronze equestrian statue until the horse's fetlock shines like the gold they lose next door. The outrageous Second Empire décor of the dining-room provided the perfect setting for famed chef Auguste Escoffier to create his outrageously elaborate sauces. The **Palais du Prince** up on Monaco Rock is a fairy-tale affair, neo-Renaissance and neo-Baroque, with a quaint **changing of the guard** — fife, drums, and all — at 11:55 A.M. every day.

CORSICA

In every sense a region apart from the rest of France, this rugged, unspoiled island offers dramatic coastlines and a wild interior of densely forested hills. The population of less than quarter of a million is concentrated mainly in the two major towns of Bastia (industrial and noisy, but with a colorful old town) and the more attractive Ajaccio.

You can alternate indolent days on the beach with some of the Mediterranean's best deep-sea diving, boat excursions around pirate coves, canoeing and fishing on inland rivers, or hikes and picnics in the mountains. For the holidaymaker, the best seaside resorts are along the indented shorelines of the west and south coasts, for which Ajaccio's airport and harbour (for the car ferry from Nice, Toulon, or Marseille) provide a convenient gateway. Give yourself plenty of driving time to reach your destination, as the roads are narrow and tortuous.

Some Hero

You wouldn't believe, from all the statues and souvenirs, and the streets named after them, that Corsica once heartily hated the whole Bonaparte clan. In the 1760s, when nearly 500 years of rule under the city-republic of Genoa was coming to an end, Carlo Maria Buonaparte fervently supported Corsican independence. But the island was ceded to France in 1768, and Carlo Maria promptly became an equally fervent supporter of Louis XV. His son Napoleon, born a year later, became a Corsican nationalist but went on, with brother Lucien, to champion the French Revolution's opposition to the island's separatism. The family house in Ajaccio was plundered to cries of "Death to the traitors of the fatherland!" Things didn't improve when Napoleon became Emperor. The city celebrated his abdication by tossing his statue into the Mediterranean.

Ajaccio

At the head of the Gulf of Ajaccio, Napoleon's birthplace is the liveliest of Corsican towns, but tourists impatient to get out to the seaside resorts are usually content with a stroll around the **port** and a pilgrimage to the **Maison Bonaparte** (Rue Saint-Charles). A guided tour of the house will tell you how, on Assumption Day (August 15) of 1769, pious mother Letizia was rushed out of church with her first birth pains. She made it no farther than a first-floor sofa to bring little Nabulio kicking and screaming into the world he was soon to conquer. The sofa you see there now is a replica, the original having been stolen during the Revolution. South of Ajaccio, the major seaside resorts are **Porticcio** and **Propriano**, both with sandy beaches and good opportunities for sailing and deep-sea diving.

☞ Bonifacio

The best way to approach this proud, old town perched high on the cliffs is by boat, past the limpid blue waters of the **Sdragonato cave** and the **Escalier du roi d'Aragon**, a staircase cut diagonally into the cliff face, used by the soldiers of the Spanish king in an abortive siege of the town in the 15th century. When you are visiting the old town on foot, you can enjoy an exhilarating walk down the staircase to the base of the cliffs and along the water's edge.

Porto-Vecchio

Surrounded by a pretty forest of cork oaks and sweet-smelling eucalyptus, the gulf surrounding Porto-Vecchio boasts an ever-expanding series of luxury resorts, the best being out on the fine sandy beaches of **Cala Rossa**. Inland, there are some beautiful excursions to be made into the forests of **l'Ospedale** and **Zonza**. The cork oaks are stripped of their valuable bark every ten years or so, baring a russet-brown trunk until the cork grows back again.

For a memorable picnic up on the lovely wild mountain pass of **Bavella**, take some of the delicious Corsican tomatoes, plus smoked liver sausage *(figatelli)* and ewe's or goat's milk cheese *(broccio)*. Be careful with the heady Corsican wines before sundown; the most enjoyable ones are the *rosés*.

Golfe de Porto

The coast of Corsica offers fun and sun for beachcombers of all ages.

Some of France's most grandiose panoramas of sea and landscape are clustered around this gulf 70 km (43 miles) north of Ajaccio. **Piana** is the most delightful of the gulf's sleepy village resorts, unspoiled by commercialization and blessed with the nearby natural wonders of **Capo Rosso** and the **Calanche**. These rugged red-granite cliffs and boulders have been hurled down to the sea by volcanic eruptions and eroded there by wind and water, forming the most bizarre and fantastic shapes.

Some of the Calanche boulders are hidden in a forest of sea pines, lying there like sleeping monsters. Over the centuries, they have been nicknamed Dog, Eagle, or Turtle, but among them you may perhaps recognize your own big-nosed geography teacher or even, along the well-marked walk of the **Chemin du Château-fort**, an unmistakably bouffant-hairstyled former prime minister. Thick-soled shoes are recommended for your walks over the rocks. Don't miss taking a **boat cruise** from the little resort town of Porto. The best one goes out to the cliff caves on the northern edge of the gulf, to the isolated fishing village of **Girolata** and the nature reserve of

Scandola — a marvellous coastal haven for eagles, bald buzzards, and other rare species nesting on the peaks of the volcanic rocks.

In the interior, drive along the winding mountain road to Evisa and the cool, quiet **Forest of Aïtone**. Off the D 84 road, just 3 km (2 miles) northeast of Evisa, is a sign reading *Piscine*. This is not a municipal chlorine-saturated swimming pool, but a series of clear, clean, natural pools formed in smooth slabs of rock by the **Cascades d'Aïtone** (waterfalls) — a sheer delight.

SOUTHWEST

The area extending from the southern edge of the Loire Valley to the Pyrénées encompasses what vote-hungry politicians call *la France profonde*, the French heartland distant in geography and spirit alike from the vanities and preoccupations of Paris. Apart from comparatively recent *autoroutes*, road access from Paris has been slow and complicated. This has been tough on the local economy, but has had the advantage of keeping the landscape blessedly unspoiled.

In and around the lovely valley of the Dordogne, Périgord beckons enticingly, with its rich cuisine, fortified towns, and fascinating cave paintings and other prehistoric remains. From the Basque country to the Mediterranean, you can explore the sunny mountains of the Pyrénées. And in between, you'll come upon the historic towns of Montpellier, Albi, and Toulouse.

Below the estuary of the Loire, the Atlantic coast is the preserve of the country's most independent-minded ports, the Protestant stronghold of La Rochelle and the proud, prosperous city of Bordeaux.

PERIGORD

This rich and fertile country is densely forested and crisscrossed by rivers flowing from the plateau of the Massif Central out to the Atlantic Ocean. Of these, the Dordogne has carved out through the centre a beautiful winding valley of gentle greenery.

In the village markets, the fruits and vegetables, mushrooms and nuts of every description bear witness to the region's self-sufficiency in food. Gourmets lament the dwindling supply of truffles snuffled out by the pigs under a special kind of oak tree, but the *pâté de foie gras* and slowly roasted *confit* of goose and duck are as succulent as ever. Even the salads of the Quercy region are all the more subtle for their dressing in walnut oil.

So many relics of Stone Age people have been found here because they favoured the abundant fish supplies in the rivers and dwellings safe from wild animals in the caves riddling the valley cliffs. With a similar concern for self-protection, the proliferation of fortresses throughout the Périgord region is a vestige of the many wars against the English, between Protestant and Catholic, and resistance to the marauding bands of brigands.

Bourges

Ancient capital of the flat region of Berry on the northern edge of Périgord, Bourges is worth a brief detour from the N 20 highway down from Orléans.

The intricate harmony of the five portals of its façade, and the peculiar grace of its silhouette, make **Cathédrale Saint-Etienne** one of the country's half-dozen Gothic masterpieces. The church is dominated by the massive nave and graceful flying buttresses linking the five chapels to the chancel (best view from the archbishop's gardens behind the cathedral). The Last Judgment portrayed on the centre portal is an example of 13th-century sculpture at its best.

The **Palais Jacques-Cœur**, a rare jewel of Gothic secular architecture, was the luxurious residence of a wealthy merchant, treasurer to Charles VII. The elegance of the palace becomes apparent only in the inner courtyard, with its seven turreted staircases and handsome balconies. The mottos engraved around the windows proclaim the self-made man: *A "vaillans (cœurs) riens impossible"* ("To valiant hearts, nothing is impossible") and *"Dire, faire, taire"* ("Say, do, and shut up"). Note the pigeon loft from which, 400 years before Reuters and Associated Press, Jacques Cœur organized a private news service using carrier pigeons.

Vallée de la Vézère

Exploring this valley that shelters the earliest signs of European civilization and man's artistic awakening is by no means a dry and dusty archaeological tour of fossils and bones. The region would in any case be idyllic for hikes and picnics. Around the caves that pockmark the cliffs overhanging the Vézère river is a green and pleasant countryside of meadows, vineyards, and orchards, and a profusion of graceful willows and poplars at the water's edge.

Montignac is the departure point for your visit to the world-famous cave paintings of **Lascaux**. Concealed and protected against atmospheric changes for 17,000 years, these awe-inspiring frescoes and engravings of bulls, horses, ibex, bison, and deer were discovered in 1940 — by four boys chasing their dog down a hole.

Within a few years, the humidity of human bodies and the exhaust fumes wafted in from passing traffic caused a rapid deterioration, and

---

Stone Age Art

Because no household tools or weapons were found near the paintings of the deep galleries, scholars have deduced that most of the French caves were not dwellings, but sanctuaries where Stone Age man depicted the beasts he hunted and probably worshipped. For his home, he preferred cave entrances or the shelter of a cliff overhang. Some of the frescoes show animals pierced with arrows or spears, perhaps a form of sympathetic magic to promote success in the hunt.

The artists depicted their potential game with red and yellow oxidized iron, powdered ochre, black charcoal, and animal fats. They blew powdered colour on to the walls of the caves through hollow bones or vegetable stalks — basically the same technique as that used by aerosol-graffiti artists in the latter-day caves of a modern subway.

---

the caves had to be closed to the general public. Now, the original caves (four galleries of 200 paintings and 1,500 engravings) can be seen only by special appointment. An authoritative guided tour in French or English is available for a maximum of *five* people each day. Write to: Directeur des Antiquités préhistoriques d'Aquitaine, 26–28, Place Gambetta, 33000 Bordeaux — but be warned that only very few applicants are granted permission to view the caves. Most visitors settle for the astonishingly realistic replica created at **Lascaux II**, which makes a satisfying and authentic-looking alternative. Anthropologists and artists have reproduced the *Salle des Taureaux* (Hall of Bulls) with 100 pictures of the animals that shared the environment of Stone Age man. Complete your visit with a side trip to **Le Thot**, where the museum has some excellent audiovisual exhibits and models of cave life; the nearby park has been turned into a zoo devoted to descendants of the animals portrayed at Lascaux.

Returning to the river, you will pass the 16th-century **Château de Losse** (where visitors can admire the Italian Renaissance furniture and tapestries) on the way to **Saint-Léon-sur-Vézère**. Surrounded by poplars and willows, the town's buff-stoned 11th-century church is a characteristic example of Périgord Romanesque.

For a wonderful view of the valley, climb to the top of **La Roque Saint-Christophe**, a spectacular long cliff 80 metres (262 feet) high, honeycombed with caves inhabited 20,000 years ago.

Les Eyzies-de-Tayac, is known, justifiably, as "*capitale de la préhistoire*." Besides its important **museum** in the remains of a medieval castle, the village is at the centre of literally dozens of major palaeolithic excavation sites, explored only since the 19th century by the French pioneers of studies in prehistory. The Cro-Magnon shelter *(Abri de Cro-Magnon)* on the north side of town is the spot where, in 1868, railway workers uncovered three 30,000-year-old human skeletons beside their flint and bone tools. Anthropologists say that these tall, large-brained men with high foreheads *(homo sapiens sapiens)* were of a physical type still to be seen in parts of southwestern France.

For cave paintings, all accessible by guided tour only, the most attractive site is the **Grotte de Font-de-Gaume**, reached by an easy walk up on a cliff above the eastern edge of town. The pictures of mammoths, bison, horses, and reindeer are between 15,000 and 40,000 years old. The **Combarelles** cave, farther to the east, is a long winding gallery where the pictures are engraved rather than painted, and very often superimposed.

The caverns of the **Grotte du Grand Roc**, to the northwest of Les Eyzies, are a natural rather than a historical phenomenon, but well worth a visit for the weirdly shaped stalagmites and stalactites and the panorama of the Vézère Valley.

☞ **Dordogne**

This valley is so beloved by British and Dutch holidaymakers that cunning travel agents often blithely extend its name to describe the whole Périgord region. For the British, its green countryside of river, meadow, copse, and hedgerow, fertilized with the blood of their ancestors in the Hundred Years' War, is a "home away from home" — with the welcome bonus of a ruined castle or two, roast goose, and walnut liqueur. The river is good for both fishing and canoeing, and if you haven't brought your own bike for exploring the back country, you can rent one at Sarlat.

Start at the confluence of the Vézère and Dordogne rivers, where the hilltop village of **Limeuil** affords a fine view of both valleys and their bridges meeting at right angles down below. Drive south away from the river to **Cadouin**, with its impressive 12th-century Cistercian **abbey**, a major Périgord Romanesque church with wooden belfry on a remarkable split pyramidal cupola. The soberly designed church contrasts with the more decorative Gothic and Renaissance sculpture of the cloister.

Back on the river, perched above a 150-metre- (490-foot-) deep ravine, the redoubt of **Beynac-et-Cazenac** is a splendid fairy-tale castle, much frequented by English troublemakers in the Middle

Ages. The barons of Beynac lost it in turn to Richard the Lion-Heart and Simon de Montfort, Earl of Leicester, before turning it into a Renaissance palace. Across the river are Beynac's rival, **Castelnaud**, in ruins, and the 15th-century castle of **Fayrac**, complete with drawbridge, battlements, and pepperpot towers nicely restored.

From **La Roque-Gageac**, you get a magnificent view of all three castles. It has won a prize as one of the most beautiful villages in the country — especially well deserved when the late-afternoon sun catches the houses' stone-tiled roofs. It's also an antiques-collectors' paradise (amateurs beware).

The mysterious Dordogne valley is a place for romantic dreamers.

Sarlat, capital of the Périgord Noir, is a lovely old town, bustling in high season but of quiet charm in spring and autumn. The **Saturday market** on the Place du Marché-aux-Oies is a joy, as are the narrow streets of the old town east of the busy Rue de la République. Look out for the Gothic and Renaissance houses on the Rue Fénelon and Rue des Consuls (especially **Hôtel Plamon**) and for the Place du Peyrou's grand **Maison de La Boétie**, across from the cathedral. An open-air summer festival is held on Place de la Liberté. And don't leave without trying that most humble and delectable delicacy *pommes sarladaises*, thin-sliced potatoes sautéed in goose fat with garlic and parsley — the sweetest death known to Western man.

Padirac's stalactites look rather forbidding. Porcelain geese invite you to try some Périgord foie gras.

Rocamadour

Since the 12th century, sightseers and religious pilgrims alike have been flocking to this spectacularly situated fortified town up on its cliff top above the Alzou river (best appreciated from the eastern vantage point of L'Hospitalet on the D 673). Founded on the tomb of a hermit, Saint Amadour, which was believed to have mystic curative powers, Rocamadour attracted Henry II of England and a number of French kings after him.

The present-day mob scene of tourists buzzing around the souvenir shops and the **Chapelle miraculeuse de Notre-Dame** captures something of the medieval frenzy. The modern visitor will no doubt prefer to get there by the elevator — rather than climb the 216 steps of the Via Sancta, which reformed heretics and other penitents were obliged to negotiate on their knees with heavy chains swathed around their neck and arms.

The great chasm *(gouffre)* of **Padirac**, 16 km (10 miles) northeast of Rocamadour, is one of Périgord's most exhilarating natural wonders. Elevators take you 100 metres (328 feet) down to a subterranean river for a delightfully spooky boat ride past gigantic stalactites and stalagmites, formed by the calcite residue and deposits of thousands of years of persistently dripping water.

ATLANTIC COAST

The major Atlantic coastal towns are more businesslike than their Mediterranean counterparts and the resorts have a stronger appeal to sailors than to beach-lovers. What the vineyards around Bordeaux lack in attractive landscape and villages (apart from Saint-Emilion) they make up for in the quality of their wines.

Built to protect the town during bitter conflict between Protestants and Catholics, La Rochelle's ramparts make a picturesque car park.

La Rochelle

One of the most handsome of France's ports, this historic bastion of Protestantism seduces the visitor with its quiet charm and dignity. Surrounded by lively cafés, with an avenue of trees along one quay, the old harbour still serves the fishing fleet and small sailboats. Its entrance is guarded by two 14th-century towers remaining from the town's fortifications. To the left, the **Tour Saint-Nicolas** served as a fortress and prison. At the foot of the **Tour de la Chaîne**, which was a gunpowder storehouse, lies the huge chain slung across to Saint-Nicolas to bar passage at night.

The grand old lighthouse (and second prison), the **Tour de la Lanterne**, now stands inland at the end of the ramparts of the Rue

Sur-les-Murs. You will find prisoners' graffiti on the walls of the graceful octagonal steeple, as you climb up to the balcony for its view over the city and the bay. The Gothic tower gate and belfry, **Porte de la Grosse-Horloge**, leads into the prosperous old merchant quarters. Note the gracefully vaulted shopping arcades and galleries of the 16th- and 17th-century houses. Don't miss the handsome Renaissance **hôtel de ville** (on Rue des Merciers) with its Italian-style courtyard, staircase, and belfry. Another elegant house is the double-gabled **Hôtel de Pontard**, hidden away at the rear of a garden at the savings bank (Caisse d'Epargne, 11, Rue des Augustins).

The **Musée des Beaux-Arts** (at 28, Rue Gargoulleau) includes an important portrait of Martin Luther by Lucas Cranach and notable canvases by Giordano and Ribera.

The oyster beds of Arcachon, west of Bordeaux.

Ile de Ré

With its gleaming white villas and smart little hotels, a sunny micro-climate, beautiful pine-shaded beaches, and succulent oysters and mussels, this cheerful island is much appreciated as a holiday resort, especially for the sailing possibilities from the harbour of its "capital," **Saint-Martin-de-Ré**. Visit the **Phare des Baleines**, a lighthouse at the western end of the island (257 steps to the view at the top). Excursions to the island depart from La Rochelle's Vieux Port.

Bordeaux

Anyone interested in ships will no doubt head for the great port to inspect the freighters and tankers from Asia, Australia, Africa, and the Americas. Guided tours by launch depart from the landing stage (embarcadère Vedettes) of the vast esplanade des Quinconces.

Landlubbers may prefer the cafés, shops, and galleries around the **Place de la Comédie**, a main centre of city life. The square is dominated by the **Grand Théâtre**, the jewel of Bordeaux's many 18th-century buildings. It is a temple-like structure of twelve Corinthian columns, its entablature adorned with statues of the Greek muses and the goddesses Juno, Venus, and Minerva. The majestic double staircase inside inspired Charles Garnier for his design of the Paris Opera House.

South of the imposing Place de la Bourse, the old **Quartier Saint-Pierre** around the church of the same name is a masterpiece of urban renewal. The once ill-famed slum has grown into a lively neighbourhood of art galleries and quaint little shops, with an open-air market on the Place Saint-Pierre. On the beautifully renovated houses along the Rue Phillippart and Rue Bahutiers, notice the grotesque masks and winged angels sculpted over the doorways.

The dimensions of the gigantic Flamboyant Gothic **Cathédrale Saint-André** closely rival those of Notre-Dame de Paris — which is a mere 6 metres (20 feet) longer and 4 metres (13 feet) wider. It has some remarkable sculpture over the porches. Inside, the extraordinary, almost blasphemous, Renaissance **bas-reliefs** on the organ loft show Jesus ascending to heaven on an eagle like a Greek god, and descending to Limbo among diabolical figures of the Underworld.

The **Musée des Beaux-Arts** (in the cours d'Albert) includes works by Veronese, Perugino, Rubens, and Van Dyck, as well as major paintings by Delacroix and Matisse.

Saint-Emilion

At the western end of the Dordogne Valley, this is undoubtedly the most attractive of the Bordeaux wine villages, not least due to the golden-tinted stone of the medieval houses around its sleepy Place du Marché. Unique in Europe, the 1,000-year-old church known as the **Eglise Monolithe** was carved out of the solid rock on which the village is built. After wandering around the old ramparts and narrow streets, take a rest in the ivy-covered ruins of the 14th-century **Cloître des Cordeliers**. The local Maison du Vin can give advice for your tour of the surrounding vineyards.

PYRENEES

The mountains that form France's natural barrier with Spain present for the most part a landscape of gentle rolling greenery. (Even the mountain streams tend more to the babbling brook than the turbulent torrent.) Tourism is little-developed and cross-country skiing is favoured — so the mountain scenery remains unspoiled by chair lifts. The Pyrénées are ideal for camping and hiking.

Biarritz

Nostalgia fans will appreciate the patina of faded grandeur of this elegant resort where Queen Victoria once promenaded along the front, Bismarck fell madly in love with the wife of a Russian ambassador, and the Prince of Wales took care of all the others. Today, hortensias

On the Biarritz promenade, the sunbathers will arrive any minute.

and tamarisks still ornament the seafront gardens — but the **Grande Plage** is no longer considered a hazard, unlike in 1900 when it was known as the *Plage des Fous* (Madmen's Beach), and fewer suicidal shots ring out from the casinos.

The Villa Eugénie, from which the wife of Napoleon III made Biarritz fashionable, has become the **Hôtel du Palais**, an extravagant monument of idle luxury.

There's an easy beach walk from the **Cap Saint-Martin** lighthouse out to the rugged **Rocher de la Vierge**. Beyond, the big waves of the Plage de la Côte des Basques are more suitable for expert surfers and windsurfers than for desultory bathers. When you're a little sun-silly, cool off at the aquarium of the **Musée de la Mer**. Or take a pleasant day trip to nearby **Bayonne**, where the **Musée Basque**, set in a 16th-century mansion, provides a valuable introduction to the folklore of the region.

Saint-Jean-de-Luz

Less well-known than Biarritz, this charming little fishing village has converted from whale to tuna (tunny) and anchovy. Similarly, it has small-scale, though no less delightful, attractions around its sheltered **harbour**. The cafés, galleries, and boutiques are lively, the artist's colony is not at all phony, and the timbered houses of the old shipbuilders' **Quartier de la Barre** are tastefully preserved.

The town's great claim to fame is the wedding of Louis XIV to the Spanish Infanta Maria Theresa in 1660; the houses that lodged them, **Maison de Louis XIV** and **Maison de l'Infante**, still stand by the port. The austere façade of the 15th-century **Eglise Saint-Jean-Baptiste**, where the wedding was celebrated, doesn't prepare you for the characteristic Basque ornament within: carved oak galleries to separate the various classes of worshippers on three sides of a single nave, with polychrome wooden vaulting and a sumptuous three-tiered gilded-and-crimson Baroque altar.

The Pays Basque invites both energetic hikers and siesta fans.

☛ Pays Basque

The fierce regional pride of the Basques is nourished in the most serene and restful landscape imaginable. Amid sunny valleys and rolling green hills, their gabled houses are immaculately maintained, gleaming white, set off by russet brown timbering. The Basques are as pious as the Bretons, and decorate the interiors of their churches with meticulous carpentry.

From Saint-Jean-de-Luz, follow the D 918 southward to **Ascain**,

No connection between Basque and any other language has ever been proven. In France it is spoken by fewer than 80,000 people.

with a village square surrounded by enchanting 17th-century houses, and a typical, old wooden-galleried church. A rack-and-pinion railway at Col de Saint-Ignace carries you 900 metres (2,950 feet) up to the top of **La Rhune** for an exhilarating view of the Atlantic Ocean and the western Pyrénées. **Sare** is a favourite stop for hikers and gourmets, or a ravenous combination of the two. You can measure the village's religious fervour by the grand Baroque altar in the church. Nor could there be a more attractive demonstration of the Basques' independent-minded nature than the main street of **Aïnhoa**, where each sturdy-beamed whitewashed house is of a different height and juts out at a different angle.

Saint-Jean-Pied-de-Port was the last stage before crossing into Spain on one of the main routes of pilgrimage to Santiago de Compostela — and you can still follow the pilgrims' path around the **ramparts**, up a stairway through Porte Saint-Jacques to the **ville haute**. Note the charming red-sandstone houses along **Rue de la Citadelle**, which leads to an old bridge across the Nive river with a pretty view of the town's Gothic church. For a panorama across the Nive Valley, climb up to the **citadel**, built by Louis XIV as a defence against a potential Spanish invasion.

Leave the D 933 at Larceveau to cut east across the **Col d'Osquich**, delightful walking and picnicking country with a constant view of the Pyrénées peaks to the south. End your tour of the Basque country at **Oloron-Sainte-Marie**, with a visit to its 12th-century **Eglise Sainte-Marie**, notable for the remarkable sculpture of medieval life on its portal in shimmering white Pyrénées marble.

Pau

This town holds a special place in French hearts as the birthplace of their beloved Henri IV, in 1553. In more modern times, after their victorious campaigns against the French in the Pyrénées, the Duke of Wellington's veterans appreciated its balmy climate and retired there to make it something of a British colony. The British provided two mayors — Taylor and O'Quinn — and left their mark with horse racing, fox hunting, and the country's first golf club.

Today, the **Château de Pau**, more Renaissance palace than fortress and restored in the 19th century, is an interesting museum of Gobelins tapestries and paraphernalia from the early life of the country's most popular king. It is difficult to distinguish legend from fact in the life of this lusty womanizer, but it's doubtful whether Henri actually did sleep in the great tortoiseshell said to be his cradle.

Stroll along the terrace at the foot of the château, known as the **Boulevard des Pyrénées**, for the region's most spectacular view of the snowcapped peaks lining the southern horizon like a white crystal necklace. The chief treasure of the town's **Musée des Beaux-Arts** is a fascinating painting by Degas, *The New Orleans Cotton Exchange.*

Saint-Bertrand-de-Comminges

A pleasant detour off the Pau-Toulouse road, this fortified hilltop town has a splendid Romanesque-Gothic **cathedral** that merits an unhurried visit. Inside, the superb 16th-century woodcarvings of the **choir stalls** make up a cheerful compendium of Pyrénées characters, high and low. The open Romanesque arcades allow the peaceful little **cloister** to take full advantage of the mountain backdrop.

Toulouse

Centre of the national aerospace industry, with a vigorous local culture and bright and breezy street life, the city has an infectious enthusiasm to it. The charm works quickly if you hang out at the cafés on **Place Wilson** or shop in the boutiques in the nicely refurbished old houses of the **Rue des Changes** and **Rue Saint-Rome**, and the second-hand book shops around the church of Saint-Sernin.

The red brick of its major monuments and old houses, the region's dominant building material, has earned Toulouse the name *la ville rose.* The structural prowess of its architects in this medium can be admired in the magnificent 11th-century **Basilique Saint-Sernin**, an undisputed masterpiece among France's Romanesque churches. On the south side, note the 12th-century **Porte Miègeville** and the vigorous sculpture of the Apostles gazing up at the Ascension of Jesus on the tympanum.

The **Eglise des Jacobins**, burial place of the philosopher and theologian Saint Thomas Aquinas, is a Gothic fortress church, with a noble tower, elegant twin-columned **cloister**, and a remarrior of polychrome beauty (subtle dark reds, pink, and bu'

The town's civic pride is given expression in the gran
and Renaissance houses of merchants who made their ic...
woad (blue dye) for the textile industry. They proclaimed their success with the highest towers they could build. The **Hôtel de Bernuy**
(1, Rue Gambetta), now a high school, reveals its splendours once
you are inside the gates. The first courtyard boasts a monumental Renaissance stone loggia and arcade, while the second courtyard, in traditional red brick, has an octagonal tower enclosing its staircase. At
the equally splendid **Hôtel d'Assézat**, set back from the Rue de Metz
and home of various scholarly academies, you can climb the
lanterned tower in order to
enjoy a panoramic view of the
city.

Situated at the corner of Rue
de Metz and Rue d'Alsace-Lorraine, in a converted medieval
monastery, the **Musée des Augustins** houses one of the richest collections of religious
sculpture in France, consisting
of an ungainly hodgepodge of
treasures recovered from the
cloister of Saint-Sernin and the
monastery of Notre-Dame de la
Daurade, both destroyed in the
19th century, and from the
cathedral of Saint-Etienne.

*Saint-Sernin basilica
towers over a Toulouse
bric-a-brac market.*

Carcassonne

This is a town for everyone who
likes fairy-tale castles. It has

served as a fortress for the Gallo-Romans, the Visigoths, Franks, and medieval French (you can see the layers of their masonry in the ramparts). You'll get the best overall view of Carcassonne from the *autoroute*; the town looks most dramatic when seen with night-time illuminations. Most people park on the east side of the old town *(la Cité)* and walk over the drawbridge of the **Porte Narbonnaise**.

But you'll get a much better feel for the medieval atmosphere of a fortified town, with its ramparts and lookout towers, if you park on the western side, by the church of Saint-Gimer, and walk up around the old **Château Comtal**. After a look at the ancient sarcophagi and medieval sculpture in the castle's little museum, take the guided tour around the parapets. If the battlements and pepperpot towers, the dungeons, moats, and drawbridges strike you as a bit over the top, put some of it down to the romantic imagination of Viollet-le-Duc. Although much is authentic, the famous 19th-century architect who masterminded the restoration work had a somewhat fanciful idea of feudal architecture and stuck on all kinds of frills and furbelows if he lacked the original plans. A blatantly outlandish example of this is the Romanesque-Gothic **Basilique Saint-Nazaire** — which Viollet-le-Duc thought was originally part of the fortifications and so blithely added battlements to the west façade. Inside the basilica, in the choir, you can see some fine 13th- and 14th-century **sculptures** and **stained-glass windows**.

Albi

This serene and cheerful town — built, like Toulouse, with red brick and so known as *Albi la Rouge* — was once the scene of brutal religious persecution. The grandiose Gothic **Cathédrale Sainte-Cécile** bears witness to that turmoil. In medieval times, Albi provided a controversial refuge for the Cathar "heretics," also known as Albigeois or Albigenses, whose austere doctrines emphasizing the simple opposition of good and evil were an implicit reproach to the luxurious life of the Church in Rome. In 1208, Pope Innocent III dispatched a military crusade to wipe out the movement that had spread to Toulouse, Carcassonne, and Béziers. Twenty-five years later, the first Inquisition was established to take care of the remnants. To impress the citizens of Albi with the reasserted power of the Roman church, the cathedral was built in 1282 as a red brick "fortress of the faith," massive enough to resist any heresy.

In the 13th-century bishop's residence, the Palais de la Berbie, the **Musée Toulouse-Lautrec** honours the painter (who was born in Albi in 1864) with the country's largest collection of his works and sketchbooks.

Montpellier

In this lively university town, at the Mediterranean end of the Southwest, the centre of city life is around the airy, bustling **place de la Comédie**.

For a quieter coffee, try the pretty **place du Marché-aux-Fleurs**, shaded by plane trees around a Henry Moore sculpture. And on the rue des Trésoriers de France and rue des Trésoriers de la Bourse, you'll discover some handsome 17th- and 18th-century **mansions** that have imposing stairways in the inner courtyards. The **Musée Fabre** (at 13, rue Montpellieret) has an outstanding art collection, including important paintings by Courbet, Delacroix, Veronese, and Zurbarán.

For many, the most enchanting spot in town is the late-17th-century **Promenade du Peyrou**, spacious classical gardens with a triumphal arch, an equestrian statue of Louis XIV, and, on a mound at the far end, a hexagonal *château d'eau* (water tower) that looks more like a love temple, providing a fine view south to the Mediterranean and north to the Cévennes mountains.

End your trip with a dip in the sea at the pleasant, unpretentious resort of **Sète**, famed for its nautical jousts in the harbour. And then, although it's quite hard going, walk up to the terrace of the little **Mont Saint-Clair** for one last view of the Pyrénées to the west and, out over the Mediterranean, to the Alpilles of Provence to the east.

WHAT TO DO

With such a weight of culture, of monuments and natural sights, it would be easy to forget that France is also a country where the good life is still to be enjoyed far from the châteaux and cathedrals. Sports are popular, the self-indulgent shopper is pampered, and night life is cultivated with that special Gallic flair. Sightseeing is only the beginning of a visit to France.

SPORTS

After years of excessive attention to intellectual pursuits, the French have turned increasingly to outdoor sports. Everybody and his grandmother are out running, jumping, hiking, and biking. For skiing and spectator sports, the most modern facilities have been installed, greatly enhanced by France's selection as host for the 1992 Winter Olympic Games, held in Haute-Savoie. The enormous diversity of climate and geography across the country means that every imaginable kind of sport is available.

Jogging seems to have graduated from fad to daily habit, and there's always a park or river bank where you can get away from the traffic and car fumes. Moreover, the large hotels increasingly have saunas and gyms to complete your work-out. Paris organizes a spring marathon along the Seine and around the Bois de Boulogne.

There's no better sport than **hiking** to get the most out of the French countryside. Every little *syndicat d'initiative* can provide you with itineraries, many of them marked in red or blue on trees or lampposts along the trail. Providing good exercise without being exhausting, some of the itineraries are guided tours for botany or geology enthusiasts.

More ambitious and experienced hikers might like to try the challenging routes known as *grandes randonnées* marked out through the Alps, the Pyrénées, and the Lubéron mountains of Provence (for details about them, contact the *Fédération Française de Randonnées Pédestres*, 64, Rue Gergovie, 75014 Paris). Even for the most modest hike, be sure to equip yourself with proper footwear, not just skimpy

Horseback riders set out on a trail ride under the noontime sun. You too can hire a horse for the day.

tennis shoes. French manufacturers have specialized in lightweight boots for summer hiking to replace the heavy clodhoppers of old.

Mountaineering novices needing training can obtain it through the Club Alpin Français, 24, Rue Launière, 75019 Paris, while the club's local branches in the resort towns of the Alps and the Pyrénées dispense advice and information to experts and novices alike.

Whether your principal means of transport is car, train, or even boat, **cycling** is ideal for excursions. You can take off into the hills on bikes rentable at some 250 railway stations throughout the country. Cycling is an especially pleasant way to tour the vineyards of Champagne, Burgundy, or Alsace.

Horseback riding is a delight in the forests of the Ile-de-France and Brittany or the area around Pau in the Pyrénées. And there are plenty of possibilities for good riding in other parts of France. The *loisir-accueil* (leisure and hospitality) department of the major regional tourist offices can tell you where to hire a horse for the day. For information about prolonged riding holidays, with accommodation and meals included, write to the Fédération Française d'Equitation, 25/27 Rue de Tolbiac, 75013 Paris.

For ecological reasons, **hunting** is declining in popularity these days, but the best "shoots" for experienced hunters (with a 48-hour licence from the local prefecture) are still available in Sologne, the Vosges, and Périgord. The season is generally from mid-September to the end of January.

Fishing is going as strong as ever: freshwater for trout and pike in the Annecy and le Bourget lakes, trout, carp, shad, and bream in the Burgundy rivers, the Dordogne, and tributaries of the Loire. Get your licence through the local *société de pêche* (fishing association). Sea fishing's better in the Atlantic than in the Mediterranean. Good deep-sea expeditions are generally advertised down at the port, most notably along the Brittany coast and at La Rochelle.

Water sports are amply catered for. The Côte d'Azur has cleaned up most of its polluted beaches so that **swimming** is much safer there these days, but you'll find the Brittany and smaller Normandy resorts much less crowded. The pollution count is tested regularly, and the percentage is displayed at local town halls. Watch out for the occasional stinging jellyfish *(méduse)* in the Mediterranean; and be careful when swimming at any of the more secluded Atlantic beaches where there are no lifeguards on regular duty. Many French municipalities have excellent Olympic-size pools, and more and more hotels are installing them, too.

Whether fishing for supper or skipping stones, there's fun to be had on the river banks.

The **wind-surfing** craze has now calmed down a little, but enthusiasts can still rent a board *(planche à voile)* in any of the major resorts. Straight **surfing** is a strictly Atlantic sport, best at Biarritz.

Sailing is growing in popularity. If price is no object, you can hire a 30-metre (100-foot) vessel with a 10-man crew down at Cannes or Antibes and, on the Atlantic coast, at the equally well-equipped Saint-Malo, La Baule, or La Rochelle. For those with their own boat, berths may be easier to find in Atlantic ports than on the Côte d'Azur.

Inland, the great boating adventure is **canoeing**, particularly in Périgord. For details of nationwide facilities and the list of navigable rivers, write to the Fédération Française de Canoë-Kayak, 17, route de Vienne, 69007 Lyon.

Back on dry land, possibilities to play **tennis** are endless, so be sure to pack a racket. Tennis courts are hard surface, in municipal parks or attached to hotels. The latter can often help you with temporary membership to private clubs.

For **golf**, bring your own home-club membership card for easier access to the best courses in the major seaside resorts — Le Touquet, Cabourg, Deauville, La Baule, Biarritz, and Mandelieu (Cannes). Around Paris, international-class courses are to be found at Fontainebleau, Chantilly, Saint-Cloud, and Saint-Nom-la-Bretèche.

Winter sports fans don't usually need a guidebook to tell them where to go. Generally speaking, the Alps are best for downhill **skiing** and the Pyrénées for

Le golf is catching on in France, among players of all ages.

cross-country *(ski de fond).* For the latter, you might also consider Corsica.

In France, only a small number of long-established ski resorts, such as Megève and Val-d'Isère, have some tradition and a village life to supplement the activity on the slopes. These are best for families who want first-class ski schools for kids and other beginners. You can write to the Association des Maires des Stations de Sports d'Hiver, 61, Boulevard Haussmann, 75008 Paris, for a list of mountain villages in the Alps and Pyrénées where the hotel and skiing facilities are relatively modest but where village life is not completely submerged by ski and *après-ski.*

Inveterate skiers tend to head for highly specialized modern winter-sports *stations* with excellent facilities, high-tech equipment, the most challenging *pistes,* and frenetic discos, but little character — Les Arcs, Tignes, La Plagne, and Avoriaz. Wherever you go for

---

Piglets and Pétanque

Perched on a borderline between sport and folklore, the grand Provençal game of boules, or pétanque, is the perfect expression of regional character. At a distance, all seems tranquil in the sandy village square, where half a dozen or more somewhat portly, gently perspiring fellows lob heavy metal balls along a shady avenue of plane trees. But draw nearer and you'll discover a ferocious combat, in which the ambient good humour barely conceals the high passions fuelled by mutual scorn, recrimination, and pastis.

The object of the game is quite simply to get the maximum number of balls as close as possible to a little wooden jack, the cochonnet (literally piglet). Good boules acquire the patina of medieval cannonballs. Players form teams of two (doublettes), three (triplettes), or four (quadrettes). They may be meticulous pointeurs, aiming close to the jack, or debonair tireurs, bombing the opponent's ball out of the way.

The most important piece of equipment is a piece of string, to determine the distance between the boules and the cochonnet and who pays for the next round of pastis.

your skiing, if you're not travelling with children, it's best to go outside the school holidays in order to avoid the crowds.

Of the spectator sports, **bicycle racing** remains extremely popular. The Tour de France in July, with its grand finale along the Champs-Elysées in Paris, is as important as a Cup Final for English football or a World Series for American baseball. Each stage of the race, which is at its most strenuous and exciting in the Alps or Pyrénées, resembles a local festival, with

Boules must be one of France's most popular sports; after all, it's suitable for most ages.

each village considering it a privilege to be blessed with the cavalcade of grimacing, groaning stars.

If **football** (soccer) is a national sport, with Marseille, Monaco, and Paris S.G. providing championship teams, **rugby** is generally considered to be at its boisterous best in the southwest of France — Béziers, Narbonne, Toulouse, and Agen being among the most famous teams. For once, the rough and tumble are all on the field rather than among the vociferous spectators.

Pelote is a Basque speciality — roughly along the lines of squash, but played with a leather-bound ball hurled at the wall with an elongated basket-glove known as a *chistera*.

The great Roman amphitheatres of Arles and Nîmes make dramatic settings for the annual summer **bullfights**.

Monte-Carlo has a major **tennis** tournament in May that's an important warm-up for Paris's French Open at Roland-Garros in June, just before Wimbledon. See if your hotel concierge can get you tickets.

In **motor racing**, the most spectacular events, in late May or early June, are the Grand Prix at Monaco and the 24-hour race at Le Mans (a day trip from the Loire Valley or Normandy).

In Paris, **horse-racing** enthusiasts go to Auteuil for the steeple-chase and Longchamp for flat racing — June and early October being the months for the great classics. Chantilly (in June) and Deauville (in August) claim equally prestigious events.

ENTERTAINMENT

While Paris is still without a doubt the undisputed major focus for theatre, classical concerts, ballet, and opera, you'll find plenty going on in the provinces, particularly in the summer when even the tiniest Provençal or Périgord village stages some kind of arts festival.

Paris After Dark

The Paris night scene has lost none of the glitter and bounce that Toulouse-Lautrec made famous at the turn of the century. The Moulin Rouge (in the Place Blanche) still puts on one of the great boisterous floor shows of Europe. The rest of Pigalle is indeed sleazy, but then it always was. Exceptions to the rule: Chez Michou (in Rue des Martyrs) remains a witty cabaret of talented transvestite imper-sonators, and the Folies-Bergère (in Rue Richer) — the music hall that launched the careers of Joséphine Baker, Maurice Chevalier, and Mistinguett — is still going strong.

Over on the Champs-Elysées, the Lido continues the grand tradi-tion of girls wearing nothing but feathers and balloons, while the Crazy Horse Saloon (in the Avenue George-V) relies just on cunning patterns of light to clothe the most beautiful naked ladies in Paris (very few of them actually French). On the Left Bank there are two floor shows that combine pretty girls and pretty transvestites in a nonstop riot of pastiche and satire: the Alcazar (Rue Mazarine) and Paradis Latin (Rue du Cardinal-Lemoine).

Festivals

This is a far-from-exhaustive list of both traditional and new cultural festivals.

January: *Avoriaz* (Savoie) science-fiction film festival; Champagne and Burgundy village processions for wine-growers' patron Saint Vincent

February (or early March): *Nice* Mardi Gras carnival

March: *Cluny* chamber music

April: *Bourges* rock music; *Strasbourg* choral music; *Arles* Easter bullfights in Roman amphitheatre

May: *Cannes* International Film Festival; *Saint-Tropez* "Bravade" religious procession; *Amiens* jazz

June: *Versailles* chamber music; *Strasbourg* music; *Honfleur* Whitsuntide Fête des Marins; *Nîmes* Whitsuntide bullfights in amphitheatre; *Paris* Festival du Marais (music and theatre); *Dijon* (until August) music and theatre, especially street theatre.

July: *Avignon* international theatre, music, opera, dance, and cinema; *Aix-en-Provence* opera; *Arles* photography seminars, exhibitions, and audiovisual shows in amphitheatre; *Montpellier* music, opera, and dance (starts last week in June); *Orange* opera in the amphitheatre; *Nice* jazz; *Bayonne* folklore*Paris* Festival Estival, music and theatre (till September); *La Rochelle* Francopholies (music festival); *Prades* Festival Pablo Casals (chamber music; until mid-August)

August: *Annecy* fireworks by the lake; *Chartres* organ recitals in cathedral; Assumption Day procession and Mass; *Aix-en-Provence* jazz; *Colmar* wine fair; *Le Touquet* chamber music

September: *Lyon* Dance Biennale; *Deauville* American film festival; *Paris* Festival d'Automne, music and theatre (till December); *Dijon* wine festival; *Mont-Saint-Michel* procession and Mass for Saint Michael

October: *Angers* avant-garde music; *Nancy* jazz; *Perpignan*

November: *Burgundy* (Beaune, Nuits-Saint-Georges, Meursault, and Chablis) wine festivals; *Dijon* gastronomy fair; *Cannes* dance

December: *Les Baux-de-Provence* Christmas Eve Fête des Bergers (shepherds) and Midnight Mass; *Strasbourg and Alsatian villages* Christmas fairs

Music

If you're a lover of **classical music**, the exciting new venue is the Opéra Bastille, praised for its acoustics rather than its architecture. Confusingly, the palatial old Paris Opéra, renamed the Opéra de Paris-Garnier, now specializes in ballet. The Orchestre de Paris often performs at the Pleyel concert hall; concerts also take place at the Salle Gaveau, the Châtelet Théâtre Musical, the glamorous Théâtre des Champs-Elysées, and in historic churches.

In the provinces, Lyon, Strasbourg, and Lille all have first-class orchestras, and the various festivals (see page 199) bring top performers from all over the world.

The French take their **jazz** much more seriously these days than Americans do. Paris has some 15 clubs, and in the summer the action is on the Côte d'Azur. Of the Paris clubs, the New Morning (Rue des Petites-Ecuries) attracts most major American and European musicians, while Le Dunois (Rue Dunois) is a modest, intimate place cultivating the avant-garde. You can hear mainstream jazz at the Bilboquet (Rue Saint-Benoît), Le Furstenberg (Rue de Buci), and the bars of the Méridien hotel (Boulevard Gouvion-Saint-Cyr) and Concorde-Lafayette (in Place du Général-Koenig). **Rock music** concerts are held at the Zénith (in La Villette, *métro* Porte de Pantin). June 21 is *la Fête de la musique* all over France, when bands perform all night long in the major cities.

Discothèques go in and out of fashion as fast as the music that's played in them. The expensive Paris discos hide out around the Champs-Elysées, notably on the Rue de Ponthieu and Avenue Matignon, while the younger crowd haunt eardrum-busters around les Halles. At the coastal resorts, the expensive discos are often attached to the casino and the big hotels.

Theatre

The Comédie-Française (in Rue de Richelieu) is the high temple of French classical drama — Molière, Racine, and Corneille — but con-

Republican Guards turn out for a grand gala at the old Paris Opéra.

tinually expands its repertory. On the Left Bank, the Odéon (in the Place de l'Odéon), now the Théâtre de l'Europe, puts on international productions, with prestigious guest companies performing in English, German, and Italian. Even with a minimum of French, playgoers can enjoy the innovative contemporary theatre under the direction of Peter Brook at the Bouffes du Nord (on Boulevard de la Chapelle), Patrice Chéreau at the suburban Théâtre des Amandiers (in Nanterre), or Ariane Mnouchkine at the Cartoucherie de Vincennes (on the Avenue de la Pyramide). The most important centres of provincial theatre include Nancy, Strasbourg, Toulouse, Lyon, Avignon, and Montpellier.

Cinema

For serious movie-fans, Paris is an unrivalled treasure island, a film-crazy town where directors and screenplay writers achieve a celebrity equal to that of star actors and actresses. Not even Los Angeles or New York can match the French capital's average of 300 different films showing each week. Practically all of them are available in at least one cinema in *VO,* an original, undubbed version with French subtitles. Study the weekly entertainment guides, *Pariscope* or *L'Officiel du Spectacle,* especially for the obscure little jewels offered by the town's two *cinémathèques* (at the Palais de Chaillot and the Centre Pompidou).

Don't be intimidated by the queues; you nearly always get in. The usherettes *(ouvreuses)* expect to be tipped, it's their only income. Give them at least 1 franc.

SHOPPING

To shop seriously in France, you need a clear plan of attack. Unless you are buying things you want to use during your vacation, such as sports equipment, it doesn't make sense to shop right at the start of your trip then have to lug your purchases around the country.

From the catwalk to the sidewalk, fashion is big business in Paris.

Paris is still a shopper's paradise, not only for the fashions, perfumes, and other luxury goods for which it has always been famous, but also for a comprehensive selection of handicrafts and gourmet delicacies that at one time could be found only in the provinces. If possible, divide your Paris stay in two, the major part at the beginning, to see the town, with a couple more days at the end of the tour to do your shopping.

Paris: The Big Stores

The two big department stores best equipped for dealing with foreigners are the **Galeries Lafayette** and **Printemps**, next door to each other on the Boulevard Haussmann. Both of them provide hosts to help non-French-speaking customers, as well as having selections from the major designers conveniently displayed in their clothes departments. Galeries Lafayette probably has the edge in the fashion department, and china and household goods, while Printemps leads in its perfume, accessories, lingerie, and vast toy and adult gifts departments.

For those who like dressing up in baker's overalls, waiter's jackets, butcher's aprons, and plumber's pants, the **Samaritaine** at the Pont-Neuf has an enormous selection of professional uniforms — 52 trades are represented.

FNAC is a chain of breezy, new-style department stores (in the Rue de Rennes, Forum des Halles, passage du Havre (across from the Gare St-Lazar and Parvis de la Défense), specializing in books, discount records, cameras, electronics, and sports goods.

Fashion

These days, the fashion pendulum occasionally swings to London, New York, Rome, or Tokyo, but Paris remains the capital for all of them and the showplace for their talents.

From the Right Bank — around the Rue du Faubourg-Saint-Honoré, avenues Montaigne and George-V, and over to the Place des Victoires and les Halles — the *haute couture* houses, together with their *prêt-à-porter* (ready-to-wear) boutiques, have spilled over to the Left Bank, around Saint-Germain-des-Prés.

Look out not only for the old school of Chanel, Dior, Givenchy, Lanvin, Saint-Laurent, Ungaro, and Louis Féraud, but the new generation of designers — Gaultier, Mugler, and Montana — and their foreign competitors (Yamamoto, Issey Miyake, Valentino, and Missoni), as well as the scores of cheaper boutiques that turn out variations on the innovators' designs. When it comes to the designers' perfumes, you'll probably get a better deal in the duty-free shop at the airport.

For leatherware, in addition to its fabled silk scarves, **Hermès** (Rue du Faubourg-Saint-Honoré and Avenue Georges-V) is an institution all on its own, catering for the well-heeled horseman/woman, globe trotter, or man- and-woman-about-town, with high-quality luggage, saddles, and boots, and the ultimate diary and address book.

While the Paris stores and boutiques may fill every clothes need you can possibly imagine, you can find good old-fashioned stuff out in the provinces — oilskins *(ciré)* or a sturdy dufflecoat *(kabig)* in Brittany, or perhaps a heavy Breton woollen sweater *(chandail breton)*. And Saint-Tropez is still renowned for sexy, imaginative casual wear.

Antiques

Don't let the mind-boggling prices asked for the genuine article deter you from antique-hunting, or at least window-shopping, among the exquisite shops of Paris's 6th and 7th *arrondissements.* The Carré Rive Gauche, a little rectangle that's bounded by the quai Voltaire and the Boulevard Saint-Germain, the Rue du Bac and the Rue des Saints-Pères, constitutes a veritable museum of ancient Egyptian, Chinese,

Shoppers browse boutique windows by day and by night.

pre-Columbian, African, and Polynesian art, as well as Louis XV, Second Empire, Art Nouveau, and Art Deco.

You'll find the prices are more manageable at the weekend **flea markets**, although many of their stalls are manned by professional antiques dealers. The *marché aux puces de Saint-Ouen* at Porte de Clignancourt groups half a dozen markets: Vernaison specializes in musical instruments, lead soldiers, old toys, buttons, brass, and tinware; Biron has mostly antique furniture; Malik is a great favourite with the young, for its nostalgic *Belle Epoque* dresses, First World War military uniforms, 1920s hats, and an amazing assortment of Americana; Paul Bert may be the place to find that undiscovered masterpiece every flea-market addict dreams. Jules Vallès is the smallest and cosiest, especially good for Art Nouveau lamps, military souvenirs, theatre costumes, and old dolls.

The **bouquinistes** (second-hand book sellers) along the Seine, most of them between the Pont Saint-Michel and the Pont des Arts, still turn up the odd rarity in periodicals as well as old books.

Even young ones enjoy consumer culture. Here in Anjou, baby chicks are for sale.

Household Goods

The old Paris food-market district of les Halles still retains its many excellent restaurant-supply shops. An astonishing array of pots and pans, kitchen knives, and other utensils can be bought at the venerable Dehillerin (18, Rue Coquillière) and MORA (13, Rue Montmartre).

Normandy and Brittany are both known for their attractive rustic pottery, while Gien, in the Loire Valley, and Limoges produce excellent chinaware. The Rue de Paradis in Paris is lined with discount shops specializing in Limoges. In the back country behind the Côte d'Azur, Vallauris is a major centre for ceramics, and nearby Biot for glassware (see page 167).

From pots and pans to ceramics and cutlery, quality kitchenware is easy to come by in France.

Gourmet Delicacies

Every region has a wealth of specialities, well displayed and easy to find. But if you do prefer to do your food shopping in Paris, the most famous luxury grocery shop is Fauchon (26, Place de la Madeleine).

You'll also find groceries specializing in regional delicacies, with self-explanatory names such as *Aux produits de Bretagne* or *Aux produits de Bourgogne*. There are street markets all over Paris — particularly useful if you want to take back some cheese or sausage on the last day of your holiday. The most colourful are on Rue Mouffetard, Place Maubert, and Rue de Seine on the Left Bank, and Rue des Martyrs, Rue Lépic, and Avenue du Président-Wilson on the Right Bank.

For wine, the best bargains in Paris are at the Nicolas chain. One of the largest selections is at Lucien Legrand (1, Rue de la Banque, as bankers and stockbrokers are notorious connoisseurs).

EATING OUT

There are some tourists who spend a holiday in France without visiting a single museum or church, and who wouldn't dream of wasting time shopping or lying on a beach. And yet they come away with tales of adventure, excitement, poetry, and romance — and the feeling they that know the country inside out. They have spent most of their time wining and dining, and the rest of it sleeping off the meals.

Not all budgets, nor waistlines, would permit such single-minded dedication to eating your way across France. But reserve at least a few evenings for that unique institution, a great French meal. As Jean Anouilh, the playwright, once said, "Everything ends this way in France — everything. Weddings, christenings, duels, burials, swindlings, diplomatic affairs — everything is a pretext for a good dinner."

Where to Eat

In the big cities, you have a wide choice: gourmet restaurants (relatively expensive); the large family-style *brasseries* or intimate *bistrots* (more moderately priced); cafés or wine bars (for a cheaper snack). Fast-food chains are very successful and need no introduction.

The fixed-price *menu* (appetizer, main course, and dessert) is often the best value, particularly in the expensive gourmet establishments, where you get an introduction to the restaurant's specialities without paying the much higher *à la carte* prices. Look, too, for the house wine *(réserve de la maison)*, usually served in carafes by the *quart* (quarter) or *demi* (half) litre.

The typical "continental" **breakfast** *(petit déjeuner)* is still croissant, brioche, or bread and butter with coffee, tea, or chocolate. Increasingly, orange juice is offered as an extra, but you must insist on *orange pressée* if you want it freshly squeezed. Big hotels offer English- and American-style breakfasts. But we recommend you go out as often as possible to the corner café — it's fascinating watching a town getting up in the morning, especially when you yourself don't have to go off to work.

Traditionally, the French **lunch** (*déjeuner*) is as important as dinner. A good alternative is a café salad, or a cheese, ham, or pâté sandwich made in a long *baguette*, or a picnic. *Charcuteries* and *traiteurs* (caterers) will pack complete meals, hot or cold. A corkscrew is more important than a credit card.

In the provinces the **evening meal** (*dîner*) is served at 8:00 or 8:30 P.M., as opposed to 8:30 or 9:00 P.M. in Paris and such favourite Parisian resorts as Deauville, Saint-Tropez, or Cannes. The French are much more relaxed than you might have expected about how you dress for dinner — and even though the smart places expect a jacket, only a very few insist on a tie.

What to Eat

Although the character of the cuisine varies so radically from region to region, there are some general notions to French eating habits that you'll find all over the country.

First things first. The **starter** (*entrée*) can comprise the simplest dishes: *crudités* — a plate of green pepper, tomatoes, carrots, celery, cucumber; or just radishes by themselves, served raw with salt and butter; *charcuterie* — various kinds of sausage and other cold meats, notably the *rosette* sausage from Lyon, *rillettes* (a soft pâté of pork or goose) from Le Mans, and ham (*jambon*) from Bayonne or Auvergne; vegetable soups (*potage*) or fish soups served with *croûtons* and a Provençal sauce of garlic and chilli pepper (*rouille*).

> There are more than 300 different kinds of cheeses in France.

Most of the big cities get their **fish** fresh every day except Monday. Trout (*truite*) is delicious *au bleu* (poached absolutely fresh), *meunière* (sautéed in butter), or *aux amandes* (sautéed with almonds). At their best, *quenelles de brochet* (pike dumplings) are light and airy. Sole and turbot take on a new meaning when served with *sauce hollandaise*, that miraculous blend of egg yolks, butter, and lemon juice with which the Dutch have only the most nominal connection.

For your **main dish**, expect the meat to be less well done than in most countries — extra-rare is *bleu*, rare *saignant*, medium *à point*, and well done *bien cuit* (and frowned upon).

Steaks *(entrecôte or tournedos)* are often served with a wine sauce *(marchand de vin)*, with shallots *(échalotes)* or — rich sin — with bone marrow *(à la moelle)*. Roast leg of lamb *(gigot d'agneau)* is also normally served pink *(rose)* unless you specify otherwise.

While each region tends to promote its own specialities, the most famous **cheeses** are readily available everywhere: the blue *Roquefort*, soft white-crusted *Camembert* or *Brie* (the crust of which you can safely remove without offending true connoisseurs), and countless goat cheeses *(fromage de chèvre)*.

For **desserts**, try a heavenly *mousse au chocolat* or diabolical *profiteroles*, those little ball-shaped éclairs filled with vanilla cream and covered with hot chocolate sauce. Or a *sorbet* (sherbet) — blackcurrant *(cassis)*, raspberry *(framboise)*, or pear *(poire)*. Or fruit tarts — apricot *(tarte aux abricots)*, strawberry *(aux fraises)*, or, most magical of all, *tarte Tatin*, hot caramelized apples baked under a pastry crust, attributed to the Tatin sisters of Sologne after one of them accidentally dropped the tart upside down on the hotplate when taking it out of the oven.

Regional Cuisine

Once acquainted with these basics, you're ready to start your tour of the regional specialities. There's no specifically Parisian cuisine, but the capital is able to offer a sample of virtually everything you'll find around the country.

Picardy, for those coming in from the north, offers its speciality, *flamique à porions*, a leek pie best served piping hot. This, with one of the region's great vegetable soups, will keep you going all the way into Paris and beyond. In Amiens, make a point of trying the traditional *pâté de canard* (duck pâté).

Alsace is rich in freshwater fish and game, and offers a subtle mixture of French, German, and even Jewish cooking — *carpe à la juive* will be recognized as gefilte fish. Wonders are performed with cabbage. *Choucroute* cooked in Riesling with juniper berries, a cup of Kirsch tossed in at the end, makes poetry out of sauerkraut. *Civet de lièvre* is a hare stew fit for a king, and braised goose with apples *(oie braisée aux pommes)* warms the cockles of the coldest heart. The powerful prince of Alsatian cheeses is the pungent *Munster*.

Burgundy, inspired by the high life led by its grand old dukes, is ideal for those with solid appetites. This wine-growing region produces the world's greatest beef stew, *bœuf bourguignon*: beef simmered in red wine for at least four hours with mushrooms, small white onions, and chunks of bacon. The tasty corn-fed poultry of Bresse is the aristocrat of French fowl — enjoy it at its simplest, roast or steamed. Charolais beef, from the lovingly tended white cattle of southern Burgundy, produces the most tender steaks. *A la dijonnaise* will usually mean a sauce of Dijon's mustard, distinctively flavoured by the sour juice of Burgundy grapes. *Jambon persillé* (parslied ham) is another Dijon speciality. *Escargots* (snails) are now mostly imported from Eastern Europe in order to meet the heavy demand, but Burgundians still make the best butter, garlic, and parsley sauce — also used with *cuisses de grenouilles* (frogs' legs) from the Dombes region. Among the cheeses of Burgundy are the moist orange-crusted *Epoisses* and *Soumaintrain*.

Normandy makes full use of its prolific dairy farms. Indeed, cream and butter are staples of the cuisine — the secret behind the sumptuous *omelette de la mère Poulard* that you'll find at Mont-Saint-Michel. The rich, slightly sour-tasting *crème fraîche* also

Saint Tropez café scene.

Planning the day's entertainment over a quiet lunch en tête-à-tête.

makes the perfect accompaniment to a hot apple pie. The local apples are also featured in flambéed partridge *(perdreau flambé aux reinettes)* and in chicken with apple-brandy sauce *(poulet au Calvados)*. The Normandy capital is famous for its *caneton à la rouennaise,* a duckling of unusually deep red meat with a spicy red-wine sauce thickened with minced duck livers. *Tripes à la mode de Caen* contains all the various compartments of a cow's stomach, plus the trotters, stewed in a bouillon. Besides the *Camembert* cheese, be sure to sample the stronger *Livarot* and square, tangy *Pont-l'Evêque.*

The art of nouvelle cuisine is to make a dessert a feast for the eye as well as the palate.

Brittany is best known for its magnificent seafood, served fresh and unadorned on a bed of crushed ice and seaweed, a *plateau de fruits de mer*. This will include oysters *(huîtres)*, various kinds of clam *(palourdes, praires)*, mussels *(moules)*, scallops *(coquilles Saint-Jacques)*, succulent prawns *(langoustines)*, periwinkles *(bigorneaux)*, large whelks *(bulots),* and chewy abalones *(ormeaux)*. Purists prefer their lobster *(homard)* simply steamed or grilled to retain its full, undisguised flavour. Lobster *à l'américaine* (or *à l'armoricaine*, in fact a Parisian invention) swims in a shellfish stock enriched with tomato, Cognac, cream, and herbs.

The area is also known for the excellence of its pancakes — *crêpes* (usually sweet) and *galettes* (mostly savoury), both traditionally served with cider rather than wine.

In the **Loire Valley**, try some of the freshwater fish (eel, trout, pike, or perch) cooked in a light *beurre blanc* (white butter sauce). A major delicacy of the region is *matelote d'anguille* (eel stewed in red wine). Angers and Tours both claim to make the best *andouillette* (tripe sausage), while *rillettes* made from duck, goose, or pork make another delectable starter. *Noisette de porc aux pruneaux* (tenderloin of pork with prunes) makes a lusty main dish. One of the best goat cheeses in the country is *Valençay*, shaped like an Aztec pyramid.

Lyon, the gastronomic capital of France, is renowned for the quality of its pork, wild game, vegetables, and fruit, while giving the common or garden onion its letters of nobility. Onion soup *(soupe à l'oignon)* is a local invention, and *à la lyonnaise* most often means that a dish is sautéed in onions. If you have a robust stomach, you may fancy the *gras-double* (tripe) or *andouille*, a sausage made of chitterlings. More genteel local dishes include, for starters, artichoke hearts *(cœurs d'artichaut)* with foie gras, or *gratin de queues d'écrevisses* (baked crayfish tails); as main dishes, leg of lamb braised for seven hours and *poularde demi-deuil* — chicken in "semi-mourning," because of the white meat and black truffles.

Too good to pass up — Brittany's seafood is among the best you're ever likely to come across.

The cuisine of **Bordeaux** naturally enough exploits its wines, the *bordelaise* sauce being made with white or red wine, shallots, and beef marrow. It is served variously with *entrecôte* steaks, boletus mushrooms *(cèpes)*, or lamprey eels *(lamproies)*. The oysters and mussels from nearby Arcachon are excellent. Try the region's Pauillac lamb *à la persillade* (cooked with parsley).

213

Provence, embracing the Côte d'Azur, marries Mediterranean seafood with garlic, olives, tomatoes, and the country's most fragrant herbs. But for a starter, have the local fresh sardines, just grilled and sprinkled with lemon. More spicy is *tapenade*, a mousse made of capers, anchovies, black olives, garlic, and lemon — delicious on toast.

From the coastal area between Marseille and Toulon comes the celebrated *bouillabaisse*, a fish stew that may contain some or all of the following: *rascasse*, John Dory, eel, red mullet, whiting, perch, spiny lobster, crabs, and other shellfish, seasoned with tomatoes, olive oil, garlic, bay leaf, parsley, pepper, and (not authentic without it) saffron. Provençal cooks also make a splendid *daube de bœuf* (beef stew with tomatoes and olives).

Périgord is famous for its *pâté de foie gras*, truffles, in ever dwindling supply, and for all the richness of goose and duck, most notably *confit d'oie* or *confit de canard*. The bird is cooked slowly in its own fat and kept for days, weeks, or even months in earthenware jars. The *confit* is used as the base of the hearty Toulouse or Castelnaudary *cassoulet*, which includes beans, pork, mutton, and sausage. And don't forget *pommes sarladaises*, potatoes sautéed in goose fat, garlic, and parsley; dandelion salad *(salade de pissenlit)* dressed with walnut oil and bits of bacon; and chestnuts, roasted and served with partridge or made into rich desserts.

Wine

If you happen to prefer red wine rather than white, you can safely and acceptably order red to go with fish; in fact a chilled Brouilly, Morgon, or Chiroubles of the Beaujolais family is an excellent accompaniment for both fish and meat. Dry Burgundy or Loire Valley whites are indeed exquisite with fish, and you can drink the Alsatian whites with anything, with absolute impunity. Beer goes particularly well with Toulouse sausage and Alsatian *choucroute*.

A few basic pointers about the classic wines:

The **Burgundy** reds divide easily into two categories, those that can be drunk relatively young — the supple *Côte de Beaune* wines of Aloxe-Corton, Pommard, and Volnay — and those that need to age a bit, the full-bodied *Côte de Nuits* wines of Vougeot, Gevrey-Chambertin, and Chambolle-Musigny. Outstanding Burgundy whites include Meursault and Puligny-Montrachet.

Bordeaux wines have four main regional divisions: Médoc, aromatic mellow red with a slight edge to it; Graves, an easy-to-drink red, dry and vigorous like the Burgundies; Saint-Emilion, dark, strong, and full-bodied; and the pale, golden Sauternes, sweet and fragrant, and perfect with foie gras. The lesser Bordeaux wines can all be drunk a couple of years old, but good ones need at least five years to mature.

> **Wine is not consumed with salads or other dishes with vinegar preparations. Combining the two could result in a strange taste.**

The **Loire Valley** produces fine dry white wines such as Vouvray and Sancerre, and robust reds such as Bourgueil and Chinon.

Of the **Côtes du Rhône** wines, the best-known red is the fragrant, deep purple Châteauneuf-du-Pape, but look out, too, for the Gigondas and Hermitage, and, for lunchtime drinking, the Tavel rosé.

The names of the delicious white wines of **Alsace** depend on the variety of grapes from which they are made — Gewürztraminer, Riesling, or Sylvaner.

For your after-dinner drink, as well as *Cognac* and the mellower *Armagnac*, there's a wide range of fruit brandies *(eaux-de-vie)* made from pear, plum, cherry, or raspberry, as well as the famous apple *Calvados*. Or, for a sparkling finish, the nation's pride and joy: Champagne, described by the connoisseurs as *aimable, fin, et élégant* ("friendly, refined, and elegant").

A votre santé!

INDEX

Aix-en-Provence 18, 154, 162, 199

Aix-les-Bains 149

Aïnhoa 187

Ajaccio 171-173

Albi 174, 190-191

Alyscamps 157-158

Amboise 121, 142

Angers 116, 139, 144-145, 199, 212

Anjou 14, 64, 205

Annecy 146, 148-149, 194, 199

Arc de Triomphe 31, 47-48, 51-53, 55, 92, 154

Arc-et-Senans 115

Arcachon 182, 213

Arles 19, 153-154, 156-158, 197, 199

Armorique, Parc régional d' 137

Arras 85, 87

Arromanches 128

Ascain 186

Autun 102, 107

Avignon 20, 43, 147, 153-154, 159-161, 199, 201

Avoriaz 196, 199

Avranches 129, 131

Azay-le-Rideau 139, 144

Bagatelle, Parc de 70

Baule 133, 138-139, 195

Baux-de-Provence 158, 199

Bavella 173

Bayeux 117, 126-129, 131

Bayonne 185, 199, 208

Beaubourg 47, 54, 73-74, 76

Beaujolais 151, 214

Beaune 102, 108-109, 111-113, 199, 215

Beaux-Arts, Ecole des 68

Belvédère d'Eze 169

Bernières 128

Besançon 115

Beynac-et-Cazenac 178

Biarritz 184-185, 195

Biot 167, 206

Blois 22, 139-142

Bonifacio 172

Bonnieux 162

Bordeaux 12, 17, 43, 99, 110, 174, 177, 181-183, 213, 215

Boulogne, Bois de 51, 70, 192

Bourges 20, 175, 199

Cabourg 124-125, 128, 195

Cadouin 178

Caen 119, 122, 126, 129, 211

Cala Rossa 172

Calanche 173

Camargue 157

Cancale 133

Canebière 165

Cannes 164-167, 195, 199, 208

Cap Fréhel 133, 135

Capo Rosso 173

Carcassonne 21, 189-191

Carnac 133, 137-138
Castelnaud 179
Castillon 152
Centre Pompidou 47, 54, 73, 202
Chablis 102-103, 199
Chambord 139, 141
Chamonix 147-148
Chantilly 46, 82-83, 195, 198
Chartres 20, 46, 80-81, 84, 117, 199
Chenonceau 139, 142-143
Cirque de Baume 116
Cirque du Fer à Cheval 116
Cité, Ile de la 47, 50, 59
Clos de Vougeot 110, 112
Clos-Lucé 142
Cluny 61-62, 76, 85, 102, 106, 108, 112-114, 199
Colmar 94, 99-102, 199
Combarelles 178
Compiègne 84
Corniches, Les 169
Courseulles 128
Côte d'Azur 12-13, 16, 40, 146-147, 164, 194-195, 200, 206, 214
Côte d'Emeraude 132-133
Côte d'Or 13, 110-111, 147
Cramant 91
Croisette 167

Deauville 123-124, 126, 195, 198-199, 208
Dieppe 119
Dijon 43-44, 85, 102, 108, 111, 199, 210
Dinard 133, 135-136

Dordogne 12, 18-19, 22, 38, 174, 178-179, 183, 194

Eiffel Tower 32, 47-50, 64, 69, 73, 120
Epernay 88-89, 91
Eyzies-de-Tayac 177
Eze 169-170

Fayrac 179
Fontainebleau 22, 82-83, 195
Fontenay, Abbaye de 105
Forum des Halles 54, 203

Gevrey-Chambertin 111-112, 215
Géode 47, 76
Girolata 173
Golfe de Porto 173
Gordes 162
Grand Canal 77, 80, 83
Grand Roc, Grotte du 178
Guimiliau 133, 136-137

Hautecombe, Abbaye de 150
Hautvillers 88, 91
Honfleur 123, 199
Houlgate 125
Huelgoat 133, 137

If, Château d' 165

Jumièges 61, 122-123

Kaysersberg 96, 99-100
Kerlescan 138
Kermario 138

Lampaul-Guimiliau church 137
Lascaux 176-177
Latin Quarter 37, 64-65
Limeuil 178
Loches 143
Losse, Château de 177
Loue, Vallée de la 116
Loue river 114, 116
Louvre 13, 22, 36, 47, 49-50,
    53, 68, 71-72, 74
Lubéron 162
Lyon 17, 19, 43, 146, 150-154,
    156, 195, 199-201, 208, 213

Madeleine, Eglise de 55, 129,
    206
Marais 32, 57-58, 74, 199
Marseille 17-18, 38, 93, 154,
    164-165, 171, 197, 214
Megève 148, 196
Menthon-Saint-Bernard 149
Ménerbes 162
Monaco 169-170, 197-198
Monolithe Eglise 184
Mont-Saint-Michel 41, 117,
    122, 129-131, 133-134, 199,
    210
Montagne Sainte-Victoire 163
Monte-Carlo 164, 169-170, 197
Montmartre 55-57, 66, 205
Montparnasse 66-67
Montpellier 174, 191, 199, 201
Montréal 104
Musée alpin 147
Musée alsacien 98
Musée Bartholdi 102
Musée Basque 185
Musée Condé 83

Musée Courbet 116
Musée d'Histoire de la ville 135
Musée d'Orsay 50, 74-75
Musée d'Unterlinden 100
Musée de Cluny 62, 76
Musée de Dieppe 119
Musée de l'Affiche 76
Musée de l'Annonciade 166
Musée de l'Histoire de France
    58
Musée de l'Homme 76
Musée de l'Oeuvre Notre-Dame
    96-97
Musée de la guerre et du raid du
    19 août 1942 119
Musée de la Mer 185
Musée de la Voiture 84
Musée de Normandie 126
Musée de Picardie 87
Musée des Arts de la mode 74
Musée des Arts décoratifs 74,
    97
Musée des Augustins 182, 189
Musée des Beaux-Arts 92, 98,
    109, 115, 122, 126, 145, 153,
    182-183, 188
Musée du Cinéma 76
Musée du Débarquement 129
Musée du Docteur-Faure 150
Musée du Second-Empire 84
Musée du Vin 112
Musée Fabre 191
Musée Guimet 76
Musée historique lorrain 92
Musée Picasso 74
Musée Rodin 76
Musée Rolin 108
Musée Toulouse-Lautrec 191

Nancy 85, 91-92, 104, 199, 201
Napoleon Bonaparte 27, 29-32, 38-39, 47, 51, 53-55, 68-69, 72, 82, 84, 86, 93, 102, 124, 142, 147, 171-172, 185
Nice 17-18, 164, 168-169, 171, 199
Nîmes 19, 153-156, 197, 199
Notre-Dame de Paris 61-62, 183
Noyers 103

Obernai 99
Oloron-Sainte-Marie 187
Omaha 128-129
Opéra Garnier 54
Oppède-le-Vieux 162
Orange 19, 153-155, 157, 163, 199, 207
Ornans 73, 116
Ouistreham-Riva-Bella 128

Padirac 180
Panthéon 66
Parish Close Road 136
Pau 187, 193
Pays Basque 16, 186
Pays d'Auge 125
Pâquier, Parc du 148
Pelote 197
Perpignan 199
Petrarch 160
Pépinière 92
Père-Lachaise cemetary 59
Phare des Baleines 182
Pharmacie du Cerf 97
Piana 173
Pointe du Grouin 133
port de pêche 119

Portail Royal 81
Porte de la Grosse-Horloge 182
Porte Miègeville 188
Porte Narbonnaise 190
Porticcio 172
Porto-Vecchio 172
Propriano 172

Reculée des Planches 116
Reims 20, 30, 85, 88-91
Ré, Ile de 182
Rhône 17, 146, 150-152, 155, 157, 160, 215
Rhune, La 186
Riquewihr 99
Rocamadour 180
Rochelle, La 23, 174, 181-182, 194-195, 199
Rocher de la Vierge 185
Rocher des Doms 160
Roque Saint-Christophe 177
Roque-Gageac 179
Rouen 21, 117, 119-122
Roussillon 162

Sacré-Cœur 57
Saint Tropez 10, 164-166, 199, 204, 208
Saint Vincent 199
Samaritaine 203
Sare 186
Sarlat 178-179
Scandola 174
Sdragonato cave 172
Senlis 46, 84
Serein, Vallée du 103
Sénéquier 166
Sète 44, 191

Sorbonne 48, 65-66
St-André Cathédrale 183
St-Bertrand-de-Comminges 188
St-Didier Eglise 161
St-Emilion 181, 183, 215
St-Etienne Cathédrale 175
St-Etienne Eglise 126
St-Eustache 52, 54
St-Germain-des-Prés 64, 67, 203
St-Jean-Baptiste Eglise 185
St-Jean-de-Luz 185-186
St-Jean-Le-Thomas 129
St-Jean-Pied-de-Port 187
St-Lazare Cathédrale 107
St-Léon-sur-Vézère 177
St-Louis-en-l'Ile 63
St-Maclou Eglise 121
St-Malo 127, 134-135, 195
St-Martin-de-Ré 182
St-Maurice Cathédrale 145
St-Maurice Eglise 148
St-Nazaire Basilique 190
St-Omer 86
St-Ouen 121-122, 205
St-Ours church 143
St-Paul-de-Vence 167
St-Pierre-et-Saint-Paul, Abbatiale 113
St-Rémy-de-Provence 159
St-Sernin Basilique 188
St-Thégonnec 133, 136
St-Trophime 157
Ste-Cécile Cathédrale 190
Ste-Chapelle 60-61
Ste-Croix Eglise 100
Ste-Jeanne-d'Arc Eglise 120

Ste-Madeleine Basilique 106-107
Ste-Marie Eglise 187
Strasbourg 17, 85, 93-94, 96-100, 199-201
Sword 19, 82, 128

Tarascon 158
Toulouse 17, 44, 174, 188-191, 197, 201, 214
Touquet, Le 86-87, 195, 199
Trophée des Alpes 170
Trouville 124-125
Trouville beach 125
Turbie 169
Turckheim 99-100

Vaches Noires 125
Vaison-la-Romaine 155
Vallauris 167, 206
Vedettes 50, 183
Vendôme–Opéra–Madeleine 54
Versailles 13, 25, 27-28, 32-33, 38, 46-47, 64, 66, 76-80, 83, 109, 113, 156, 199
Vézelay 102, 105-107
Vézère, Vallée de la 176
Vieux Bassin 123
Vieux Port 165-166, 182
Village Noir 162
Vimoutiers 126

Zonza 172

HANDY TRAVEL TIPS

An A–Z Summary of Practical Information

A Accommodation 222
Airports 223
B Bicycle and Moped
Hire 224
C Camping 224
Car Hire 225
Climate and
Clothing 225
Communications 226
Complaints 227
Crime and Theft 228
Customs and Entry
Formalities 228
D Driving 229
E Electric Current 231
Embassies and
Consulates 231
Emergencies 232
Etiquette 232
G Getting to France 233
Guides and
Interpreters 235
H Hairdressers and
Barbers 235
Health and Medical
Care 235
Hitch-hiking 236
L Lost Property 236

M Maps 237
Minitel 237
Money Matters 237
N Newspapers and
Magazines 238
P Photography and
Video 238
Police 239
Prices 239
Public Holidays 240
R Radio and TV 240
Religious
Services 240
Restaurants 241
T Time
Differences 243
Tipping 243
Toilets 243
Tourist Information
Offices 244
Transport 245
U Useful Expressions
246
W Water 247
Weights and
Measures 248
Y Youth Hostels 248

A

ACCOMMODATION *(See also* CAMPING, YOUTH HOSTELS.*)*

Hotels. Hotels throughout France are officially classified from one star to four-star luxury establishments. For advance reservations, especially during holiday periods, you can obtain lists of officially approved hotels throughout the country from the French national tourist offices (see page 244).

On the spot, tourist offices and *syndicats d'initiative* can supply local hotel lists. Note that a hotel labelled simply *Hôtel* may not have a restaurant, especially in big towns. The *Accueil de France* offices, located in tourist offices in the cities, will make room reservations for a small fee.

Major airports and railway stations have hotel reservation desks. In the arrivals hall of Paris's Roissy-Charles-de-Gaulle airport, a push-button system gives you free access to a broad selection of hotels for reservations throughout Paris.

Châteaux-Hôtels de France. These converted châteaux, covering the whole of France, are an expensive but worthwhile romantic alternative, notably in the Loire Valley. They are listed — in a directory available from tourist offices — together with **Relais de Campagne**, a similar chain offering a wider variety of hotels in country settings, with ratings from two to four stars (some of them genuine, old-time stagecoach inns).

Logis de France and **Auberges de France** are government-approved hotels, often outside towns, many with character and charm. A free directory can be obtained from the French national tourist offices before leaving (you have to pay for it on the spot). *Logis* are in the one- and two-star bracket; *auberges* are smaller, simpler establishments.

Pensions may be either small hotels or guest houses. They are generally family-owned and provide meals.

Gîtes de France; gîtes ruraux. These are officially sponsored, (sparsely) furnished holiday cottages or flats (apartments). Rental costs include all charges. Sleeping arrangements may be in dormitories.

House rental. Local tourist offices *(syndicats d'initiative)* can recommend agencies with complete lists of houses and apartments to let. You need to reserve well ahead.

a double / single room	**une chambre pour deux personnes / une personne**
with / without bath / shower	**avec / sans baignoire / douche**
with a double bed/twin beds	**avec un grand lit/deux lits**
What's the rate per night?	**Quel est le prix pour une nuit?**
I'm looking for a flat (apartment) to rent for a month.	**Je cherche un appartement à louer pour un mois.**

Note: The *hôtel de ville* is not a hotel but the town hall.

AIRPORTS *(aéroport)*

Paris is the major gateway to France, but many international flights operate to other big cities. All French airports have duty-free shops and efficient transport to the town centre.

Paris is served by two airports: Roissy-Charles-de-Gaulle, which is about 25 km (15 miles) northeast of the city; and Orly, about 16 km (10 miles) to the south. Most intercontinental flights use the ultra-modern Roissy. For general information at Roissy airport, phone 01.48.62.22.80.

Roissy and Orly are linked by coach. In normal traffic conditions, the journey between airports takes about an hour and a quarter. You can also get a coach from Roissy to the place de l'Étoile terminal in Paris, and one from Orly to the Invalides terminal. Both journeys take at least 40 minutes. The coaches leave frequently between 6 am and 11 pm.

Trains from the Gare du Nord to Roissy (RER line B) leave every 15 minutes and take 35 minutes. From the Quai d'Orsay, Saint-Michel, or the Gare d'Austerlitz (RER line C) to Orly takes 40 to 60 minutes. Trains run frequently from early morning to late at night.

Taxis from the airport to the centre of Paris are expensive for single passengers but worthwhile for three.

Where's the bus for...?	**D'où part le bus pour...?**
Can you help me with my luggage?	**Pouvez-vous m'aider à porter mes bagages?**
How much is that?	**Combien est-ce que ça coûte?**

B

BICYCLE and MOPED HIRE *(location de bicyclettes/mobylettes)*

Cycling is a highly popular sport in France, and it's possible to hire bikes *(bicyclette or vélo)* in many of the traditional tourist spots, such as Brittany and the Côte d'Azur. Try the station of the nearest town, or enquire at your local tourist office. You will need your passport or identity card, and you'll have to pay a deposit, unless you hold a major credit card.

Mopeds *(mobylette)* are sometimes available for hire as well (same conditions as for bikes). Minimum age to ride a moped is 14; for scooters from 50 to 125 cc, it is 16 ; over 125 cc, it's 18. Crash helmets are compulsory. Enquire about rentals at your hotel or the local tourist office.

I'd like to hire a bicycle. **Je voudrais louer une bicyclette.**

for one day/a week **pour une journée / une semaine**

C

CAMPING

Campsites are officially graded from one to four stars. There are approximately 9,000 sites in France, including more than 100 in the Paris area. During peak season it's advisable to make reservations well in advance, and in the Midi it's essential. It's quite a good idea to have an up-to-date camping card, or *carte de camping*, which will give you third-party insurance and sometimes a discount.

Free camping *(camping sauvage)* is not allowed. If you want to camp on private property, you must first get permission from the owner.

For information about camping, consult the special leaflet issued by the French national tourist offices. You can get your camping card, renewable annually, from either:

Fédération française de camping et de caravaning, 78, rue de Rivoli, 75004 Paris; tel. 01.42.72.84.08

or

Camping Club de France, 218, bd. Saint-Germain, 75007 Paris; tel. 01.45.48.30.03.

Have you room for a tent/ a caravan? **Avez-vous de la place pour une tente / une caravane?**

May we camp on your land?	**Pouvons-nous camper sur votre terrain?**

CAR HIRE *(location de voitures)* (See also DRIVING.)

All major car-hire firms in France offer French-made cars, and sometimes foreign, too. Locally based firms generally charge less than the international companies, but you may have to turn the car in where you took it out. There are some good deals to be had if you book your car together with your plane or train ticket.

To hire a car you must produce a valid driving licence (held for at least one year) and your passport. Depending on the model and the hiring firm, the minimum age for renting a car varies from 21 to 25. If you pay by a major credit card you do not have to pay the usual advance deposit payment. In fact, many firms only accept payment by credit card. Third-party insurance is usually automatically included; for an additional fee per day you can obtain full insurance coverage.

I'd like to hire a car	**Je voudrais louer une voiture**
tomorrow.	**demain.**
for one day / a week	**pour une journée / une semaine**
unlimited mileage	**kilométrage illimité**
Please include full insurance.	**Avec assurance tous risques, s'il vous plaît.**

CLIMATE and CLOTHING

Broadly, the farther south you go the warmer it is. The northern and western areas of France (including Paris) enjoy a temperate climate. The region to the east and in the interior Massif Central has warmer summers and colder winters. The Mediterranean coastal area is marked by hot, dry summers and mild, showery winters. With the exception of this coast, rainfall is sporadic all year round, with most precipitation between January and April and least in August and September. Snow can be a problem in winter, but mostly in mountain areas.

Paris weather is usually good. Once it gets started, much later in April than Cole Porter told us, the spring is unbeatable. Summer is often hot but not scorching, autumn gloriously romantic and gently warm, winter quite supportable. Paris under snow, a rare event, is spectacular.

France

Except in winter, medium-weight attire is usually adequate. You are likely to need rainwear at any time of the year.

Clothes for restaurants are much less formal than you might have imagined. The French like to look *good*, whether casual or formal. Ties for men and dresses for women are rarely compulsory. Avoid shorts in cathedrals, and keep your beach wear for the beach.

COMMUNICATIONS

Post office *(bureau de poste)*. You can identify French post offices by a sign with a stylized blue bird and/or the words *La Poste* or *PTT*. In cities, the main post office is open from 8 am to 5 PM weekdays and 8 am to noon on Saturdays. In Paris, the Poste du Louvre is open 24 hours a day, 7 days a week. You'll find it at 52, rue de Louvre, 75001 Paris, tel. 01.40.28.20.00.

Letter boxes are painted yellow and often set into a wall. Stamps can be bought at post offices and *tabacs* (tobacconists).

Poste restante (general delivery). If you don't know where you'll be staying, you can have your mail addressed to you c/o *poste restante* in any town. Towns with more than one post office keep mail at the main office *(poste principale)*. You'll have to show your passport to retrieve your mail.

Telegrams *(télégramme)*. All local post offices accept telegrams, domestic or overseas. You may also dictate a telegram over the telephone: for France, dial 3655; for countries outside France, dial 08.00.33.44.11.

Faxes *(télécopie)*. Major post offices have public fax machines. You can often use those at your hotel, but the charges will be higher.

Telephone *(téléphone)*. Long-distance and international calls can be made from any phone box. If you make a call from your hotel, a café, or a restaurant, charges could be much higher than from a public telephone.

Nowadays most pay phones are card operated. You can buy phonecards at post offices, railway ticket counters, and shops recognizable by a "Télécarte" sign; they are available for 40 F or 120 F charge units.

For long-distance calls within France, there are no area codes (you just dial the 10-digit number of the person you want to call). For information, dial 12.

To ring abroad from France, dial 00 followed, after the change of tone, by the country's number (listed in all boxes), the area code, and the subscriber's number. To reach the operator dial 00, then 33, followed by the country's number (U.K. 44, U.S. and Canada 1). If you don't know the telephone number of the subscriber, dial 00.33.12, followed by the code number of the country in question. It's cheaper to make long-distance calls after 9:30PM.

Minitels. Minitels (see page 237) are available for public use, at all post offices and can be used for everything — from looking up phone numbers to making bookings and ordering goods.

express (special delivery)	**exprès**
airmail	**par avion**
registered	**recommandé**
A stamp for this letter/postcard, please.	**Un timbre pour cette lettre/carte, s'il vous plaît.**
I want to send a telegram to...	**J'aimerais envoyer un télégramme à...**
Have you any mail for...?	**Avez-vous du courrier pour...?**
Can you get me this number in...?	**Pouvez-vous me donner ce numéro à...?**

COMPLAINTS

Hotels and restaurants. To avoid unpleasant scenes with waiters or hotel employees, ask to see the manager *(maître d'hôtel* or *directeur)* immediately. If you fail to obtain on-the-spot satisfaction, you can refer the matter to the nearest police station *(commissariat de police)*. If the police are not able to help, apply to the regional administration offices *(préfecture* or *sous-préfecture)*, asking for the *service du tourisme*.

Bad merchandise. Within about ten days of purchase a store will usually exchange faulty merchandise (if you have the receipt), but you will hardly ever get your money back.

I'd like to make a complaint.	**J'aimerais faire une réclamation.**

CRIME and THEFT *(délit; vol)*

The entertainment districts of Paris, Nice, Marseille, and Lyon are places to be wary in. Keep to well-lit streets at night and watch your wallet, especially in crowded buses or trains.

If you have items of real value, keep them in the hotel safe and obtain a receipt for them; it's a good idea to leave large sums of money and your passport there as well. Don't leave valuables visible in your parked car. Any loss or theft should be reported at once to the nearest *commissariat de police* or *gendarmerie* (see POLICE).

Keep a photocopy of your plane tickets and other personal documents, with a note of the phone and telex numbers of your travel agent: it could come in useful in case of loss or theft.

My ticket/wallet/passport has been stolen.	**On a volé mon billet / portefeuille/passeport.**

CUSTOMS *(douane)* and ENTRY FORMALITIES

Nationals of EU countries and Switzerland need only a valid passport or identity document to enter France. Nationals from Canada, New Zealand, and the USA require passports whilst Australian and South African nationals must obtain a visa. For the latest information on entry requirements, contact the French embassy in your country.

As France belongs to the European Union (EU), free exchange of non-duty-free goods for personal use is permitted between France and the UK and Eire. However, duty-free items are still subject to restrictions: again, check before you go.

For residents of non-EU countries, restrictions when going home are as follows:

Currency restrictions. There's no limit on the amount of local or foreign currencies or traveller's cheques that can be brought into France, but amounts in banknotes exceeding 50,000 French francs (or equivalent) should be declared if you intend to export them.

Currency restrictions. There's no limit on the import or export of local or foreign currencies or traveller's cheques, but amounts exceeding 50,000 French francs or equivalent must be declared.

I've nothing to declare.	**Je n'ai rien à déclarer.**
It's for my own use.	**C'est pour mon usage personnel.**

D

DRIVING (See also CAR HIRE.)

To take your car into France you will need:

- International Driving Permit or your national driving licence
- Car registration papers
- Insurance coverage (a green card is no longer obligatory, but comprehensive insurance coverage is advisable)
- Nationality plate or sticker
- Red warning triangle
- A set of spare bulbs

Drivers and passengers of cars fitted with seat belts are required by law to wear them. Children under 12 must stay in the back seat.

Regulations. As elsewhere on the Continent, drive on the right, overtake (pass) on the left, yield right-of-way to all vehicles coming from the right (except on roundabouts/traffic circles) unless otherwise indicated.

Speed limits. On dry roads: 130km/h (around 80mph) on toll motorways (expressways), 110km/h (68mph) on dual carriageways (divided highways), 90km/h (56mph) on all other roads, and 50km/h (31mph) in built-up areas. When roads are wet, the limit on motorways is reduced to 110km/h, and all other limits are reduced by 10km/h (6mph). Don't exceed speed limits; all roads are patrolled.

Road conditions: French roads, all of them with greatly improved surfaces, are designated by an A, standing for *autoroute* (motorway); an N for *nationale*, national highway; a D for *départementale,* or regional road; and a V for a local road *(chemin vicinal)*. The *nationales* invariably prove too narrow during peak holiday periods: around July 1 and 14, August 1 and 15, and September 1.

Motorways in France are privately owned, with sizeable tolls *(péage)* charged according to vehicle size and distance travelled. All amenities (restaurants, toilets, service stations, etc.) are available, plus orange SOS telephones. For a more leisurely drive, take the alternative routes *(itinéraire bis)* signposted by arrows: a green arrow on a white background indicates north–south, while the opposite direction is shown by a white arrow on a green background.

France

Parking. In town centres, you will find that parking places have their own individual meter or you will be required to display a ticket obtained from a machine (*horodateur*) which will allow you to park for a specific period of time. Some streets have alternate parking on either side of the street according to which half of the month it is (the dates are marked on the signs). Fines for parking violations are heavy; in serious cases your car may be towed away or have a wheel clamp attached.

Breakdowns. Switch on flashing warning lights, and place a warning triangle 50 metres (about 50 yards) behind the car. Call the *gendarmerie*, who will send a breakdown service. It's wise to have internationally valid breakdown insurance, and to obtain an estimate *before* repairs are done. Sales tax will be added.

Fuel and oil. Fuel — now increasingly self-service — is available in super (97 octane), super unleaded (95 octane and 98 octane), and diesel. It is rare to find normal (90 octane). All grades of motor oils are on sale. Service-station attendants expect to be tipped.

Road signs. Most road signs are the standard pictographs used throughout Europe, but you may encounter these written signs as well:

Accotements non stabilisés	*Soft shoulders*
Chaussée déformée	*Bad road surface*
Déviation	*Diversion (detour)*
Gravillons	*Loose gravel*
Impasse	*Cul-de-sac (dead end)*
Nids-de-poule	*Pot-holes*
Priorité à droite	*Yield to traffic from right*
Ralentir	*Slow down*
Rappel	*Reminder*
Route Dangereuse	*Dangerous road*
Sauf riverains	*No entry except for residents*
Sens unique	*One-way street*
Serrez à droite/gauche	*Keep right/left*
Sortie de camions	*Lorry (truck) exit*
Stationnement interdit	*No parking*
Véhicules lents	*Slow vehicles*

driving licence	**permis de conduire**
car registration papers	**carte grise**
Full tank, please.	**Le plein, s'il vous plaît.**
super/diesel/lead-free	**super/gas-oil/sans plomb**
Check the oil/tyres/battery, please	**Veuillez contrôler l'huile/ les pneus/la batterie.**
I've had a breakdown.	**Ma voiture est en panne.**

ELECTRIC CURRENT

The 220-volt, 50-cycle AC is now almost universal, though 110 volts may still be encountered. If you bring your own electrical appliances, buy a Continental adaptor plug before leaving home (round pins, not square).

What's the voltage — 110 or 220?	**Quel est le voltage — cent dix ou deux cent vingt?**
an adapter plug	**un adapteur**
a battery	**une pile**

EMBASSIES and CONSULATES *(ambassade; consulat)*

Contact your embassy or consulate when in trouble (loss of passport, problems with the police, serious accident). Opening times vary, so it's best to phone first. All embassies are in Paris. There are consulates in other major cities, listed in the phone book *(bottin* or *annuaire)* under "Consulats."

Australia (embassy/consulate)	4, rue Jean-Rey, Paris 15e; tel. 01.40.59.33.00
Canada (embassy)	35, av. Montaigne, Paris 8e; tel. 01.44.43.29.00
Eire (consulate)	12, av. Foch (enter from 4, rue Rude), Paris 16e; tel. 01.44.17.67.00
New Zealand (embassy/chancellery)	7 ter, rue Léonard-de-Vinci, Paris 16e; tel. 01.45.24.11
South Africa (chancellery/consulate)	59, quai d'Orsay, Paris 7e; tel. 01.45.55.92.37

France

United Kingdom (consulate)	135, rue Faubourg St. Honoré, tel. 01.44.51.31.00
USA (embassy)	2, rue Saint-Florentin, Paris 1er; tel. 01.40.39.82.92

Where's the embassy/consulate?	**Où se trouve l'ambassade/ le consulat?**
I'd like to phone the... embassy.	**Je voudrais téléphoner à l'ambassade...**
American/British/ Canadian/Irish	**américaine/britannique/ canadienne/irlandaise**

EMERGENCIES *(urgence)*

For genuine emergencies, you can obtain assistance in any part of France by dialling 15 for ambulance, 17 for the police *(police secours),* or 18 for the fire brigade *(pompiers)* or for such emergencies as drowning.

See also other entries in this section, such as EMBASSIES AND CONSULATES, HEALTH AND MEDICAL CARE, POLICE, etc.

Though we hope you'll never need them, here are a few key words you might like to learn in advance:

Careful!	**Attention!**
Fire!	**Au feu!**
Help!	**Au secours!**
Stop thief!	**Au voleur!**
Can you help me?	**Pouvez-vous m'aider?**

ETIQUETTE

The French tend to be polite and well-heeled. "Monsieur" and "Madame" are usually appended to greetings, and a certain formality, or reserve, is expected of visitors, and this applies to attire as well. Shorts and other skimpy clothing are out of place not only in churches but also on the streets of most places other than resorts and in all but the most casual restaurants.

G

GETTING TO FRANCE

See a good travel agent well before your planned departure date for help with your timetable, budget, and personal requirements.

BY AIR

Scheduled flights

Paris is the major gateway to France, although a number of international flights operate to Lyon, Nice, and many other cities, including Ajaccio, Bastia, and Calvi in Corsica. To avoid having to travel miles from point of departure to point of arrival, it's worth looking into regional possibilities.

Paris is served by two intercontinental airports, Roissy-Charles-de-Gaulle and Orly (see page 223). The average journey time between Paris and Johannesburg is 14 hours, London 1 hour, New York 8 hours (or less than 4 hours by Concorde), Toronto 9 hours.

Charter flights and package tours

From the U.K. and Eire. Most tour operators charter seats on scheduled flights at a reduced price as part of a package deal which could include a weekend or a couple of weeks' stay in Paris or elsewhere, or any number of special-interest holidays or short breaks.

From North America. Paris is the starting point for many tours of France. Wine-tasting, gourmet, and cooking tours, as well as tours of the châteaux, are included in package deals leaving from over a dozen American and Canadian cities. You can also choose from fly/drive and fly/rail schemes.

From Australia and New Zealand. Package deals for Paris are offered by certain airlines. You can also travel by independent arrangement or go on an air-and-car-hire arrangement.

From South Africa. There are excursion fares and numerous package deals that include Paris and other European sights.

BY CAR

Cross-channel ferry operators offer plenty of special deals at competitive prices, particularly with the advent of the Channel tunnel. A good travel agent will help you to find the most suitable ferry for your destination. Travel via the tunnel is quicker and more convenient than by ferry, with frequent departures each way, 24 hours a day, and no pre-booking necessary, but prices are likely to remain high for some time.

BY BUS

Regular services operate from London to Paris (via Calais). Numerous lines join Paris with regional cities such as Bordeaux, Lyon, or Nice.

BY RAIL

All the main lines converge on Paris. There's an excellent network of ultra-rapid express trains, the TGVs *(Train à Grande Vitesse)*. First-class and second-class fares are available; advance booking is compulsory (a supplement is payable on certain trains). Paris–Lille takes 1 hour; Paris–Lyon 2 hours; Paris–Besançon $2^{1/2}$ hours; and Lille–Lyon 5 hours. Auto-train services *(Trains Autos Couchettes)* are also available from all major towns.

The journey from London to Paris takes from 6 to 11 hours with a ferry crossing, only 3 hours via the tunnel. From the Boulogne hoverport, there's a 2-hour, 20-minute turbo-train service to Paris (Gare du Nord).

Tickets. Visitors from abroad can buy a *France-Vacances Pass*, valid for specified periods of unlimited travel on first or second class, with reductions on the Paris transport network and one or two days free car rental (with first class only), depending on type of card.

Anyone under 26 years of age can buy an *InterRail* card, which allows one month's unlimited second-class travel through a large number of European countries as well as Morocco. A restricted version of the pass is now available, covering one, two, or three zones; France, Belgium, Netherlands, and Luxembourg constitute one zone. A version of the *InterRail* card is also currently available for those over 26, valid for 15 days or 1 month. The *Freedom pass* enables you to buy vouchers for unlimited travel in the country or countries of your choice, on any 3, 5, or 10 days in the month.

People living outside Europe and North Africa can purchase a *Eurailpass* for unlimited rail travel in 16 European countries, including France, as well as passes for travel exclusively within France or within France and selected other countries. This pass must be obtained before leaving home.

GUIDES and INTERPRETERS *(guide; interprète)*

Syndicats d'initiative (see TOURIST INFORMATION OFFICES) can help you find qualified guides and interpreters. Guides engaged all day should be offered lunch. It's customary to tip the guide.

We'd like an English-speaking guide.	**Nous aimerions un guide parlant anglais.**
I need an English interpreter.	**J'ai besoin d'un interprète anglais.**

H

HAIRDRESSERS and BARBERS *(coiffeur)*

Prices vary widely according to the class of establishment, but rates are usually displayed in the window. Most hairdressers are closed on Monday.

I'd like...	**Je voudrais…**
a haircut	**une coupe**
a shampoo and set	**un shampooing et une mise en plis**
a blow-dry	**un brushing**
Don't cut it too short (here).	**Pas trop court (ici).**
A little more off (here).	**Un peu plus court (ici).**

HEALTH and MEDICAL CARE (See also EMERGENCIES.)

Make sure your health insurance covers illness or accident on holiday. Your insurance representative, automobile association, or travel agent can give you details of special travel insurance.

Visitors from EU countries with corresponding health insurance facilities are entitled to medical and hospital treatment under the French social security system. Before leaving home, make sure you find out about the forms(s) required to obtain this benefit. Doctors who belong to the French social security system *(médecin conventionné)* charge the minimum.

The stomach trouble that hits many travellers is generally not due to drinking tap water, which is safe in towns all over France. Fatigue, too much sun, change of diet, and too much food and drink are the causes of most minor complaints. Serious gastro-intestinal problems lasting more than a day or two should be looked after by a doctor. Don't be surprised if

France

a doctor prescribes suppositories; in France, they're considered the best and fastest way of getting drugs into the bloodstream.

Chemists or **drugstores** are easily recognized by a green cross. The personnel is helpful in dealing with minor ailments but often don't speak English. Telephone numbers for SOS doctors in large towns are listed in local directories.

Where's the nearest (all-night) chemist?	**Où se trouve la pharmacie (de garde) la plus proche?**
I need a doctor/dentist.	**Il me faut un médecin/dentiste.**
I feel sick.	**J'ai mal au coeur.**
I've a headache.	**J'ai mal à la tête.**
stomach ache	**mal à l'estomac**
fever	**de la fièvre**

HITCH-HIKING *(auto-stop)*

This is permitted everywhere except on motorways (expressways). If you do hitch-hike, it's always wiser to go in pairs. It's easier to get a lift if you hold up a big piece of card with your destination marked on it.

Can you give us a lift to…?	**Pouvez-vous nous emmener à…?**

LOST PROPERTY

Restaurants and café personnel are usually honest about keeping forgotten or lost objects until the owner reclaims them. In the case of wallets, they will probably turn them over to the nearest *commissariat de police*.

The main lost property office *(Service des Objets trouvés)* in Paris is at 36, rue des Morillons, 75015 Paris; tel. 01.45.31.98.11.

I've lost my handbag/wallet/passport.	**J'ai perdu mon sac/portefeuille/passeport.**

M

MAPS

Small street maps *(plan)* are given away at tourist offices and by many hotels. You can buy detailed country or regional maps *(carte)* in book-shops and at newsstands.

MINITEL

The Minitel, a computer network linked to telephone service, has invaded most French homes and public buildings. It's used for everything from looking up phone numbers to booking theatre tickets or ordering a case of Bordeaux. A little brochure — "'Passeport Tourisme Minitel" — with operating instructions in English and a list of useful codes is available from tourist offices. Some of the 7,000 services are in English.

MONEY MATTERS

Currency *(monnaie).* For currency restrictions, see CUSTOMS AND ENTRY REGULATIONS. The *franc*, France's monetary unit (abbreviated F or FF), is divided into 100 *centimes*. Coins come in denominations of 5, 10, 20, and 50 centimes and 1, 2, 5, 10, and 20 francs. Banknotes: 20, 50, 100, 200, and 500 francs.

Banks and currency-exchange offices *(banque; bureau de change).* Hours may vary, but most banks are open Monday to Friday from 8:30 or 9:30 am to noon and 1:30 to 4:30 PM. Some currency-exchange offices operate on Saturdays. Your hotel will usually change currency or trav-eller's cheques into francs, but the rate is not favourable — nor is it in shops where traveller's cheques are accepted. Always take your passport along when you go to change money. Note that small towns don't always have banks. Throughout France you will find ATM machines from which you can withdraw funds (in francs) from your bank account at home.

Credit cards *(carte de crédit)* are acceptable in an increasing number of hotels, restaurants, shops, etc. Visa and MasterCard are accepted much more often than American Express.

Traveller's cheques *(chèque de voyage*, sometimes referred to as "*trave-lair")* are accepted throughout France, but always have some ready cash with you, too. **Eurocheques** are also accepted in many stores and restau-rants; some places add a small percentage to cover bank charges.

France

Sales tax *(TVA,* pronounced *tay-vay-ah).* The sales (value-added) tax is imposed on almost all goods and services. In hotels and restaurants, this is accompanied by a service charge (see TIPPING).

Visitors returning home to a non-EU country can have the TVA refunded if their purchases in a single store add up to at least 1,200 F. Fill out a form and give a copy to the customs when leaving France for the refund to be sent to your home.

Could you give me some change?	**Pouvez-vous me donner de la monnaie?**
I want to change some pounds/dollars.	**Je voudrais changer des livres sterling/des dollars.**
Do you accept traveller's cheques?	**Acceptez-vous les chèques de voyage?**
Can I pay with this credit card?	**Puis-je payer avec cette carte de crédit?**

N

NEWSPAPERS and MAGAZINES

In addition to French national and local newspapers, you'll find the Paris-based *International Herald Tribune, Wall Street Journal,* and many English daily papers in major cities all over France, usually on publication day.

For the best information on what's on in Paris, buy the weekly magazine *Pariscope* or the *Officiel des spectacles.* In the provinces, the *syndicat d'initiative* often publishes a similar, smaller periodical. Magazines in many languages are available at larger newsstands.

Have you any English-language newspapers?	**Avez-vous des journaux en anglais?**

P

PHOTOGRAPHY and VIDEO

Film *(pellicule)* and video cassettes are widely available in France, though they tend to be much more expensive than they are in North America, as is processing. When buying video cassettes make sure they are compatible with your equipment.

POLICE

Despite what the French say about their police, most outsiders find them friendly, intelligent, and helpful to tourists. In case of need, dial 17 anywhere in France for police help. In cities and large towns you'll see the blue-uniformed *police municipale*, the local police force who keep order, investigate crime and direct traffic. In the country, *gendarmes* are responsible for traffic control and crime investigation.

Where's the nearest police station?	**Où est le poste de police le plus proche?**

PRICES

To give you an idea of what to expect, below are some average prices in French francs (F). However, inflation inevitably makes them *approximate*, and there are considerable regional and seasonal differences.

Airport transfers. Air France coach to Orly 45 F, Air France coach to Roissy 55 F; Orlybus 30 F, Roissybus 35 F. Train to Orly 86 F, train (RER) to Roissy 46 F. Taxi to Orly approximately 160 F, to Roissy approximately 210 F.

Camping. 90–150 F for four persons with tent, 110–170 F with caravan (trailer).

Car hire (international company; weekly rates with unlimited mileage). *Clio* 287 F per day, 4.60 F per km, 1,930 F per week. *Renault 19* 355 F per day, 5.20 F per km, 2,680 F per week. *Renault Safrane* 533 F per day, 8 F per km, 4,200 F per week. *Renault Espace* 867 F per day, 10 F per km, 5,075 F per week. Taxes and insurance included.

Cigarettes. French, 9–15 F for a packet of 20; foreign brands, 13–20 F for 20; cigars, 30–60 F each.

Entertainment. Cinema 45 F; admission to discotheque (including first drink) 80–150; casino admission 80 F; cabaret 200–640 F.

Guides. 900–1,100 F for half day.

Hairdressers. *Man's* haircut 95 F and up. *Woman's* haircut and blow-dry 150 F and up, manicure 60 F and up.

Hotels (price of double room). ****L 1,200–2,700 F; **** 900–1,500 F; *** 500–900 F; ** 350–600 F; * 150–400 F.

France

Meals and drinks. Continental breakfast: in a hotel 50–150 F, in a café 30–60 F. Lunch/dinner: tourist menu 60–80 F, for a meal in a fairly good establishment 150–200 F. Coffee 8–12 F, whisky or cocktail 35–60 F beer/soft drink 13–40 F, Cognac 35–60 F, bottle of wine 45 F and up.

Museums. 17–40 F.

Youth hostels. 100 F per night in Paris; 50 F elsewhere.

PUBLIC HOLIDAYS

The following are French national holidays — inevitable sources of traffic jams on the eve. When a national holiday falls on a Tuesday or Thursday, the French often take the Monday or Friday off to make a long weekend, which is referred to as *faire le pont*.

January 1	*Jour de l'an*	New Year's Day
May 1	*Fête du Travail*	Labour Day
May 8	*Armistice 1945*	Victory Day
July 14	*Fête nationale*	Bastille Day
August 15	*Assomption*	Assumption
November 1	*Toussaint*	All Saint's Day
November 11	*Armistice 1918*	Armistice Day
December 25	*Noël*	Christmas Day
Movable Dates:	*Lundi de Pâques*	Easter Monday
	Ascension	Ascension
	Lundi de Pentecôte	Whit Monday

R

RADIO and TV *(radio; télévision)*

The principal TV channels are France 1, 2, 3M6, and the cultural channel ARTE. Canal Plus and cable TV are available only on subscription. All programmes (except for a few late-night foreign films, usually on Fridays and Sundays) are in French. The news is broadcast at 1 PM, 8 pm and around 11 pm; films usually start at 8:40 pm. You can easily tune in to BBC programmes on short or medium-wave radios.

RELIGIOUS SERVICES *(office religieux)*

France is predominantly Roman Catholic. Times of mass are always posted at church entrances, and on green roadside signboards at the entrance to towns and villages. Hotel receptionists, policemen, and tourist-office personnel can supply further information.

Where is the Protestant church/ the synagogue?	**Où se trouve le temple/ la synagogue?**
What time is mass/the service?	**A quelle heure commence la messe/le culte?**

RESTAURANTS

Eating well is one of the most important aspects of life in France. **Breakfast** *(le petit déjeuner)* normally consists of a big bowl of milky coffee (chocolate for the children), plus either flaky *croissants, brioche,* or slices of fresh *baguette*, with butter and jam. The French often dunk their *tartine* — bread, butter, jam, and all — into their coffee. **Lunch** *(le déjeuner)* is served between noon and 2 p m. It can be a lengthy affair, with *hors d'œuvre*, main dish, salad (generally just lettuce and dressing), cheese, and dessert. **Dinner** *(le dîner)*, served from 8 to 10 p m, resembles lunch but can go on for hours. Children usually have a snack *(le goûter, le quatre-heures)* at 4 p m to fill in the gap.

There are many types of place to eat and drink. **Cafés** serve wine, beer and spirits, soft drinks, tea and coffee. Some of them sell snacks, such as ham or cheese sandwiches — substantial affairs made from half a *baguette*. In the morning there is usually a basket of croissants on the table; you can help yourself, then tell the waiter how many you've taken when you pay. A **bistrot** is a small café-restaurant serving simple meals, usually dishes of the day *(plats du jour)* placarded outside in whitewash on a blackboard. Beware of the sign "Steak Frites," which is usually a passport to indifferent food. A **brasserie** is a larger café-restaurant, with copious local dishes. In the country you will see **auberges** (inns), **hostelleries,** and **relais de campagne**; they serve full meals, and often superb food. Prices vary, but the menu, complete with prices, should be posted outside. **Restaurants** are classified by travel agencies, automobile associations, and gastronomic guilds with a variety of codes — stars, knives and forks, chef's hats, and so on. Look at the number plates on the cars in the car park — if they're mostly local, you can suppose that it's a good restaurant. An empty dining room with waiters lolling around suggests that there may be something wrong. On motorways you'll see the sign **Restoroute**; table and/or cafeteria service is available in these establishments. A **relais routier** is roughly equivalent to a roadside diner, often frequented by lorry drivers. The food here can be excellent, if you hit the right place.

France

To help you reserve a table...

I'd like to reserve a table
for two/three/four people.

J'aimerais réserver une table pour
deux / trois / quatre personnes.

Do you have a set menu?

Avez-vous un menu du jour?

... and decipher the menu

à l'alsacienne	*with sauerkraut and pork*
à l'ancienne	*with wine sauce, carrots, onions and mushrooms*
à l'anglaise	*boiled*
à la bordelaise	*with wine sauce, shallots, mushrooms and marrow*
à la bourguignonne	*with mushrooms, pearl onions and red-wine sauce*
à la broche	*spit-roasted*
en croûte	*in a pastry crust*
en daube	*casseroled*
aux duxelles	*with minced mushrooms, white wine, herbs*
à la flamande	*cooked in beer*
à la forestière	*with mushrooms, potatoes and bacon*
à la lorraine	*braised in red wine with red cabbage*
à la lyonnaise	*with onions*
à la Mirabeau	*with anchovies, olives, tarragon*
à la niçoise	*with garlic, anchovies, olives, onions, tomatoes*
à la normande	*with butter and fresh cream or with apples and cider*
Parmentier	*with potatoes*
printanière	*with spring vegetables*
à la provençale	*with garlic, onions, herbs, olives, oil and tomatoes*

T

TIME DIFFERENCES

France follows Central European Time (Greenwich Mean Time + 1). In the spring clocks are put forward 1 hour, and back 1 hour in autumn. If your country does the same, the time difference is constant for most of the year.

What time is it?   **Quelle heure est-il?**

New York	London	**Paris**	Sydney	Auckland
6A.M.	11A.M.	**noon**	8P.M.	10P.M.

TIPPING

A 15% service charge is generally included automatically in hotel and restaurant bills. Rounding off the overall bill by a few francs helps round off friendships with waiters, too. It is considered normal to hand bellboys, doormen, and filling station attendants etc. a coin or two for their services.

Porter, per bag	4-5 F
Hotel maid, per week	50-100F
Lavatory attendant	2F
Waiter	1-10% (optional)
Taxi driver	10-15%
Hairdresser/barber	10%
Tour guide	10%

TOILETS *(toilettes)*

Public conveniences in France range from the "footpad and hole-in-the-ground" variety to luxury three-star facilities, which you can usually predict by the general cleanliness of the establishment. It's advisable to use toilets in cafés rather than any public facilities, though facilities operated by municipalities can be very clean. A saucer with small change on it means that a tip is expected.

A comparatively recent innovation is the *Sanisette*: a cream-painted, cylindrical metal contraption, looking something like a telephone booth. You insert 2 francs in the slot to open the door. When you come out, the whole thing is swilled, scrubbed, and polished, ready for the next person.

France

Don't let young children go into a *Sanisette* alone — they may not be able to open the lock to get out.

Women's toilets are marked *Dames* or *Femmes*; men's are marked either *Messieurs* or *Hommes*.

Where are the toilets please?   **Où sont les toilettes, s'il vous plaît?**

TOURIST INFORMATION OFFICES
(office de tourisme/syndicat d'initiative)

French national tourist offices abroad can help you plan your holiday and will supply you with a wide range of informative brochures and maps.

Australia	BNP Building, 12th Floor, 12 Castlereagh Street, Sydney, NSW 2000; tel. (2) 231–5244
Canada	1981, McGill College Avenue, Esso Tower, Suite 490, Montreal, Que. H3A 2W9; tel. (514) 288-4264
	30, St Patrick Street, Suite 700, Toronto, Ontario M5T 3A3; tel. (416) 593-4723
United Kingdom	178, Piccadilly, London W1V OAL; tel. (0171) 493-5174
U.S.A.	444 Madison Avenue, 16th Floor, New York, NY 10020; tel. (212) 838-7800
	676 N. Michigan Avenue, Suite 3360, Chicago, IL 60611-2836; tel. (312) 751–7800
	9454 Wilshire Boulevard, Suite 715, Beverly Hills, CA 90212-2967; tel. (310) 271–2693

On the spot, each sizeable town or tourist goal has its own *syndicat d'initiative*. They are invaluable sources of information, from maps to local hotel lists and other miscellaneous items. The personnel (often English-speaking) are extremely helpful. They don't recommend restaurants or make hotel reservations (unless there is an *Accueil de France* service). Call "France-on-Call" (1-900-990-0040) for tourist information.

Syndicats d'initiative are usually found near the town centre, opposite the main church, and often have a branch at the railway station. Opening hours vary, but the general rule is 8:30 or 9 am to noon and from 2 to 6 or 7 PM, every day except Sunday.

The main tourist office in Paris is at:

127, avenue des Champs-Elysées, 75008 Paris; tel. 01.49.52.53.54.

TRANSPORT

Buses *(autobus, autocar)*. Large towns and cities have urban bus services — a particularly good way to get around and sightsee as you go. Inter-city bus services are efficient, comfortable, inexpensive, and fairly frequent; the terminals are often situated close to the railway station, where you'll find timetables and other information.

Taxis. In large towns, there are taxi stands at the stations as well as in the centre, or you can hail a cab in the street. They're available only when the "Taxi" sign is *fully* lit up. Taxis can be called by telephone everywhere — local tourist brochures give the phone numbers. Rates vary from place to place. If you have a good distance to go, ask the fare beforehand.

Métro. Paris's underground (subway) is one of the world's most efficient and fastest, and a lot cleaner than those in London or New York. Express lines (RER) get you across town in about 15 minutes, with a few stops in between. Buy a book of 10 tickets *(carnet)*, available for first or second class, if you plan to take the *métro* several times. There are also special tourist tickets, called *Paris Visite*, for one, three, or five days, allowing unlimited travel on bus or first-class *métro*, and a day ticket, *Formule 1*, valid for second-class métro, RER, buses, suburban trains, and the Montmartre funicular.

Trains. SNCF *(Société nationale des chemins de fer français)*, the French national railways, run fast, clean, and efficient trains. They have excellent regular services, often backed up by a network of SNCF-operated bus and coach services. (See also page 234).

Planes. France's principal domestic airline, Air Inter, and other short-haul carriers fly between Paris and 28 regional airports, and link some provincial cities with each other. The number of flights is increased in summer.

single (one-way)	**aller simple**
return (round-trip)	**aller-retour**

France

first/second class	**première / seconde classe**
I'd like to make seat reservations	**J'aimerais réserver des places.**

USEFUL EXPRESSIONS

You'll find the French are much more welcoming to tourists who make an effort to speak French, even if it's only the odd word.

The Berlitz phrase book *French for Travellers* covers almost all the situations that you're likely to encounter during your travels in France. The Berlitz French-English / English-French pocket dictionary contains a 12,500-word glossary of each language, plus a menu-reader supplement.

Good morning/Good afternoon	**Bonjour.**
Good afternoon/Good evening	**Bonsoir.**
Goodbye	**Au revoir.**
Is there anyone here who speaks English?	**Y a-t-il quelqu'un ici qui parle anglais?**
Speak slowly, please.	**Doucement, s'il vous plaît.**
yes / no	**oui / non**
please/thank you	**s'il vous plaît/merci**
excuse me	**excusez-moi**
you're welcome	**je vous en prie**
where/when/how	**où / quand / comment**
how much	**combien**
yesterday/today/tomorrow	**hier/aujourd'hui / demain**
day/week/month/year	**jour/semaine / mois / année**
left/right	**gauche/droite**
up/down	**en haut/en bas**
good / bad	**bon / mauvais**
big/small	**grand / petit**
cheap/expensive	**bon marché / cher**
hot/cold	**chaud / froid**
old / new	**vieux / neuf**

open / closed	**ouvert / fermé**
free (vacant) / occupied	**libre / occupé**
early / late	**tôt / tard**

beach	**la plage**	*path*	**le chemin**
bridge	**le pont**	*river*	**la rivière**
church	**l'église**	*road*	**la route**
cliff	**la falaise**	*sea*	**la mer**
garden	**le jardin**	*shop*	**le magasin**
hill	**la colline**	*square*	**la place**
house	**la maison**	*station*	**la gare**
lake	**le lac**	*street*	**la rue**
market	**le marché**	*town*	**la ville**
mountain	**la montagne**	*village*	**le village**
museum	**le musée**	*vineyard*	**le vignoble**

Sunday	**dimanche**	*Thursday*	**jeudi**
Monday	**lundi**	*Friday*	**vendredi**
Tuesday	**mardi**	*Saturday*	**samedi**
Wednesday	**mercredi**		

W

WATER *(eau)*

Tap water is safe — and sometimes even tasty — throughout the country, unless it's marked *eau non potable* ("not safe for drinking"). The French drink mineral water; it's a good thirst quencher and helps to digest meals. Keep a bottle in the car.

a bottle of mineral water	**une bouteille d'eau minérale**
fizzy (carbonated)	**gazeuse**
still (non-carbonated)	**non gazeuse**
is this drinking water?	**Est-ce de l'eau potable?**

WEIGHTS and MEASURES

France uses the metric system.

Length

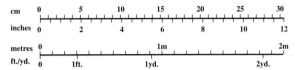

Temperature

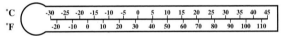

Fluid measures

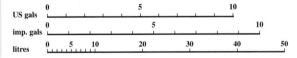

Distance

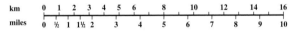

Y

YOUTH HOSTELS *(auberge de jeunesse)*

There are about 200 youth hostels in France, well scattered throughout the country, with varying facilities. Your national youth hostel association can give you all the details. Alternatively, you can contact:

Fédération unie des auberges de jeunesse,
9, rue Brantôme, 75003 Paris; tel. 01.48.04.70.40.

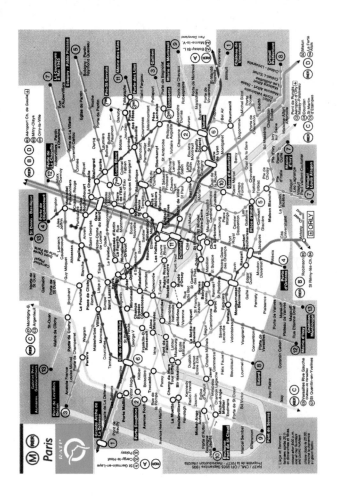

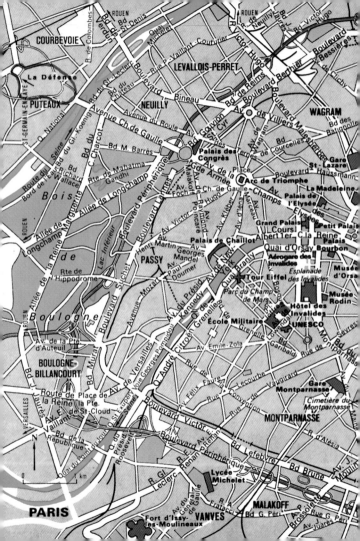

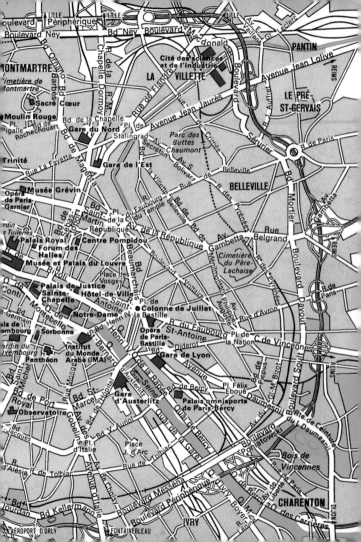

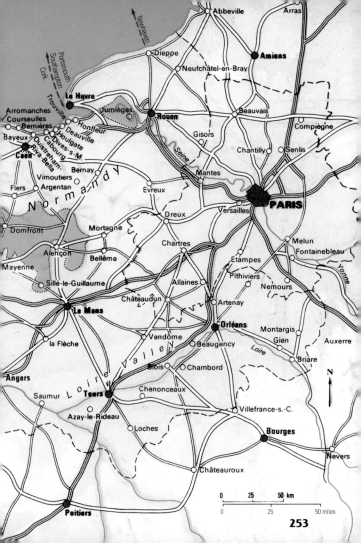

SOUTH

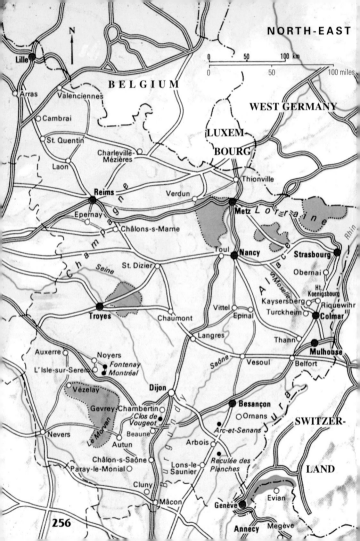